MW00908416

The Men of Match

Memoirs of a CyberDating Maven

— Nancy Beckons —

Disclaimer: All characters are based on real experiences of the author. All names are fictitious.

AUTHOR: Nancy Beckons

ISBN-10: 1937632075
ISBN-13: 978-1-937632-07-6
Library of Congress Control Number: 2012933418

Dedication

For My Readers:

I wrote this for each and every one of you—to entertain, fascinate and keep you immersed in suspense. Start at the beginning or choose a chapter and leave behind your every day stresses as you indulge in mine with laughter and disbelief!

My experiences have been funny, sad, sweet and frightening. All in all, I loved the interactions and my own growth that I experienced. As a little girl, I never dreamed that dating would be like this. I hope you enjoy my story as much as I have compiling it and I would ask each one of you to share your stories with me. Together, we will write the next book!

Nancy Beckons
http://facebook.com/nancybeckons
http://www.nancybeckons.com
http://twitter.com/nancybeckons

Table of Contents

♡

PART ONE: *Let Me Introduce You*

♡

PART TWO: My First Three Match Experiences

♡

PART THREE: Asking and Giving Advice

Acknowledgements

Since starting my two and one half year journey on Match in late 2008 I had no idea that it would evolve into writing a book about my adventures with Match Men. What I did discover was how much I truly enjoy entertaining others through my own comical experiences, and most poignantly, comedy of errors. Most important, was how this book has led to an amazing self-transformation. Like many of us I remain a work in progress. But I can truly say that I am getting closer to completing that full circle represented by the glorious fifty-acre hayfield where, to this day, I conduct my rewarding daily walk-run meditation workouts.

Anyone can probably state with nearly one hundred percent accuracy that, *life is not a straight line.* In 2008 I was bound for Santa Fe, New Mexico to start a new life as an equestrian instructor teaching kids and adults. Working with horses and the people who love them has been my lifelong passion. Then, as if a swarm of locusts made their way across our country the economy was in collapse. Like many of you I lost my new opportunity. In its place I discovered for myself a new passion I didn't know I had—writing this book here in the beautiful rolling horse country of Ocala, Florida, located in the north central region of the state.

Through cyberdating, I began journaling some of my experiences in an effort to better understand what was going on in my relationships with men. Soon enough this memoir was born. Throughout I have made wonderful new acquaintances like never before. At the same time some of my relationships with friends of both sexes have deepened and others have been lost to the wind. Most notable are my more solidified friendships I now have with men. In writing this book one of my biggest hopes is that the trials and tribulations of my experiences will help readers navigate through many different facets of themselves. Another hope is that my readers will have many memorable laughs despite some startling sad moments toward the end. As you read along one thing will become evident—some of the stories herein could easily be yours!

I would like to pay special thanks to all of the individuals below for their generosity, help and guidance. With the greatest amount of appreciation I want to acknowledge the following for helping me to turn my dream into a reality:

Thank you Cris Wanzer for the beautiful job in formatting my book. You made all the difference in the way this book came to its completion. Thank you for your expertise, and for taking the time to educate a first timer at long distance. Your wonderful manner kept me especially motivated.

Thank you Rick Ford, my "how to guru" at CdsDirect.com and staff. Without your knowledge of self-publishing and the internet I would be as lost as many other writers who self-publish. Thank you for helping to market my book using the latest methods.

Special thanks to four of my male friends, and better ones through this book. Most noteworthy was in lending me your ears, offering feedback, and spirited debate regarding the male perspective. To:

Jamie Ghidossi, my best friend, anchor, and understanding love who assisted me throughout,
Dale Culver, for continuing to believe in me,
John McGreevy, for encouraging me to write this book and keeping me inspired to the end, and

Keith Gibson, a very special Match Man who helped bring me back into spirit to complete this book and who selflessly took the time to perform a marathon edit as well.

To girlfriends:

Patty, Jessica, Jennifer, and Mary (the most wonderful soul I've met), and
Edie, 99% available by phone when I needed someone to talk to... WOW.

When the chips were down my most heartfelt moments and greatest joy come from these three:

Bella, my most cherished beauty (thank you for keeping my butt in shape, too), and
Annie, my most precious gift for our long history together,
Finally, that fifty-acre glorious hayfield—my nature connection.
You have all been an energizing source to my inner soul.

Thank you Lara for suggesting me to change back the title of this book to reflect my mission—a book about The Men of Match, and one to be enjoyed by both men and women alike.

Lastly, to Oprah and OWN for helping me understand the true meaning of the rock on my cocktail table inscribed with "HOPE." Your lifeclasses are like diamonds raining on me—sparkling, clear, and full of love.

A Letter to My Readers

Let's go on a road trip and like it, not dread it! There are no barriers, there is no fear.

— Dr. Wayne Dyer

When it comes to romance, many have said, *Men just don't get it!* These famous words were uttered by Dr. Phil one night while I was watching the Conan O'Brien Show. This particular episode was a repeat and aired live during the days leading up to Valentine's Day. In reply to Conan's question about what men should do for women on Valentine's Day, to illustrate the dilemma most men face in choosing a Valentine's gift Dr. Phil used chocolates to illustrate his point. He said if you give a woman a box of chocolates for Valentine's Day, she might not like it because it might make her fat. On the other hand, if you don't come up with the gift of chocolates, she might be upset that she *didn't* get those. (Poor guys!) You are damned if you do and damned if you don't.

Men often say that the hardest thing to figure out when it comes to women and romance is what will make them happy. That was certainly true for the men I dated on Match.com. This online dating website is the ideal medium for men when it comes to dating women. They choose a screen name to provide themselves with anonymity and they can behave in various ways which cater to the mood of the moment. They do not have to reply to women even after the cooing and wooing are over. Finally, there are no repercussions for their less-than-best actions. Men can choose to be the good, the bad or the ugly. Women can be desperate or discerning. (Of course, it works both ways for both sexes!) Based on my experiences, I advise any woman involved in internet dating to be discerning. I was active with Match.com over a three year period. I feel both qualified and compelled to answer two questions every woman involved in computer dating wants to ask: *Who are The Men of Match?*...and *What is it like searching for a soul mate in cyberspace?*

Most of the Match Men I've dated are sincere in seeking companionship but (more often than not) it is the few jerks that rise to the top who leave lasting impressions on women. Are they any different than the men who choose not to use the internet as their dating platform? Are these men more desperate to catch a date than other single, divorced or widowed men who are not involved in computer matching? YES. One unique feature separating them from the mainstream is they know the internet will showcase hundreds of women for them, or even a thousand plus if they choose to go global. After all, men are visual creatures. Using the web presents different circumstances for each sex. I found that the internet approach to dating sometimes reveals the entire core of a man. For example, the back and forth emailing can push men to a point of no return; should things get uncomfortable or too personal they can simply vanish all together. On the other hand, emailing also brings out some of the more disappointing truths about why they joined in the first place. I'll discuss these a little later. Thankfully, at any point in time, a woman can make the important decision to go on a date or move on to the next one in line.

Internet dating is a great concept, but when it comes to reality, it is far from ideal. One problem is that there are more numbers of less attractive and appealing men on the site than women (I've checked out the competition). At the same time several Match Men have informed me about their harrowing experiences involving women scammers and gold diggers. Such is life today. Legitimate women such as myself must dig hard and put forth much effort to find the better prospects. On the other hand, the lesser men make Match.com their home for two years or more. They come across well on paper with their sterling descriptions and are always ready to pounce on the doorsteps of new unsuspecting female subscribers. With the passage of time some of these Match Men improve their otherwise iffy approaches with women. There are others who continue screwing up enough that they continue to drift about. The women who are of the same cloth might also learn some things. The forums tell all.

For any woman searching for or responding to men on Match.com, another problem is the con-man. This sort presents himself so well you spend a lot of time communicating with him until one day, with no warning, he, too can vanish in a flash! Either he's found out you're on to him or you're not rich enough for his agenda! Some get angry when they are discovered by someone such as myself who doesn't hesitate to call their bluff! Then there are Match Men who pursue women as persistently as a Jack Russell terrier trying to sell themselves as the best date ever. Personally, I dislike pressure. I have met numerous sorts of Match Men, some of which I have described above. In the flash of a single moment, some of them simply change their minds about committing to a date. Is it cold feet?…could be, I guess. Others might have been looking for a pen-pal. Maybe there are just so many women out there to choose from they think, why buy the cow when you can drink the milk?

I liken Match.com to the biggest wine-tasting event at the best vineyard in the world. Members of both sexes from around the globe join to network and find that special someone. Men can be kids in a candy store before they commit to a single date. For example they can look at all of the candy, pick up each piece and play with it, and like a wine tasting event they can sample the goods and put it down never to return to that wine. No explanation, no call to break it off, no thank you but this isn't going to work.

I joined Match.com following my divorce. It wasn't my style to try an online dating service but I figured I had nothing to lose but the subscription fee—at the time $51 bought a three-month subscription. What I did not realize is the time and effort each member spends pursuing searches.

When subscribing to Match.com, the first thing you do is to choose a screen name, a password and then answer a lot of questions about yourself and what you want in a soul mate. Next are housekeeping requirements: submitting a primary photo; writing an essay or self-portrait describing what kind of a person you are, and who you are looking for. In my opinion Match.com uses a format that is easily navigated—whether it is searching for matches, seeing who has viewed you, or checking your message inbox. Also, Match.com gives you several standard *no-thank-you* responses to choose from when rejecting the advances of Match Men. The connections page, WOW, instantly shows photos of the men who have given you a *wink,* indicating they might like to get to know you better. Then it is up to the woman whether or not to reply.

I have had over one hundred men view my narrative self-portrait in a 24-hour period, producing and average of five *winks* and over ten emails per day. It is nearly impossible to reply back to everyone unless you want to make finding your perfect match a full-time job (for some, that's exactly how they see it). Some men and women on Match.com are well discerning in taking care to contact only those they are genuinely interested in. And some come across as desperate, looking for a soul mate RIGHT NOW!

The chapters and stories that follow chronicle my own personal experiences with men I searched out and men who searched *me* out. From the pilot who was looking for his mile-high-club-mate, to the man who was proud to show how physically fit his body was but would never bare his face for anyone to see, the Men of Match evoked in me every emotion imaginable. I have detailed entertaining insights I wrote to myself about what I wanted to avoid from future dates. They relate to the little red flags that some of us choose to ignore early in a relationship because we believe that those signs are mere imperfections in the human existence. They also prove valuable for anyone involved in internet dating.

If you can learn to approach the cyberdating arena with a sense of humor, some of the more unbelievable stories will leave you laughing like the ones I have written about in this book. There is something to say about not giving up on the opposite sex in spite of the trials and tribulations inflicted on us in the sometimes unnerving game of dating. Making an effort is everything. The stars of *American Idol* became successes because they made the effort to get to the audition. Prior to the audition they spent most of their lives practicing for the moment they had envisioned. Many of my Match Men seemed to forget their practice or maybe they were always this way. But some of them were special each in a unique way.

I have experienced over and over again that men will be men and some of them just don't get it! Women of all ages and walks of life will relate to the unspoken truths in this book. I hope you enjoy the stories and be assured every one of them did happen. By the way many more happened, but I had to limit this book to the more notable highlights of my adventures!

Whether or not cyberdating works out, you might conclude it's better to take some action in life than to do nothing. There's always a next time. New doors open up after old ones close. After making a tremendous effort, I thought I had found my soul mate. Instead, I was thrown the curve ball of my life and learned something radically different about true love. In my final journey on Match I found *in the most painful way* that various qualities of what we imagine to be our ideal soul mate are not necessarily appropriately ranked. To my surprise, the most important one, chemistry I found does *not* always reign number one!

— PART ONE —
Let Me Introduce You...

— CHAPTER ONE —

Who Are The Men of Match?

I love the following actual introductory emails. Some of them are funny and others you find yourself thinking: You can't find a Match… Go Figure! I have to wonder who the Match Men are
…In Their Own Words (typos and all):

Didn't you know……that all men are imposters for the first two weeks of a relationship? Eventually you'll come to find us out, and who we really are.

So who *wouldn't* want to meet a man who claims to be an imposter from the start?

Here I am: please find me! I'm trying this again. I've had some good luck, with Match.com, and even had a relationship for a while, but it just couldn't go the distance. I would love to find the right girl, and with luck, be the right guy for her.

I need to tell you that the photos in my profile are a couple of years old. Since they were taken I have gained 70 lbs., gone completely bald, gotten several facial tattoos and piercings and developed a strange and annoying limp. Other than that, I haven't changed a bit! How about you?

My mach huh….Who knows I haven't found anyone to put up with me yet. Been single all my life. Had long relationships but they all ran thare course.

Boy Scout meets mercenary….*a true and loyal friend and a ruthless enemy. Faithful lover with a quick disconnect if not happy. A Templar Knight in a modern world…saving the good and, well, not very tolerant of the bad.*

Love Bends The Mind! (What more can anyone say about love?)

Subject: How to capture the attention…of a beautiful woman from the computer…
Hmmm…quite the challenge. And you probably only get one shot at making that first impression so absolutely no pressure…right! :) Well here goes. When I saw your profile I stopped immediately- you have very pretty engaging eyes. And are a stunningly attractive woman. So my attention was caught. Then I read your profile and it was very well written (you have no idea) and evidenced a very intelligent educated lady. Then I learned how successful and passionate you are about your career and interests- and as a former professional athlete (golf does that count?) I was very impressed. I very much appreciate a woman with varied interests who is well balanced-and that seems to be incredibly difficult to find. So after reading your profile-twice! Lol…I felt compelled to introduce myself. My name is Brett. I am a successful professional who is very athletic passionate fit fun and genuine (my PR guy keeps pushing me to be immodest! :)
So to recap-fun passionate good guy is very intrigued by a beautiful successful fit diverse woman- takes a chance and says hello. Now he sits on pins and needles seeing if she replies favorably! If this does nothing more than put the smallest smile on your face I just had a good day and you should definitely e-mail me back! Have a fantastic day.

Subject: Nice Profile!
You look great too. Most of the women on here look like they just got out of prison for murdering their husband while on crack...a French fry short of being a Happy Meal. Hope you are doing well. I started this ride with the somewhat reserved hope that I might meet someone in Savannah. Then, I added 10 miles, then 25, 50, 100...now 200. I am about to throw the towel in and bag it. However...my search mileage criteria has increased with the size of asses and deplorable women that respond on here. Why is it that all the good looking girls live a ways away and the lab rats seem to be closer. Just a thought. I wonder if it's the same for the girls, or is it a match.com scam that keeps you searching...and paying.

Avast Me Lass! OK Ms Youthful, confident, sexy great package, what's the catch? If something sounds and looks too good to be true, it usually is. You're really a Match plant, the infamous escaped black widow mass murderer, you were a man till the sex change was completed last months, you look nothing like your photos and really live in Nigeria, you secretly do Polish crossword puzzles in bed at night by flashlight under the covers while eating crackers, or...? :)

My response and perhaps the best advice I could give some of these Match Men?

Even fools seem to be wise if they keep quiet; if they don't speak, they appear to understand.
— New Century Bible, Proverbs 17:28

Ready or Not, Proceed With Caution!
Intercoastal navigation uses buoys with lights and bells. Some have horns; others are flashing. They don't mean "Don't enter. They mean, Take it slow here.

Flags mean just that. Take it slow.

—A Match Man

Shortly after my divorce and at a family relative's suggestion, I joined the Match.com site. I had known him to be cautious about certain things, but if he was on Match at one time I figured this dating site must have possibilities. Prior to subscribing, I had been with one man for thirteen years, and married once, to the same. Following a decade of marriage I felt as though I had been living in an isolated black hole somewhere in space while the social mores of American life were experiencing a gradual decline. I was now the poster woman for the current dating scene. My two-year search for a soul mate on Match.com was a huge eye-opener. I was not prepared for what I was going to learn and all the things that went on!

The first revelation was that the lifestyle of men and women is not what it used to be. Today, most people, particularly singles, live in their own isolated microcosms. Then there is the never-ending busy lifestyle which also keeps many of us in an increasingly isolated lifestyle. This leaves little time to meet and socialize with others. We have less time to be friends in a traditional sense. One day, my friend Jessica explained our relationship in a text message this way: *We might not see or talk to each other for six months straight, but we still remain the truest of friends.* That seems to be the new way of life. Community spirit and respect for others has been on the decline, unless you've landed in one of those ever shrinking pockets of the country where people are real instead of battery-operated. Our lifestyles challenge us to find love in the right places. How do we do that? I believe that going online is a necessity now in order to find a potential mate. Ultimately, whether you find friends, lovers or a pen pal, online is the best bet for communicating on a personal level and socializing with others.

The traditional routes for meeting and forming social networks—bars, grocery markets, the workplace, organizations and special-interest groups, or walking your dog still exist. But we no longer always have time to hang around these places to meet. In taking a reprieve from my own isolation I resumed church-going for a bit in an attempt to regain an important perspective that I felt I had lost pertaining to my roots as a country girl from northwest Connecticut (I'm still searching for that something). Therefore, I chose a church near my home specifically to restore my faith. Inside or outside of the House of God, I pray most every day and offer thanks and appreciation to that higher power for all that I am and have. Call it my own individual spirituality.

What about our hi-tech lifestyle where analog is now extinct and digital pervades every aspect of our minds, bodies and souls? The symptoms of a stressful life have become more and more evident; and DIGITAL! Those same symptoms now tug us back to our inner core wishing for the simple life. Today's survival tools include meditation, yoga, organic food, and the ayurvedic lifestyle (the use of medicinal herbs, diet and exercise). Other healthy directions have made a strong comeback to increasing numbers of people who reject the status quo. I continue to live *not* by The Golden Rule alone (as many Match Men say they do in their profiles), but by the uplifting words of hope and faith. The golden rule gets broken all the time, many times by those who claim to stand by it. As many people do, I struggle at times with maintaining the strength sometimes needed to function normally despite the sometimes crippling effects of an auto-immune disease. Following the stress of divorce and the loss of a job before the Christmas Holiday season I was left *crashed and burned.* At my lowest point I chose to make a conscious decision to let the sun shine in on me and literally began walking about in life (call it getting out of the house). Every day I would take part of the day and dedicate it to my health. As difficult as it was at first I set out at the pace of a leisurely walk to breath in the fresh air. Along the way I would come into contact with new people and places. I felt like the female version of James Taylor's song, *Walking Man,* continually on the move physically and mentally. I set out in a kind of meditative silence walking from place to place then moving on to a different one.

Moving to North Central Florida in the late 1990s was a decision based on improving my health. Again, impaired by a condition affecting my metabolism, I needed the warm climate of Florida where the sun shines more than other places and where the winters are moderate. My choice was to live in the wide open spaces of horse country, to breathe unpolluted air, smell fresh country hay, and take in the peacefulness of nature to quiet the stresses of everyday life. I wanted the longer days to spend quality time outdoors meditating, exercising, praying, and living in a positive spirit. And when my health did not fare so well, there was always the knowledge that I could participate in two of my most favorite activities: walk/run workouts and watching the horses romp and play endlessly in the countryside. Also, I enjoyed the simple pleasures of driving along country roads that sometimes wound through the most magical of places. Of course, *Life* is more enjoyable to be shared with someone special—*a soul mate.*

After my experiences with internet dating for the past two years, my advice to women who are interested in finding their soul mates online is simple: no matter how difficult the process can sometimes be, *don't give up!* The next match might be the one you've been longing to meet! And if he isn't, you will have learned more about *yourself...and MEN!* My personal transformation was worth the laughter, tears and joy as I journeyed through three phases: initial naivety about the cyberdating world, to frustrations with the opposite sex, and finally, to a clean break from my past. The latter took place following a painful episode involving my last Match Man. In the aftermath, I completed a full circle allowing me to come back to my true identity, freer from baggage, and more understanding of the opposite sex. I am still learning to relax more, see things for what they truly are, and not take matters between the two sexes so seriously. As some of us do during emotionally painful episodes, *instead of shutting down from life and dwelling in personal regret*, I have chosen to take that venerable leap forward with the hope of improving my ways (especially staying more positive). It has always been my wish to make a worthy passage in this life. Also, I have come to accept things for the way they are. As a result, I can say that my experiences with cyberdating have left me loving more freely now and without so many of the self-imposed limits we conveniently create for ourselves.

The next best part of having been on Match.com is that I have begun accepting men for the silly creatures they really are. (It makes me laugh so hard at times!) The beginning of this journey and its ending are two separate worlds. How you come out on the other side is entirely up to you. Remember, it's the same way for men, too, as they go through similar struggles that we women have all experienced in the curious world of love. Below is an email I received from a Match Man describing his own fears and uncertainties in forging ahead to find his life's soul mate.

I have buoys of my own to remind me things aren't what they seem, and to beware when the wind changes…and yet I sail. I will not sit at home because I've met women I could regret—some who have taken and several who may have caused some pain, or even some damage. And yet I sail. I may never find what I'm looking for, and yet I sail.

Like him, I continue to sail, keeping in mind that at any time that magic moment might become one of blissful permanence.

What Are Match Men Looking For?

Most of the Men of Match look fantastic on paper. Are they too good to be true? From my experience, YES. With cyberdating, until you have graduated to the phone, it is difficult to determine whether a Match Man wrote his own profile or asked a woman-friend to write it for him. If there are numerous typos, it's a good bet that he wrote it himself! (Or, at least he did the typing.)

There's an old song, I've been told, which dates back to World War II about how men feel about women. The chorus goes like this: *Bless them all! Bless them all...the long and the short, and the tall!*

There's no explaining what attracts a man to a certain woman. Yet the perfect match for what most men want usually falls into one of the following categories:

Type One: Looking for a Dream Girl

She's what ninety-nine percent of men are looking for on Match.com. She must be petite or tall, svelte or voluptuous, dark or light-skinned, blonde and blue-eyed or brunette, or both, and either brainless or brainy. Lacking in intelligence and good sense is usually one of the qualities I have found that that most men *don't* want. There is a small percentage, though, who prefer a mum flower. Other common factors most men both desire and require are women who are not overly overweight, women who are younger than they are, and to quote from several, *no drama in their bags.* If you read a Match profile that doesn't mention his dream girl, he will qualify you through emails or the phone, if you get that far.

The common denominator that most men say they require in their dream girl, and something we women also are looking for is chemistry. Chemistry dictates that a woman will sweep him off his feet. The funny thing is that many Match Men I have interacted with fail in their efforts to find their dream girls because in reality they are more fiction than fact. I believe it goes one of two ways for men: some refuse to accept the notion that dream girls are a myth, and others just might believe what leprechauns have to say.

As long as dream girls with brains and beauty remain single, she ideal will remain just that: an ideal to be chased after. And, as long as the mystery is perpetuated in men's minds, men will never stop searching out women hoping to find their perfect match. It's all about hope...and the excitement of what's around the next turn.

Type Two: Looking for Sex

These are Match Men who want casual sex. Most write in their profiles that they are looking for a genuine relationship (what other case can they make to get a woman?). Let's face it; most men out there claim they are looking for a real relationship. Most probably are. Others perceive any internet dating site as the best venue to view tons of different women. Endless eye-candy! Men get to be the kids in the candy store. What a place to be! What many Match Men *say* turns out to be quite different from their actions and behavior. The Casual Sex type is simply looking to have sex in a similar quest to find the woman of his dreams. The great news for these men is that they get to sample what women might be like through email communications. Also convenient: if a Match Man happens to make a date with you, then changes his mind, he can choose to hide his entire profile. Where does this leave a woman? It leaves her starting over, and hopefully a bit wiser. Even if the shoe is on the other foot (the woman as the aggressor), it leaves her in a tough position because reading through profiles is all about sorting through the mess. How does anyone on match begin to determine who's good, who's bad, who's honest, and who's the bad boy of the day or week?

Here's an example of a Match Man I dated just once and then discovered he was actively playing more than one field!

The Polo Player

He had the physique and fitness of many polo players, instantly conjuring up the image of a womanizer. In reality, this Match Man was just lonely. He had told me so during a weak moment. He said he wanted to find a life partner to share in his activities. This revelation came just moments before he was to jump into the saddle of one of his horses to play the first chukker of a polo game. He had invited me to watch. I only knew this Match Man through what he had written in his profile. On the outside, he was cute and had a goofy kind of humor which I would later learn served to mask his otherwise *bad-boy* side. More than anything, his quirky humor reflected a vulnerable side and a quality many women (including myself) find attractive. The fact that he admitted to his loneliness was a good sign, too. Finally, he mentioned something about volunteering for Meals on Wheels. How endearing was that?

It didn't take long to find out that Mr. Polo was playing the field doubly so. He was going out regularly on numerous dates so that he didn't have to come home strictly to animals—his two dogs and four horses. Perhaps his claim that he was looking to find a life partner was partly true. That is what I needed to determine.

His Match headliner read:
Underrated and unloved [wa-wa-wa] amateur comedian seeks partner, sidekick or audience member. Never delay joy.

Was this Match Man just a funny guy or something else? In several communications with him by cell and emails, I found he was much more lonesome than average. Having an incessant need for company drove him to go on dates every night of the week! Following his initial interest in me, I wrote back with an invitation for a date, and left my phone number. This was not my usual mode but it seemed natural at the time. Here was his response.

I have a date already tonight and tomorrow. I'm heading for the Midnight Rodeo/Zanzibar for some dancing and grinding tonight. Maybe at Club Cloud 9 tomorrow, but we'll see. I have a date then also. Don't think anything is going on with either, but it's a fun night out. Dancing alone sucks and a guy may get the s&^t out of him for being a fag. I almost hit a guy at Z two weeks ago who hit on my date three times. The third time he asked me to do a threesome. What an a--h---! Good thing he got lost after that (which was my advice to him).

Either you like old guys with animals or you are a sales agent for Cloud 9! Sooooooooooooooooo which is it? I like the direct approach, so thanks. Been on Match long? What's your work? Tell me about your horseback riding. Well, gotta go. Your turn. Ben

I didn't write back because I found him to be a little too off-beat for me. It was also troublesome that he made a point of saying he disliked talking on the phone. When he finally did call me several days later I asked him about that. His response was that familiar inaudible garble. But I decided to give him a chance anyway. After all, I found his humor to be a good thing.

His next email:
Thanks for writing back. We both have an offbeat sense of humor, huh? Glad to know that. Sorry I came off a

bit heavy. I went there a week ago Sunday for their big party night at 10 PM and WE WERE THE ONLY COUPLE THERE! I felt bad, embarrassed, dumb, whatever other negative adjective you wish to use.....oh well. Funny now...

I remember timeless beauty. I winked a yo once. You rejected me! Beatch! Kidding. Haha You are quite beautiful, I would like to call you. I;m a lousy tyoist as you can see, I also hate to talk on the phone but will make an exception for yourself. BUT JUST TIS ONCE! HAHA. Call u tonight? Enjoy your day. Have fun, Namaste

I found it interesting that he signed, *Namaste,* a Hindu greeting commonly used in yoga involving a slight bow and performed as a gesture to acknowledge individual divinity.

The next evening my Polo Player Match Man called on his cell and leaving me a singing voice mail:

I'm picking up good vibrations. She's give me x-citation. Hey, so you don't answer your phone when strange men who call well that's...that's smart. This is a strange man. He this is K. How are u, and I hope all is well I hope...you had a fun day..I am uh just going tout to visit with a friend , that oddly enough is from the town that I grew up in...so just back from there and supposedly she brought me some special sauce from Hot dog Annie's so we're gonna go have some hot dogs and bring me up to speed on what's happening up in the old hood. So Hope u have a nice evening and call me back if you dare...har har har yep yep. Good night hope all goes well...pause...Oh, maybe I should give you my number 123-4567. I Now you have no reason..to not call since u don't have it There, I've covered all my bases so it's up to you. Bye.

He phoned me again a couple of days later to invite me to a polo match he was playing in. He would be leaving in twenty minutes! Again, I found his humor to be endearing. Also, feeling a bit lonely, the spontaneity of an invitation had some excitement to it. In haste I found myself out the door asking, *what's better this moment than an exciting polo game?* And for that moment, my instincts were on hold.

At the polo farm where the game was to be played, the horse trailers were parked in the area where the players were preparing to play. At my Match Man's trailer, there was a little feuding going on between him and his female groom. I tried to dismiss it just as Mr. Polo Player was attempting to keep down the noise level. The polo game was entertaining with people and horses abounding. Aside from the pleasant social gathering, I enjoyed an opportunity to warm up one of the horses before the game. As the game came to a close and I was preparing to leave this Match Man told me two things: he reiterated his loneliness living by himself, and he said he would like to find a woman who liked horses as much as him.

In my early days of dating, those two statements would have drawn me to him without hesitation. My Match refined instincts now were telling me otherwise. Subconsciously, I sensed a little red flag—that he was using these statements to appeal to me (you had to be there).

At the end of the evening, when everyone was back at their horse trailers packing up to leave, this Match Man fired his female groom on the spot for being intoxicated (talk about drama!). Apparently, this was not the first time she had been drinking on the job. I thought this Match Man might have found his horse friend, ME, on the spot, too, to double as his polo caddy! I wasn't proud for having such a negative thought. However, earlier in the evening my Match Man polo player didn't seem interested in anything more than HIM! I felt uncomfortable being around this sort, so I told him it was time for me to leave. Then and there, I had made my decision not to go on another date with him. He sensed my silence and typical of an awkward situation offered no response back. As I got into my car and began pulling out, he mustered the courage to walk up to my window at the last possible moment and asked if he could call me. He used a flirty wink with his charming blue eyes that I am sure he had done hundreds of times with other women. My cool response was, *Perhaps.*

The next day he emailed me:

Hey punkin! How r u this morn? I fell asleep as soon as I hit the pillow. Glad you had fun last night. Nice having you, you seem very sweet. Maybe next time we can chat more. But maybe then you won't like me so much! Some men should be seen and not heard, right? I am tied up tonight and thru most or all of the weekend, but are you around for lunch this week??

Contrary to my earlier decision, I emailed back a week later for a possible Friday date for coffee. I just had to see where this story was going! The next day he called and sounding ever so polite he said that he would take me any place I wanted to go. I didn't return his call for several days, but when I did he called back immediately with his usual offbeat humor. I asked him how it was that he was so busy from mid-week through the weekend that he did not have one hour for a date. Sidetracking me with an unrelated question, again, I pressed, *Do you have a bunch of dates lined up or is it work-related?* Finally, he confessed he had dates every night of the week! I replied, *What... am I your lunch girl?* He said he had only met me four days ago. (We had met on the polo field over a week before!) So I bade a courteous goodbye to this rather benign goofy polo pup. He did have great blue eyes though!

Type Three: Looking to Feed His Ego

Men love having the attention of a woman. When a beautiful woman directs her attention to a man, it's like drinking a perfect cocktail. Of course, I don't know many women who dislike attention from a man, *except when he is rude and obnoxious*, even if the man is not the greatest looking dude.

Remaining online with Match is a good way for men to feed their egos. That is another reason why internet dating sites are here to stay. Men have emailed me the most glorious, attention-getting messages so that they might receive a plate full of appreciation and gratitude back. Time permitting I did reply back to some of the more gracious comments with a courteous, *Thank you.* Most of them really weren't looking for a date, and they hailed as far away as California, Oregon and Washington. Nonetheless, these Match Men insisted upon commenting on how pretty my smile was or some other *wow factor* that grabbed their attention. Some of them sounded like true gentlemen, and I'm sure they were. Would they qualify as pen pals? No. They simply were in it for the validation of an attractive lady who responded back (don't we all need that from time to time?). It simply made their day! Here are some:

Hi , just want you to know you're a very sexy and pretty Lady, we are too far, but sometimes you just need to tell someone they're a 10!

You are beautiful!!!!!!!!!!!!!!!!!!!!!! I am not online anymore and very choosy about who I write to and you are WOW!!!!!!!!!

Type Four: Looking for a Pen Pal

In my estimation, this type of man is not worth the time to write back, unless you *are* seeking a pen pal. Chances are he won't tell you what he wants. So why waste your time? You'll never get the chance to meet him. I found that out with Colorado Man: His screen name contained the operative word *bachelor*. Following two months of numerous emails and IM chats, it finally dawned on me that bachelor man was just a pen pal. He might have been afraid of commitment because, despite his excuses for not meeting he still wanted to get to know me. After two years on Match he's still there. An incessant texter, he must have amassed a library by now with volumes of IM's to women.

There are more reasons why some men take to the emails, too for an extended period of time. It is a fact that some haven't even moved to the city they list as their location. Until they relocate they could be anywhere in the country. Another reason for taking the pen-pal route is loneliness. Like any of us who are feeling aloneness, some men make themselves feel good by emailing attractive women. It is the hope that every so often just one might respond to him (the same ego-booster described earlier with type three). In the end, pen pals are just that. They give compliments and inundate her inbox with mail messages, again, in the hopes of getting a conversation going.

I have found that there are those Match Men who really do wish to compliment a woman they find attractive. They might be shy or have a problem with rejection. Therefore, being pen pals is a way of lessening potential hurt. Again, the majority of men are simply validating their egos when an attractive woman responds. The question remains: how many of these are really looking to find a woman to date? And how many of these don't have enough confidence to think they could get a date with an attractive woman? It makes me wonder about the kind of havoc that goes through men's minds during the pre-dating stages. (It can't be easy!) Here are some emails I've received from Match Men, *you guessed it*, were written for whatever reasons—all good:

Subject: *Good Morning*
Nice profile, well stated, and beautiful pictures. You exude such elegance, grace and intelligence. I just wanted to tell you how much your style is admired. Best wishes in finding a partner that complements your life.
Quite a hike from Bradenton. Dale (with no photo)

My reply to him was:
Might u be seeking a reference from me? Lol.

Another Match Man wrote:
I would say your pretty HOT!! Love your pics!! Nice bod!!! I wish you weren't so far away from NM cause I would love to hook up with you. I can tell that you are breaking some hearts in FL with your good looks....

Another Match Man:
Now how could you even compare another man with me...there is no comparison!! Look at the profile...look at the pictures...now think about it can another guy really stack up! Let me help you in the analysis. OK maybe he has a pretty face, but does he really anything else to offer...does he make you laugh like this message...does he have any substance or is he just another pretty face.... The one and only, Barry

Another Match Man:
Did you add some pics to your profile???? You are soooo sexy!!!! So why is it that a sexy, hot, good-lookin lady like yourself is not hooked up with a boyfriend? By the way I like your horse pic...its cute! As far as me, I was married before (very young) and after we separated I really focused on my career. I have had girlfriends over the years but no one who really "rock-my-world"! My career has come to a point that I am happy and I am really trying to find the one that I can share my life with. That being said

my life is still a little crazy sometime with work. I do try to balance it with playing racketball a couple of times a week and finished a dance class that left many women in this city with sore feet. I would love to chat with you over the phone, if you would care to share your digits with me, but if you have falled for the "used car salesman" and he has sweep you off your feet, I would have to be a little disappointed in your character judgment. By the way my personal email is:_____. Talk to you soon,

His next email went:
Hey, what happen to you?? Robert

Me to Match Man:
I've been busy dating—out to dinner, out to Daytona swimming at the beach. I had the best fresh caught pure crab meat cakes for lunch, too. It was great to hit the ocean—water temperature was perfect!

Match Man to me:
That sounds like a great time and some gooood food!! I can't remember the seafood place, but down on the Keys there's this place that has some great sea food. I spent a little time at the Keys and got my "open water" scuba cert. I was like swimming in a large aquarium and was a great experience except for the jelly fish encounter. Anyway, glad you had a good time.

Me to Match Man:
What's your story, Robert—can u tell me u haven't met anyone in the last week or so? Or, perhaps u really don't want to? I must say, I think u might be guilty of pen-paling with me...lol

<u>Match Man to me</u>:

My story...just looking for the right person. Your very interesting to chat with. 'So tell me a little about what you do? Did you live your whole life in FL? Big Bro is in SF do you have other siblings? I am off to DC at the end of this month and visiting my folks in OH on the way back. Talk with you soon, Robert

Type Five: The Players

The Players I have met are generally wealthy. Most have said that money is not everything. From where most others sit, they seem to have it all. So what is missing? Is it something all the money in the world cannot buy? Yes, if you are talking about happiness. With all they have in terms of wealth it makes sense that the players turn to women for happiness. And, they usually do so on their terms. For most, maintaining control is important. One of them (he coins himself an *oddball)* told me from the beginning that the words *commitment, relationship* and *marriage* are stranger than fiction to him!

All men have different personalities, but the real players are driven by one overriding concern: making a lot of money. (It allows them to be in the player's seat!) In my attempt to get to the bottom of the players, I believe that finding the woman of their dreams has a lot to do with the *degree* of their wealth and attractiveness. Many are looking for near-perfection in a woman. Yet they don't place the same importance on that attribute when it comes TO THEM! Also, there is self-entitlement, in light of their financial status, you know. Finally, privacy plays a part: the richer they are, the more private and sometimes lonelier they are. (It usually *is* at the top!) So a beautiful woman who sweeps them off their feet *is* the icing on the cake, and, the pinnacle of power, control, and fortune that players *must have* in their life.

— CHAPTER TWO —

Guys, Listen Up!

I would say the three biggest *Don'ts* for anyone (man or woman) who wants to meet someone on Match.com are these:

- Don't wear sunglasses in your photo, especially mirror ones.
- Don't omit your primary photo.
- And, please don't use poor grammar with numerous typos.

These are definite turn-offs, especially for women. So men, listen up! We need to see your eyes early, often and we need to know you have enough education to write a proper paragraph or at least use a spell checker!

Lose the Mirror Sunglasses!

There are Match Men who post a photo of themselves but deliberately hide part of their faces by donning dark shades. Other than trying to be funny, what are they hiding from? I have seldom asked why they do this and find it odd. Don't they know that the eyes are the window of the soul? (Or maybe that's *why* they're trying to hide their eyes!) I wonder if some of these Match Men are the peeping toms of cyberspace?

A second mistake is not posting a primary photo. There are a variety of reasons men do not post a photo on Match.com; some are too lazy to go out and get a photo taken; some do not want anyone (especially those who know them) to know that they are on Match; or, they are married and looking for a discreet affair. A small percentage of men might hesitate to post a photo if they feel they are not attractive or are disfigured in any way.

The absence of a primary photo is not a good thing when one of the first things about looking for a potential mate has to do with physical appearance. The upside of posting photos is Match.com makes it so easy. There is no worry about resizing a large volume photo. Match Men without photos commonly email a standard line to one who interests them: *I will send you a picture using private email Here is my address.* In the early stages of my sojourn on Match, I would reply to those without photos: *No photo, no interest.* I figured if he is willing to send me photos via private email he can certainly post the same photos on Match. After all, I don't know this dude, I have no idea what he looks like, and I am certainly not going to give out my private email address to him. Should they reply back they generally do so with notable embarrassment.

More Match Men than you would guess don shades in their primary photos. Many times, I've found this to be a simple case of shyness. Here is one of my favorites whom I named, *My Mirror Sunglasses Match Man.* In a humorous fashion, I wrote to him:

Hi, Your opener should really be: I'm a cool, super dude. The glasses are nice (look new) but you know how it goes: The eyes have it! Let's see them, Mr. Cool.

He mused back:
Didn't you know that all men have lying eyes?

This Match Man's response was not what I expected in light of other things reflected in his profile. At first sight, his screen name, *Lackadaisical* was unappealing to me. Where's the energy, and was that a nickname from his earlier days? Also, there were a couple of lines he wrote in his profile that were demeaning to women:

I am not into heavy intelligent conversation as I deal with that during the work day. I am interested in someone light and breezy and not looking for a long-term commitment at this time.

Since my Mirror Sunglass Match Man *was honest* about being into mindless-types over intelligence, I don't understand why he continued to pursue me. Did he think opposites attract here? When I dropped off from him, he wrote me a couple more times. I did not respond. Two months later, I found this in my box:

Hey, _____ (not sure what name your now going by)
I'm leaving match. On the 20th and one of my disappointments is that I couldn't convince you to meet me. I am glad you discarded the "roses are red violets are blue" headliner and went back to "you get to choose".....much more intriguing!!!"

I did finally get to see this Match Man's eyes. Out of curiosity I gave him my hotmail address. Turns out, his eyes did *not* meet the pleasant mystery of my expectations. The dark shades did serve a point in hiding this Match Man's otherwise attractive physical attributes.

The Fireman Who Didn't Want to be the Laughing Stock

Not posting a photo for the next Match Man had to do with the obvious. He emailed:

*I read your profile and saw your photo as you will see my photo is not posted. I am a retired Fireman from GA and **if the guys in the firehouse ever saw my photo posted here I would never live it down.***
I travel to you are twice per week and I would like to but you dinner. At a restaurant of your choice this way you

have a comfort level that will make our meeting easier. I will send it to personal e-mail addresses only.

Bad Grammar

Lastly, there is the poor use of the English language. It would be worthwhile for some Match Men to put a little more effort in losing the bad grammar. Perhaps that is a tall order for some:

hello, I just got this durn thing to work a little, no picture yet but will figure out shortly. I am 51 also but you are way prettier than I am. I was wondering if you had lived here long as I went to h.s. until 11 grade then had to move to orphanage but moved back long time ago. I also like to dance to rock mostly but did learn some 2 step in ark when I went to college a long time ago. I don't know how this site works so I will just send you this and see if we could chatalittleuntil then or if never again stay pretty and happy------Tommy

A final note on the subject of language has to do with regional dialects. The one below from a southern Match Man whom I found to be rather funny yet forthright in the effort he made to connect with me. To him I say, *Whatever floats one's boat.* It just didn't happen to float mine:

Hi My name is Doug, Yes Im 65 but have a problem feeling it, Im active fun, I love the beach, I have been along for a good while, You woud fine me a lot of fun, lot of help around the house, I am a Christian, often that makes a difference in a womans life, I have no bad habits, maybe you might give me a holler, *THAT'S SOUTHERN* for a email.

— CHAPTER THREE —

The Best and Funniest Profiles

It doesn't take a rocket scientist to figure out that writing a decent profile is one of the most important ways to attract better dates. A well written one requires that you be your own best promoter. If you do not have marketing skills, I would suggest getting someone qualified in that area to assist you. If you have less than good grammar, seriously, *really* don't write your own profile. However, if you are looking to meet a like person without the best grammar, then *do* write it yourself.

Many men are not skilled at writing or with grammar. Those who get their friends to do the job are either smart, or they have smarter friends. The few Match Men I have been on dates with who *did* dictate what they wanted written (by their secretaries) were, indeed, dictator types. I don't wish to repeat those dates. One of them turned out to be one of the meanest persons I've ever dated…and, he called himself *GoodtimeJim*!

None of Us Are Angels

The best written profile is my all-time favorite from a Match Man I longed to meet. Unfortunately for me, he lived three quarters of the way across the country in Santa Fe, New Mexico. I spoke with him a few times by cell phone and I even contemplated making a trip out West to visit a family relative to meet him. He happened to be a British Art Gallery owner. Down to his romantic screen name—*yourkingofhearts,* and British accent, I found him ever so appealing:

His Headliner:

You are gorgeous, beautiful beyond compare. But your secret is that you are even more beautiful from within! We deserve to find each other.

His Written Profile:

None of us are angels. I am looking for someone to enhance and bring out the best in me, as I will do for you. Life is very short, I would love to spend it with someone I am totally in love with, and vice versa. That feeling of knowing—This is the one; my life is complete—has to be the most amazing experience we could ever dream of. To also prove to the world it can happen and it does exist. We are the proof! We will not take life too seriously, and be ever grateful for what we have, and what we can achieve together. My cup is always half full, my attitude is always positive. I would like my other half to feed off of that, and live life together to the max.

The next Match Man was especially creative in pulling off a top-ten list as well as any late-night comedian. What set him apart from the other 99% of Match Men was that his list unveiled an innate understanding of some qualities women like in men—humor and truth here! It didn't hurt either that he was drop dead handsome and sexy in his photo. His profile read:

I'm looking for a woman who can truthfully say:

10. I know what a touchdown is, but I prefer tackling you at halftime.

9. I can cook and that doesn't mean Lean Cuisine.

8. I will encourage you to have man time.

7. When your daughter gets dressed up I will always tell her she looks beautiful.

6. I have a hot tub.

5. I understand you are simple creatures; football, beer, and sex is all you need.

4. I will laugh at your jokes.

3. I won't turn into June Cleaver, but I will pick up your dry cleaning for you.

2. You will never doubt that I love you.

1. I won't tell you how to drive.

P.S. If you love to love then you've met your match. You will always feel loved. I never want you to doubt I am crazy about you!

Looking back, my instincts had raised a red flag about this Match Man. His initial email to me below read noticeably different in style than did his clever profile:

Subject: Hello Gorgeous

Hello Wonderful Woman. How are you doing today? I'm Matt, Wow you are so amazing and cool...your portrait caught my eye so I decided to communicate with you and see how things work out. I'm 46 years old...got 1 son named Peter 10 years old so awesome and good that I have a little son in my life...lol. I love children so much and I really want to have them with me at all time...I'm into construction and repair of oil and gas pipelines for 127 years. I'm from Florida, presently in Nigeria on a commercial and residential building contracts execution with a construction company. I am looking for a woman with golden heart and wonderful smile to make my day every morning and night.

Curious to see how smart he really was I chose to email him with the same excitement that numerous other women may have, too. I did not get a reply back. Instead, shortly thereafter, I received a message in my inbox from Match (somewhat a rare occurrence). They informed me that this top-ten list Match Man was a scam artist from Nigeria. The message cautioned anyone who had communicated with him to beware of giving out *any* information. Before I could view this Match Man's profile for a second time, Match had already removed it from their website.

There are other offbeat profiles in which men choose to set themselves apart from the mainstream. While some might see the humor in the one below, it remains my least favorite because this Match Man was my most annoying date on Match.

In His Own Words:
My idea of the perfect date is sitting on lawn chairs next to the barn sharing a nice glass of prune juice with a beautiful woman, and watching the grass grow, while listening to the harmonious sounds of my farm animals. We would neck and hold hands.

Another example of my least-liked profiles comes from a Match Man who considers himself ordinary yet is looking for a special kind of woman. I still wonder how that works!

His Headliner: *Average Joe looking for that special someone*
I am an active person who likes to get out and do things. My favorites are going out for dinner, dancing, a concert, or just staying home to read or watch a good movie. I enjoy...spending time with friends, intelligent conversation, or quality time with that someone special...whether it's just going for a walk, a museum, or a night on the town.

Here's a memorable headliner:
Never above you. Never below you. Always beside you. I am looking for a woman that feels the same way.

Finally, here is one of the funniest written profiles from *ADozenKisses:*

Hello, I am a sex addict.

Yes, I am addicted to sex and chocolate. My psychologist said that I should post this problem publicly because that will be the first step in curing it (not that I really want to). She also said that it may help someone else discover that they have many of the same issues and that's a good thing. Now don't get me wrong, I only like fine chocolate, Belgium, Swiss and some others. I am sophisticated. What are you thinking? If the first thing that popped into your head was, I wonder what type of sex he likes then maybe you should contact me. You may have some of the same issues and I can help. I started out reading many of your profiles and must admit they were VERY BORING. I want somebody honest. I want somebody fun that makes me laugh. Oh my God! They sound like a high school girl's diary. Give me a break. Now don't get me wrong. I have nothing against younger women, in fact I really like them. I just get along better with the young ones with a brain. Now, getting back to my issues. I found out about this problem, if you want to call it that, because I noticed that I was getting headaches, neck aches and my back would hurt. I also noticed that sometimes my feet would hurt. After seeing doctors and finding nothing wrong, I'm in great shape, I decided to see a psychologist. The psychologist told me that the next time I experience a pain in the neck to try some chocolate and sex and see if this works. It did. She said my symptoms were not uncommon for this type of addiction and said that many people have the same problem but don't know it and they go through life not knowing what is causing their problems. We all know that being honest and fun has nothing to do with the way someone looks so if your profile says you are looking for someone honest and fun but you find yourself only clicking on the pictures of people you find attractive and sexy you are either being dishonest or you may be suffering from a similar affliction. While I am not an expert, she did show me how to recognize signs of this in people's facial expressions and to distinguish this from other issues. So if I detect some of the indication of this problem in your pictures, I may contact you. Please remember that I am taking a great chance in publicly exposing my problem and am doing this for your benefit as well. So, if you are experiencing any of these symptoms you should contact me. I can help. I really can. BTW everything else you hear from me is factual. Update: My subscription will end July 19. It has been entertaining and educational. If you are interested...write to me at......and then the little at sign and then outlet dot com with no spaces of course.

— PART TWO —
My First Three Match Experiences

— CHAPTER FOUR —

The Journey Begins...

Through my initial dating journeys on Match.com I began making some interesting discoveries about myself and about the search for a soul mate. I characterize this period as the first leg of my journey. Unknown to me at the time, some of my beginning discoveries eventually led me down the road to a more critical self awareness. One revelation was that my own perspective of who I am today in 2012, is enormously different from that of who I was when I began in 2008. Did I come out for the better? YES. In 2009, I would be cycling through the second leg of my journey and one which was marked by much frustration and disappointment with the opposite sex. Finally, in January, 2010 after signing off of Match for a third time I was oblivious to what the last leg of my journey would present. During this period (through May, 21, 2011) I held fast and hard to the concept of a silver lining—believing that I had found my soul mate. However, the opposite would become my reality. Through the darkest of times the last leg of my journey would become a launching pad for the completion of my self-transformation. And in the end, there *was* a silver lining!

Despite all of the ups and downs of on-line dating, I would characterize most of my cyberdating journey as more positive. Looking back, two questions loomed large in my mind: *Who would think that I might come out a great deal wiser regarding the male gender?* And, coming from a less technological generation, *who could imagine ever meeting a soul mate in cyberspace?* At the time I felt certain that choosing the world's largest online dating site was the smartest way to go.

One of the most important things about posting my profile was in having high quality photos to accompany my written profile. Appearance surely makes or breaks a deal with men. To this day, I am baffled at how many profiles exist on either side with no primary photos. Let's face it, men *are* visual creatures. Added to that I made changes to my Match profile several times by coming up with new catchy headliners. They were like exercises in sales and marketing. The practice paid off because my written profile elicited more positive responses and the quality of my dates improved. What the beholder interprets on the other end never fails to tell you how good (or how bad) a job you did. Therefore, I paid close attention to the responses of Match Men.

Over the past two years, through the eyes, dates and written responses of my Match Men, I collected tremendous information about the behavioral approaches between men and women. How valuable is that? As disappointing and daunting as some of my relationships were, everything eventually sorted itself out to its rightful ending including my last Match Man, a woman abuser. As a result, I've gone from being a true novice around men to a kind of cyberdating maven. In addition, I can say with sincere satisfaction that I am a more evolved individual, too. Surrounded now by more genuine women friends, I have also forged more quality friendships with new men as well as strengthening some older ones. I admit that some of my friendships with heterosexual men remain better served from a distance (in miles!) I still maintain, *Who says men and women can't be friends?*—as Billy Crystal and Meg Ryan famously debated in, *When Harry Met Sally.* Times definitely have changed and more men and women today have become more of just that.

Again, creating a well written profile over time proved to be a most beneficial learning experience for me. My first headliner and rather short profile went:

You might have created me—in your profile.

Imagine the idyllic picture of jogging around the perimeter of a farmer's hayfield, the wonderful smell of huge rolls of hay that have just been baled...the footing soft, the going easy. NOW...envision soaking up the gorgeous views and smells of nature that span over a mile in all directions. Open your eyes, and there I am.

One example of many responses I received went:

IMAGINE...not a bad concept. Initially sounds trite but proves to be profound.

A second headliner I used was:
Looking to Settle Up...Not Down.

One of many responses to that was:
You have one of the most clever headliners. Of all the profiles I have seen up here, I like witty.

Finally, a third headliner I used was:
You get to search...but I get to choose.

Responses to that went:
Take care and choose as you like!

Hi there. You do get to choose but that's okay. Sometimes it's nice not having to worry as much because I trust your and other women's intuition.

*Re: Things U say in your profile:
I like you (gut feeling).*

Your profile & pix are fabulous. You are stunning, actually gorgeous.

(For Author's earlier profiles, see Conclusion, Chapter 34)

In Less Than Sixty Seconds

Two months into Match.com, I was experiencing a rather dull period. In as much as I was receiving an endless number of winks and emails none of the Match Men I communicated with caught my eye. My inbox was so inundated that rarely did I conduct my own searches. I was thinking that all of the men available to me had made their appearance through their own searches. Then, one below came along. I named him, *In less than sixty seconds* because after meeting him he left the poorest impression in that amount of time.

On paper this Match Man looked pretty good—a young admirer with serious potential. Unlike many others, his profile was well written, and his specs read well: a bit young at 40, and blonde and blue-eyed. In his photo, he looked as cute as a button. Although he was seeking a woman between the ages of 27 and 45, he was eager to meet me several years his senior. My mind questioned the age issue. It was always at the back of my mind because people were certain that I was younger by over a decade. I concluded there should be no problem with my age because I was confident at being a great catch. Shrugging off the cautionary thought, I was excited to meet this Match Man. There was the convenience factor, too, both of us from the same town. We made a date to meet following several email exchanges.

Match Man to me:

> *I see you are on line. It's a nice day shall we meet at the Gazebo on the square?*
> *Reggie*

I agreed to meet and he wrote:

Hi, Nancy. How is your day going? I guess in 4 hrs. we will actually meet. Are yu sure you don't want to talk first? Reggie

Initially appearing considerate, I decided further communications wasn't necessary. We decided upon a location and a final communication from him was brief:

See you there. I'm wearing jeans and an Adidas t shirt. Reggie

I drove down to the city square just ten minutes from my home. It was the end of winter and the weather hinted of a spring fling; sunny with a clean and crisp feeling in the air. The setting seemed perfect. There was the privacy of park benches nestled in the shade alongside a busy cosmopolitan atmosphere. Parking on all four sides of the square made it convenient to drive completely around so I could catch a glimpse of him beforehand. As I nervously waited at the traffic light, I noticed a man walking on the corner. Was it him? No. I scanned another. This one *was* wearing an Adidas t-shirt and talking to the hot dog vendor on the corner. His hair appeared too dark to be the man I was looking for. At that moment, I realized how common these T-shirts were and they appeared everywhere. As I drove closer, I doubted this was him because the man looked more like 50 with salt and pepper hair. He appeared to be in good physical shape though. I continued to ask myself whether it indeed could be him, even though he looked markedly different from his picture. My instincts were trying to tell me something.

There were no other men in sight. I had to find a parking space. I called him on my cell. As my phone rang him up I watched the man standing beside the hot dog vendor pick up his phone. Did I have on the wrong glasses? It was too soon to tell because I was still a bit far away.

Alas, it *was* him! I watched as he confirmed over the phone that he was the one standing alongside the hot dog vendor. I told him I was driving past him at that moment. He glanced at me in confirmation and I continued around the square to park. A novice cyberdater, I was relieved that this part was over.

We found our way to a cozy outdoor café to sit and talk. Startled by his older appearance I commented to him that I did not recognize him from his online photo. A confession rolled out that he used someone else's photo! And he said it as if there was no harm in what he did! Turns out this Match Man was fifty years old, not forty. In total disbelief, I asked him why he did that. His reason was that he had too many older women coming after him. I could have ended things at that moment but I was curious. So I decided to sit down for coffee to see what else he had to say. I just had to know just where some of these Match Men were coming from!

For every five minutes of the hour we spent together, I sipped my coffee while my opinion of this Match Man deteriorated. Fast-talking and sarcastic he made assumptions and harsh judgments about most everything. So loudly opinionated he was including his joking around about his ex-wife. Call it *rude, crude and socially unacceptable*. Displaying a smirk on his face, he recounted how lucky he was in divorcing her before she was diagnosed with brain cancer and became a financial liability to him. I asked why he had divorced her in the first place. He replied, *she didn't like to cook anymore, clean house, or have sex.* My thoughts were: *whew, get me out of here, pronto!*

Literally, in less than sixty seconds (upon finding out about his fake photo) this Match Man had conveyed to me that familiar feeling of dread. When I was leaving, this imposter insisted on driving me across the square so I didn't have to dodge traffic while walking to my car. Of course, he had a reason—he wanted to attempt that pushy kiss. Upon getting out of his car, he attempted just that! Politely, but firmly, I declined with a solid, *No.* I stepped away from his vehicle and left. When he emailed me the next day, I responded by telling him how unamused I was by his sarcasms. Taking a defensive stand he quipped that I wasn't his type. I quickly concluded that his response was an obvious reproach for my having rejected him.

I thought I'd never hear from this Match Man again, but it was only a matter of time before he would be back on my computer steps for another futile try.

— CHAPTER FIVE —

An Englishman in France

Following this date, I was in need of a breath of fresh air. The next time I opened up my inbox, I noticed one who called himself, *Sleepless4u*. It reminded me of the movie, *Sleepless in Seattle*.

Sleepless In France

This Match Man was living abroad. His headliner read, *An Englishman living in France*. As paradoxical as it seemed this international call dazzled me. Although I have relatives living in France, I would never use that as a reason for dating a Match Man especially at such a great distance. Therefore, my first three Match experiences made an interesting reference point for all that lay ahead on my journey through Matchland.

When the going gets rough, sometimes all we want is a great fantasy to relish until we're ready to get back to reality. My Match Man in France was just the cure until the fear of another impending imposter was well behind me. It was time to go international.

Odd as it was that this Match Man was British and living in France, to my surprise he told me that he barely knew a word of French! He was attractive, well spoken with good manners, and could trace his ancestry to a United States President. Through his work he had met the British Royal Family several times.

He referred to himself as a workaholic. That wasn't exactly the best turn-on for a woman. Did I care? No. I was living a fun fantasy with him that would eventually find its ending when the conversation ran its course. This interactive fantasy went on for two weeks. One day he emailed me that he needed someone to tell him when to stop working! Having worked in the design industry for his entire life he was a prominent magazine designer for several well known British magazines. He had only recently transitioned to designing books. He told me he had suddenly decided to leave England and move to a quaint little cottage in the French countryside. How life changing and romantic was that!

For a fleeting moment, I questioned, should I book a flight to Paris and take off for a few days on a French countryside vacation? If distance was a deal-breaker for a relationship, this was it. Our emails continued this way:

Match Man to me:
Hi, Nancy

I didn't really expect a reply but I'm pleased that you did. My work is interesting, particularly the photography part. I take photos on life in France for a couple of magazines in England. The last one was about a vineyard. I also do some aerial photography. That's the really fun bit! Why did I move to France? Well it seemed like a very good idea and that's it really. I can be a bit compulsive sometimes. Not sure if that's a good thing, but it makes life a bit more exciting.

I can't believe your age…you look 37. You might think about modeling. I have worked in advertising and if I was on the selection panel, I would certainly choose you!

Hello, Nancy

My town is sort of in the middle of France. It is a bit like England in the winter. However, the summer is wonderful and the weather is warming up already. I keep finding lizards walking around the kitchen and I have rescued a few from the cats.

I live next to a large forest, in a rather quaint cottage surrounded by farmland. If you want to e-mail me the address is xxxxxxx. But I will understand if you prefer not to do that! I could send you some photos.

I am trying to learn French, but I don't have a talent for languages. Editing books and listening to language learning CDs at the same time tends to scramble the brain. My problem is that I have so much work that I never seem to find the time to just sit and learn.

What is it like where you live? I have only been to the USA once...changed planes in Chicago on my way to Costa Rica to write and take pictures for an article, for a magazine. I have always wanted to see if it is just like in the movies.

I do have a very interesting American ancestor...you will definitely have heard of him! Best wishes...

Hi, Nancy,

Sorry I've been out photographing people and trying to get some exercise...I spend too much time at my computer!

I'm back and well and truly chained to it now. Thanks for your compliments...it's what keeps artists going!

I am more than happy to keep in contact with you. You seem to be rather wonderful.

Best wishes....

Sleepless4u was an exhilarating change from the doldrums of dating American men. The fantasy of living in a cute cottage in a beautiful forest in France away from the turmoil of the world was too captivating. It was nice to rest in this dream until the reality of being so far away cast its shadow on me. And that was it for my British sweetheart.

— CHAPTER SIX —

He Turned Me into a Poet
and
SecondNatureMan

Early in my Match journey, I came upon a Match Man who literally turned me into a poet! That I could hear melody, rhythm and verse still remains a mystery. Through our connections with others sometimes we live a life we never knew possible. For bringing out the poetry in me, he will always be one of my brightest memories on Match.

His screen name was *SecondNatureMan*, and his headliner was a catchy, *Here, There and Everywhere.* I found my poetry Match Man to be unusually fun, intriguing and the most inspiring of all the dates I've had on Match. Even though our chemistry was not particularly strong, there was a vibrant intellectual connection between us. That connection made me feel alive, in wonderful spirit, and positively charged. Yet that powerful interaction, *chemistry* was not present. There were other powerful forces which kept us communicating for several weeks, though. Eventually our journey would come to an end but not without the most wonderful memory of a shining light.

Adding more ways to describe my *SecondNatureMan,* he was creative, stimulating, very kind and down-to-earth. He summed up his ideal match through a song he wrote and posted it as his written profile. Having searched ME out, his first email to me sprang from curiosity regarding my passion for horses. Taking a creative approach he asked me the following hypothetical question, *If you were an animal would you want to be a horse?* I responded *Yes*, and in turn asked him what he would be. *An otter,* he replied. The next thing I knew he was asking me to write a poem about an otter. I did just that. I had seen an otter just once at a private zoo in Millbrook, New York. The zoo housed him at the riverbed habitat which flowed through the area's hilly terrain. When I came upon him at the zoo's entrance, the otter had me in a trance with his effortless swimming. I watched from high above on a wooden bridge. This endearing creature left me with an indelible impression. Unknowingly, this Match Man had my creative juices flowing and so my poem about this otter memory was born:

The Otter
I've seen an otter just once in my life,
The impression it left on me was more than just nice.
Most exciting, I say, with not a trivial concern.

He was by himself, in the purest of mountain spring,
Swimming so gracefully that I wanted to sing.
Let me tell you exactly how it was.

His face so cute he was endearing to watch,
And his eyes were half closed dreaming a lot,
Totally focused on the pleasure of his swim.

Through the water he glided, oh so smooth,
Up and down he would also move.
There was a rhythm he had which held me in delight.

His motion was swift as he dove so deep,
He came up so quick it was anything but meek.
A worthy showoff he was in his state of fame.

This otter, oh so smooth, active, and full of bliss,
It would be a shame for anyone to miss.
The water his life, the world his true spirit.

My Second Nature Match Man loved this poem and he encouraged me to write another about the herb, mint. I was on a roll! It went like this:

Mint

There are many flavors of mint that abound,
But there is just one that I find to be the perfect
balance,
And one that surely will not make me feel tightly
wound.

It is not too strong, bitter, or especially too mint,
Walk by it outside and see it in its natural form,
untouched
How it pleases the senses and leaves freshness within.

This kind I describe breathes new life in drinkers of
tea,
And Kentucky Derby fans love its racy verve in their
Juleps.
It has large leaves and perfect patterns, just look and
see.

Dried Mediterranean mint is less potent and best in
salads,
Crumbled gently to release its romantically delicate
airs.
The taste will arouse your senses, suddenly, I hear
ballads.

Peppermint mixed with menthol or camphor is another
story all together.
It must be used sparingly lest it interrupt any liking for
mint.
We've all experienced it at times we are feeling under
the weather.

Of the two, mild wintergreen or potent peppermint,
which one right now?
I think it all comes down to the mood and desire of the
moment.

SecondNatureMan was as delighted over this poem as I was in disbelief over writing it!

My mint poem led to being invited for a date at Cypress Garden's attraction in Winter Garden, Florida. I accepted while wondering who this Match Man was that envisioned himself as an otter. He turned out to be the creator of one of the amusement attractions! When I arrived at Cypress Gardens, a VIP pass was waiting for me at the gate. I felt like royalty as security ushered me in through a side entrance gate. The attraction he had created consisted of a live person transformed into an ethereal like statue, and spray-painted in grey paint to simulate a stone like appearance. Gradually she came to life in slow, robotic-like movements. The surreal aspect of the attraction had spectators visibly in awe, and so was I.

Before the show began, I did not know that a special surprise was awaiting. I had been told to arrive well before the attraction began. My surprise was going backstage to observe the details of the attraction's creation!

This Match Man was such an inspiration to me that I continued writing poetry long after we said our good-byes. The subjects of the poems I wrote were representative of my feelings during the first leg of my journey on Match.

Although our date went well, again, there were no sparks. Also, it was a given that our differing lifestyles and the distance between us presented obstacles. Two weeks later the news arrived that he had found his dream girl on Match. How exciting he was for propelling me into doing things all creative. I was both happy and jealous (in a good way) that he had found his soul mate so quickly and effortlessly. Afterall, he gave me a precious gift: *the awareness that there are times when we are our own greatest mystery, and the things we are capable of achieving when we are encouraged to unleash our talents.*

His parting words:

Hi Nancy,
Sorry it's taken me awhile to get back to you. I had a good time with you [on our date] and thank you for the compliments on my work. I'm really glad you enjoyed your day with me.
Well, although I really enjoyed your company I have to say that distance is a factor with me. More to the point, I went out with someone and really had my head turned around. I took my profile off Match and want to give this a go. It's what I've been waiting and hoping for.
I really hope you get the chance to meet your soul mate as I think I may have found mine. It would be such a triumph of spirit for the wonderful person you are .
So thank you very much for connecting with me. It was a real pleasure!
Take care, Bob

Match Inspired Poems!

Riding high from my poetry Match Man I found myself in the most positive mind frame—that things could only get better in coming closer to finding my soul mate. For now, I continued to be immersed in poetry and verse, this time for the Match Man of my dreams:

My Perfect Match Man
There is but one Match Man who I would call my perfect Match,
His kind is so worth knowing, I beg you tell you why.
He hath so much mirth, intelligence and spirit, I continuously sigh.

Such a woman's friend he is because he understands so much,
About a woman's joys, her wishes and needs, there's no limit to his scope.
He's entertaining, bright, good-looking and articulate, he has so much hope.

Sometimes I wonder, what if I had not met him when I did?
He has enhanced my life so greatly when I have supported him most.
He brings my self-confidence to the fore that I just want to make a toast.

If I were not in the best of ways mentally or physically and he asked for help,
My ailments would never stop me from supporting him in time of need.
He's the best man a God could create, as if planted from his own unique seed.

I hope he takes all that I say to him in the best of spirit, and I mean it,
And I hope he tells me when I need to be of lighter cheer.
Then he will prove his qualities of a Match Man to me who is so dear.

So, my perfect Match Man, do you not realize how uplifting you are to me?
I hate to see you feel down even if it is for a moment or more.
Because if you felt happy all of the time how would you know your inner core?

When I was not seeing many good prospects for what seemed like a long stretch (three months) on Match, it was a letdown.

In reflecting my disappointment the next poem felt more like emptying out my soul in emotion. Still in poetry mode, these were my last two:

Don't Make Me Cry
I want to find a Match Man who doesn't make me cry,
So hard to find, the journey so long on a site such as Match.
Every time I meet a new Match Man I think he could be the one,

With the wisdom and understanding of how not to make a woman cry.
At first sight he seems so bright, so fresh, so personal and kind,
As time goes by, that all fades leaving tears in my eyes for the things he can no longer hide.

Who are these men who make women cry, and know little about their joy?
I have come to learn that what will be, will always be with these Match Men.
They have issues like you and me, and so much more than the whole world knows.

With all their tics, eccentricities, and drama from their past,
They have become faint ghosts now that I have found my own way,
And when my spirit weakens, I know how to stay alone and just be okay.

Time went on and still, I found no worthwhile dates to choose from. Feeling futile in my journey I decided to take a break from Match.com. Just as some become addicted to on-line dating, I was feeling worn down. This probably wouldn't be my first. One day, during a crisp winter's jog around my favorite 50-acre hay field, I thought back to my *SecondNatureMan* for the inspiration he brought me. A positive charge was ignited and this final poem rolled out as I ran alongside the beauty of the framed countryside:

Recharge
The rolled bales of hay are gone,
The season has come to a close.
But life will go on and on.

The field now lies dormant and quiet,
As if to take a rest for the winter.
And recharge for the Spring riot.

The birds have changed their patterns,
Sounding out their new melodies.
Who's to say that all this really matters?

It matters because of life's constant change,
In maintaining its balance of vital forces.
They include light, darkness, wind, and rain.

The rolled bales of hay are gone,
The field is resting now.
It almost makes you want to yawn.

A new season awaits around the turn,
Will it be growth like you've never seen before?
Or will there be hard lessons from which to learn?

— PART THREE —
Asking and Giving Advice

— CHAPTER SEVEN —

A Funny Thing Happened...
and
The Advice Seeker

Who knew that when I went on this date I was going to be giving advice to a Match Man on the verge of heartbreak? Upon meeting for coffee he confessed that he sought me out just for that reason—advice. He was a large-volume stock trader. I thought these men were made of tough stuff! Perhaps, if he were in hedge funds. LOL! Initially, my feelings were mixed when I made the decision to meet him over coffee at a nearby Starbucks. I didn't think he wasn't my type, however, as time went on I was becoming more confused about just what my type was. His specs went along the lines that he was a few pounds overweight, had three kids living with him, and he was interested in moving to the Cayman Islands.

Looking back, might my overriding interest in meeting this man be in learning something new about the stock market? As for the Cayman Islands, I'm thinking that the only reason to move there is to establish a secret numbered account to hide money. Perhaps living in a paradise away from the stresses of life, too! The two problems associated with this scenario is that years ago I thought I read something in the newspapers about the United States government cracking down on numbered accounts in an agreement made between the two countries. Even if one wanted to move to the islands for the laid back lifestyle, there are numerous other desirable places to live. Don't get me wrong, the Cayman's are beautiful especially if you are into the flat sand bar terrain, beautiful sea and coral reefs, and of course the banks with their anonymous accounts.

Like all stock traders this Match Man talked fast and skated through a multitude of topics in a matter of seconds. Not quite finished with his day of trades he was still talking on the phone in the sweltering Florida heat outside his brand new, bright red jeep as I pulled into Starbucks. He greeted me waving a slip of paper with codes and numbers in a format similar to ticker tape. He was apologetic that he needed to make one more call before we walked through the door. I told him it was fine. What could I say when, at that very moment my attention focused on a mouth-watering green tea frappuccino (a favorite) piled high with whipped cream served to the customer standing before me? My quick order to the barista went; *I'll have the same please, but easy on the whipped cream.* Finished with my order, this Match Man's initial words, *Have you ever been in trouble?* caught me off guard. Not knowing why he asked I responded, *What kind of trouble?* He said, *Like the IRS.* I responded back with a quick no, but figured he had had a recent run-in with the IRS.

As we sat down, I felt relieved to be at Starbucks drinking this perfect dessert. Anything said to me at the moment, good or bad, wasn't even relevant considering the heat outside and my intense frappuccino focus. Then he complimented me on my looks and I politely returned the same. Then came the weight issue. It was obvious to anyone who saw him that he was carrying an extra 50 pounds. He communicated that he was very self-conscious, noting it might an obstacle to his success in finding his dream girl. During our lively chat, I decided to come clean with him about how different we were and that I was meeting him more out of curiosity. At least I was being honest. It was almost as if a sigh of relief came over him as he began what was to be a lengthy discussion regarding an attractive petite dark-haired woman similar to me in stature and looks. This woman had captivated this Match Man's interest over a year ago. In making a poor attempt to characterize their relationship as friends he was dying to tell someone his ongoing story about her. Now I was on the receiving end of what was probably a long line of listeners. (You know the heart break scenario!) Recently he said he flew her down with him to Paradise Island in the Bahamas for a romantic getaway. There was one problem though— their relationship was not well-defined *beyond* friends. However, this stockbroker Match Man definitely had it bad for her. I was thinking that his lady friend obviously knew this but decided the island get-away was more important. During their trip, this attractive nutritional consultant (who had her own TV show) ran into a cute dude on the beach. The man turned out to be a recently divorced cop. As the two cavorted together, the attractive hunk made his move. A romance between them was in the making, and within an eyeshot of HIM!

At once, this advice seeking Match Man pulled out his cell phone to show me three pictures of her. I was quite surprised to see her paired with the cute cop. I asked how he could take a picture of the two of them and carry on. He told me that when she came back to their beach spot where they had been basking in the Bahamian sun, she asked if she could spend some time with her new *friend,* as she called him. With some reluctance this Match Man approved!

Thinking that this Match Man and his lady were simply friends now, I asked him what the real story was behind their trip together. He explained he was so in love with this petite beauty but felt compelled to let her pursue another male friendship in the hope that she would eventually see him as the better catch. I responded, *Dude, you are fooling yourself! A woman who flirts with another man while on vacation with you crosses way over an acceptable line!* And he agreed. I asked him why he was doing this to himself. The expression on his face told all. It became clear that the reason I was sitting in front of this Match Man was because I was willing to share my advice while resembling his love interest in most every way: size, features and hair color. Was this comic relief or what? So I gave him this piece of advice: *she doesn't love you, she was simply in it for a paid-for vacation!*

The Match Man commented that his love interest would describe men she was attracted to as having killer bodies. My advice to him was to lose some weight, otherwise, stop the self-torture and break off from this female heart throb. Such simple commonsense advice (something he should already known) gave him little relief. In finding a way to make him feel better I changed the subject and asked for his own male perspective about a Match Man I had been seeing recently for two weeks (*The Player*, Chapter 24). I asked my advice seeker about this loner who, at a moment's notice expressed great interest in taking me out to a new restaurant. Then, after patiently waiting for more than a week for that special restaurant outing to happen, nothing ever did come of it and soon enough we were dining back at a regular haunt. What did my advice seeker have to say about this? A long pause followed. This only confirmed what I have already learned about the male species: they sometimes volunteer making plans with women and then forget to follow up. How disappointing! Wishing to see the better in this new romantic interest of mine, I ended the pause, saying, *I'll have to see what happens.* I wondered if I was deluding myself the same way he was. We both agreed we would wait to see how things sorted out. At that point, our date was over, but we'd be curious to know how things ended up for the other.

I knew that we would talk and perhaps meet again. As strangely as our paths had crossed we had this similarity: being true to helping one another. In parting, I got a text message from him thanking me for listening and sharing advice.

A week rolled by and I did receive a text message from him about meeting again. Not choosing to take on the role of therapist I did not reply back. This leads me to the next chapter in which I offer my own insights to men regarding *what women want* and *what women don't want* in relationships with men.

— CHAPTER EIGHT —

What Women Want

It's like a football game. Men have to have a strategic plan to get the catch and it goes like this: He tried three times and then it was the fourth down and long, and time to drop back and punt. Rather than give up and punt, he comes back at a different angle.

—As told by a male friend

The Inside Scoop

Men, here's the inside scoop: There are times when what a man *wants* to do for a woman and what a woman *needs* from him are as dissimilar as the planets are as far apart from one other.

Let's start with compliments. Compliments are king. Just a month into our relationship one Match Man commented to me, *You're a top five per center.* Without knowing the exact meaning of that, it sounded great and I was on cloud nine. Making a woman feel like a million dollars by complimenting her in such a grand way will surely capture her interest. It's the great start to every relationship. But compliments end there. They are too easy, and women are sometimes suspect about them. On the other hand, capturing one's heart is a different matter altogether. But that can take a great deal more effort.

I asked the Match Man above (a doctor) exactly what he meant by his *five per center* remark. He answered: *you possess all of the highest qualities in a person, beauty from within and beauty from the outside.* WOW! If that were not enough, he referred to me as, a more *highly evolved* individual because of the daily grind I would make most days in maintaining my physical and mental health with good diet, exercise and maintaining a positive outlook. What he didn't know was that I began doing all of this because of an autoimmune disease I wished to keep at bay. And, I liked it for the rewards that payed off. As genuine as he was with his compliments, though, it was obvious how smitten he was. Thanking him generously I asked, *Then, why do you think I am still single?* He responded, *You haven't yet found a man worthy of you.* He, too, considered himself to be in the top five-percentile of humans because of how highly evolved he claimed to be. Could it be the doctor factor? I pondered some of the self-aggrandizing statements he made about himself after having spent a lifetime of one-hundred-hour work-weeks as an MD which ultimately led to the failure of his marriage. To his credit, his recent retirement of two years had given him time to stop and reflect on decades past. It seems that amount of time gave him the right to say he had evolved. Perhaps, because in another breath he commented about how his teenage sons repeatedly told him that he didn't have a clue about women. Then there was his own self-admission and revelation enough that he did indeed experience trouble attracting women and maintaining relationships with them. My belief is that it takes many years to attain a level of spiritual growth for improvement unless you are a monk and dedicated to a single focus. However, recognition is a first step and this Match Man had made a recognizable start.

It is no secret that men consider themselves to be *simple* creatures and women to be the *complicated* sex. Controversy abounds over this subject as women make claims to the contrary. I believe the significant difference between the sexes is all to do with the emotions that women more freely express than men, and which makes us *appear* more complicated. We, too make claims that men make *us* complicated. My answer to men: *Men can choose or not choose to deal simply with our emotional sensitivities.* For example, take the expression of joy on a woman's face when she receives a simple bouquet of flowers. Whether the flowers are roses or another kind is not as important as the point that he is thinking of her.

What about the simple respect given to a woman through a phone call or message the day after a wonderful night out the evening before? Is that really so complicated? So guys, please be yourself, give a woman the respect she desires and requires and tell her how you really feel. My advice: Honesty and respect are two of the best ways in winning a woman's heart. Lastly, please don't confuse being yourself with always attempting to be on your *best behavior.* Women see through *best behavior* because we have personally witnessed it hundreds of times through our friends, and done it ourselves! I see the good news between the sexes as represented by the common ground existing between us. For example, women like many of the same things men do—a romantic walk on the beach, attending a concert, sports activities, or a private dinner for two with candlelight and wine. Suggesting these things and following through, yes, follow through with them is what's most welcoming to the heart of a woman, too.

Aside from simple compliments and romantic gestures, why is it that men sometimes feel unappreciated when they go to great lengths to do something nice for a woman? Again, I believe such trouble arises from the dichotomy between what men set their mind to do and what they are lacking in understanding regarding a woman's individual needs. If men could grasp this concept, I truly believe that many troubled relationships might fare better. This concept certainly goes both ways. Here is my own best example of this:

Three weeks into my relationship with a Match Man, he went to great lengths to plan an event at his home on an evening that I told him would not work well for me.

However, postponing the occasion for another evening wasn't an option for him. He was on a single-minded mission to plan this surprise for me (perhaps he needed it more?) and only a major earthquake would cause it *not* to go as planned! This Match Man had been in high gear businesswise and was obviously stressed (I was unaware at the time). It seemed he could not steer out of his own way. Not enough time and stress are two ingredients that foreshadowed the disappointment for both of us at the end of an evening designed to impress.

The special night this Match Man planned was a creative, fun *Island Night* complete with tropical drinks and home-cooked island dinner. I found it a bit intriguing that he wasn't experienced in the kitchen. The thought that he would be going to such great lengths and laboring over untested recipes was a little frightening. What a magnificent credit for his effort, though. At the beginning of our island adventure, I was seated on the makeshift sand on an impromptu beach with coconuts and other fruits adorning the dining platform. There was a blown-up palm tree as part of the back-drop that he confessed took the greater part of an hour to inflate. (Without an air compressor, I can imagine how deflated his lungs must be!) Nevertheless, the tropical atmosphere he created was unmatched considering the wintery cold night outside. My Match Man had taken several hours to prepare this perfect island dinner for two. I was taken aback!

This special night began well with a joyous element of surprise and moved to good food and company. He did lots of talking and seemed on a high. As the evening progressed there was a gradual change—tropical rum drinks were having their full effect having flowed all evening long on *his* side of the beach. Suddenly there was an unusual *mission* that this Match Man had: he began grilling me with personal questions and delving into what he defined, *the inner core of who you are.* After consuming a number of drinks (just one for me) the final curtain call was upon us. Both tired by now, my answers to his intensely personal questions were not forthcoming enough to put all of his questions to rest. He became noticeably upset. The questions continued and things deteriorated between us. He had succeeded in alienating me. The end result was that a special night (which I truly appreciated intitially) became a most unfavorable memory.

My hard won advice that I have to offer men from this experience is that a two-way exchange of acceptance goes a long way regarding contentment between the sexes. What I also learned is that there are times when men go overboard trying to impress women when it is hardly appropriate. Try to get to know who she is. It seems there are times each of us does things that make sense only to us and not another. This scenario can lead to both being unappreciated, or worse, cause a clash between two as reflected above. Then, what made sense to this Match Man was not mindful of my own spoken needs regarding my difficult schedule that evening as well as my comfort level in attending that evening. Therefore, my advice for men is that they might make better use of their instincts when it comes to making a splash for a woman. You might ask, *What it is that you both appreciate?* and not just what you alone wish to do for her. *So guys, try remembering that a single-minded focus on your happy mission with a woman can sometimes put you in stormy waters!*

— CHAPTER NINE —

What Women Don't Want

In giving advice seek to help and not to please your friend.

— Solon (circa 550 B.C.)

That men on the whole do not communicate things about their private lives with other men the way women do with other women sometimes makes it virtually impossible for them to really understand women. I am giving it my best shot here. For those of you who think knowing what women want is complicated, it really isn't. Here is a list of some things *we women simply don't like or want.* You might know about some others in your own experiences, too.

A Top Ten List
Men with little or no imagination.
Try suggesting fun things to do (such as activities or trips). Imagination is important to women. Getting treated to lunches and dinners one after another can get old. How about a spa date, or, if money is a concern, give her the gift of a simple manicure.

Men who leave all the decisions to the woman.
Why is it that so many men leave it up to the woman? Where to go to dinner or making plans to do something is not hard to do and many women like it when a man makes a suggestion. Unless she specifies a place of her own choosing or it's a surprise you know she'll like, confirm with her about going there. More than not she will probably

say yes. If any of you are worried about taking the blame if the food turns out badly or the service at the restaurant is bad, please don't fret. Men who use this rationale are afraid to make a mistake. If she takes you to task for making a bad decision then she's not worth it. Don't we all make mistakes from time to time?

Men who don't know the difference between red and yellow roses.

Where did etiquette go? If a man sends a woman a dozen red roses in the early stages of a relationship when he doesn't know how she feels about him, it sends the wrong message. Yellow roses symbolize the beginning of a friendship, so if it is to be roses, give yellow ones early. Otherwise, she might think all you really have on your mind is sex. Better yet, forget roses all together and choose a seasonal arrangement. Don't forget, women do love receiving flowers.

Men who don't believe in romance.

Turn up the volume here. Every woman *loves romancing* even if she has told you otherwise. She just doesn't want to hurt your feelings. Even if you've already shown that you're not the most romantic type, keep trying. She sees other good traits in you or she would already be gone.

Men who say they use coupons when they shop for food.

They're good and it shows you are thrifty. Personally I don't want to know about it. Just because you have two growing boys to feed is a great reason but it is a turn-off. I'm thinking, *Am I richer than he is? Could he ever take care of me when I'm in need?* That can be a scary concept. If you *do* use coupons it's probably best not to make a spectacle of it.

Men who make a woman fight for her rights.

You've made a mistake or done something bad or stupid to a woman and then you turn the whole matter around so *she* looks like a bad person? How dare you?

Men who don't have much to offer.

There are always a few of these around. You take us out to dinner a few times and then expect to have sex with us? What else do you have in your bag? And you're not even that attractive! To give it straight - some of you snore like a freight train and when you have sex with us, who cleans up?

Men who think that women do not want to be taken care of.

Of course we do, even in this day of so-called equality. The big difference between now and then is that now we want to establish our own careers and financial independence for our own happiness. This improves our relationships with men. If men have no interest whatsoever in taking care of women, then why would men expect *women* to take care of *them?*

Men who focus on themselves much more than on a woman.

No explanation here other than one-way streets dead-end faster than you know it.

Men who don't know enough to give a woman something she says she likes.

Most women love to shop. Let's say that a woman says she loves the skin products at a certain store. What she's saying is that she likes shopping there. Try telling her how you like the way her skin feels; so soft, smooth and silky. Tell her how much you like the way she takes care of it. Surprise her with a gift certificate to the store and tell her to go knock herself out because you know it will make her day.

One last thing men might want to note: A genuinely spoken compliment to a woman never cancels out accumulated mistakes you might have made with her. Rightful actions must follow good words. Right or wrong, the more you allow your ego to get in the way of the relationship, the less empowered a woman feels. When that happens, sorry guys, but you've lost. Be yourself and don't think too hard. Good luck.

— PART FOUR —
Romance at Every Degree

— CHAPTER TEN —

Three True Romantics of Match

The Irish poet and dramatist, Oscar Wilde wrote, *If you are not too long, I will wait for you all of my life.* The five Match Men who follow exhibit a similar passion.

If you are looking to obtain the best insight into a genuine romantic, it goes like this: with ease they freely express their emotions on paper for their beholden. Unguarded, they don't leave much out. My first romantic Match Man did just that.

My Hawaiian Pirate

He was from Hawaii and his screen name was Pirate Pat. Not only did he write *the love letter of all letters* to me, but he wanted me to know that he had placed me at the top of all of the beauties on the island!

Every woman should have a letter like this written to her at least once in her life. It seems inconceivable that this pirate Match Man could not find one eligible beauty for himself on the entire island of Hawaii! The amount of time it took him to write his letter would convince me to have it framed and hung on a wall in my house. I would pass it by several times a day and have it there for all to see including my pets.

The question remains, should I have made a date with this pirate to go on an island vacation? After entertaining the idea I stopped short of booking a flight. Perhaps he was going through a similar stretch of fantasy that I had experienced earlier with *Sleepless4u,* (My Englishman in France, Chapter 5). As adventurous as it sounded, the thought of traveling to Hawaii to meet an unknown was risky, morally conflicting, and he never proposed paying for a ticket. Still, it was exciting being on the receiving end of such romantic rapture. Here's how it went:

<u>Pirate Pat's email to me:</u>
"Wherever you stand be the soul of that place." *Rumi*
*Aloha Goddess alassatheart~(*my *screen name at the time). You are an Epiphany deserving of worship! I shall build an altar to you and your goddess name will be "Ho'o puakea" (the color of sunset clouds). You are like a comet in my night sky filling my eyes with wonder and star dust. I just had to write and say hello. You are the reason why we continue to swim this vast internet sea for the promise of someone like you. You give us hope. Lately, I feel like Gilligan without the company of MaryAnn or Ginger." So I contemplate returning to the mainland. With a little encouragement, this pirate could be persuaded to pillage your village and take you for ransom. (SMILE) Please visit my profile and see if any bubbles are generated from your chemistry set. Would like to explore walking the plank with you and descending into the depths of possibilities. MaryAnne Williamson said, "It does not serve the world to dream small." After all life is either a great adventure or nothing at all. "It is all the work of the ticking crocodile. Time is chasing after all of us." Peter Pan*

I hope to hear from you soon and thank you for the serendipity of you here on match! Let's conspire and see what is around the next bend in the road. The bible does instruct one when he finds a pearl of great value in the field, that one is to give all to possess it! Indeed, Pirates do know hidden treasure when they come upon it.

With love, every fear is overcome and it no longer is a fear. What we thought would be a boundary that we couldn't trespass becomes the horizon for an exciting journey into worlds uncharted. Fear often makes us protective of something that our ego holds dear: In offering this piece of ourselves on the altar of love, we perform a

*powerful ritual of sacrifice, sacrum facere, 'to make holy".
In the sight of love every offering is sacred - what we lose
of ego, we gain in heart. RUMI
Pirate Pat
Ps You should be kissed, and often and by someone who
knows how! Rhett Butler in Gone with the Wind. If kissing
was an Olympic Sport, we would medal in it! The dream
was always running ahead of me.*

My reply to Pirate Pat:
  *Where are all those beach beauties hiding on your
island?*

Pirate Pat to me:
  *Aloha Lassatheart,
  What beauties? There are 62,000 residents on the
whole island and believe me eligible mates are slim to
none. Just look on the website. YIKES. Regardless, your
comet has streaked over my night sky filling my eyes with
stardust. Around and around I go, dizzy with the joy of your
reality. You are proof that God exists for no mere mortal
could have imagined the likes of you. Now, I know angel's
feet have touched the ground. Where do you have your
wings dry cleaned and fluffed. This Pirate is thirsty for a
grog of conversation with you. Shall we conspire to explore
the possibility?
  Hope to hear from you soon.
  Your most loyal fan, Pat*

  And sadly I did not return that *grog of conversation* to
my Hawaiian pirate.

The Really Feely *Wow* Man

  Visual seems to be king with men. When they see a
beautiful woman feelings bombard them. Many men hold
back masking their true feelings. Instead, they maintain an

emotionally void expression considered to be the accepted mode of behavior. Few others are bursting at the seams. Like my pirate, they'll take your breath away or they will literally let it all hang out in a kind of desperation.

My *Wow* match man below was such a man. His example of going to the extreme in expressing his feelings highlights some similarities between the sexes. At certain points in men's lives I have seen some exhibit that rare release of emotion and expression which causes them to verbalize their feelings over the top. How nice it is to know that men *can* articulate their innermost emotions and feelings to women. Somewhere in between what both sexes are taught growing up it's good to know that there is an acceptable middle ground which gives these three romantics the opportunity to do just that. The anonymity of cyberspace makes it more possible to do that, too!

For me, one of the best ways a man can communicate his true feelings for a woman is through poetry. Even if he is not a poet he can always choose another way. A true effort is everything. Just listen to the intensity of emotions coming from this Match Man and guys, tell me if you've ever felt like this:

Wow!!!! Lead me not into temptation, heaven help me to be strong. I can't fight all that I'm feeling, and I can't do it alone. Help me break this spell that I'm under, guide my feet and hold me tight. I need 10,000 angels watching over me tonight. One need not look towards the heavens to find an angel for I have one here before me. If I ever saw an angel, it was in your eyes. I'll sweep you off your feet, and make God regret he left an angel behind, you know what Heaven's lost without you if I were an angel... I would choose to watch over you can we please chat if you don't mind. My Email is....it's also as my IM messenger Oh less I forget My Name is Ray. Well I got to go now... hope to hear from you soon NB: My membership will end today and we could never get to talk to each other anymore. Please email me to that my e-mail address so I can send you my picture and that of my son have a nice day and GOD bless you and your family. Ray

Married and Seeking Love in the Wrong Place

My third Match Man romantic was seeking something that I could never give him—an affair with a married man, HIM. His plea to be with me led me to take on the role of therapist. Feeling his pain through the internet waves, I felt compelled to oblige for a very short time, and surprising myself. Initially emailing a negative reply to him he responded back with this:

My hope was to have company of a woman like you once a month is all I wanted ...to feel alive again...to dance again...to feel your scent as we danced ...yes I am a hopeless romantic!!

It was mindboggling at how enamored this Match Man appeared to be with me that he would go to such lengths to expose the personal details of his own married life below. However, I do credit him for his initial honesty and straightforwardness regarding his marital status, and his desire for seeking a discreet relationship. As disconcerting as it was I told him how I felt and he responding:

Subject: YOU ARE AMAZING!

I know I am NOT want you are seeking and you have made that quite clear. Your discomfort with a married man relationship is meritorious and again speaks volumes about the lady you are. I admire that about you as should all who read your profile. I am writing first of all to tell you that you are rare and stunningly attractive. Your profile is well written and well said. There are men on here that will be very happy just to get a chance with you and that is for certain...you will screen well as you should but at some point you must trust your instincts that have guided you all these years so far. At some point you will have to TRUST and hope you will not be deceived....or hurt as a result. Secondly, I am writing to say that men like me and there are many, for age notwithstanding, are legally married and for reasons that are also meritorious in principle and righteous in fact, may not be "married" for many, many years and dared to seek the possibility of experiencing the warmth, happiness and excitement that a gentleman remembered once filled his life and wants to once again. The assumption is, and rightly so, that a married man is a louse and a cheater and a creep looking to exploit his selfish wants at the expense of anyone in his way. That is not always the case at all. Sometimes there are reasons and it's so sad that because a man chooses to be honest and state his legal married state, that good women won't even give him the time of day or any consideration at all. Yet so many women while waiting for their divorce to be final or still pending will go on here and seek a man but not say they are still legally married ......why? well because men would think a woman who is married is on here has no interest in a relationship that is grounded in mutual respect and caring for each other knowing that both may still have separate lives but take joy in the life they create for their special relationship.

Finally, I simply want to suggest that maybe...just maybe you would re consider and ask "why" rather than eliminate from your search men who would be happy to treat you like the princess you are and make your days that much happier.

This email to you requires no response at all since I am NOT writing this for me or for your consideration...that would make my writing self serving and suspect as to my sincerity. So please, I understand your views and accept them for the noble cause they impart. But all is never what it seems and sometimes just turning over a rock may reveal amazing things you otherwise would never see. Please have a wonderful life in your search. You won't be on here for long ...you are simply too nice NOT to be taken soon. Warm regards...

My response to this married Match Man went:

I appreciate your taking the time to write your thoughts, and thank you for your compliments. Considering a married man for the reasons you stated to for "happy times" would never be an option -- it would destroy my spirit.

I am happy w who I am and unlike many who stay in loveless marriages, I can't imagine living in perpetual pain as you do. I do not understand it.

Match Man to me:

Thank you, Nancy for your response. I understand your point of view. I would never ever want to hurt you or anyone ....I am not cruel nor am I unfeeling for others especially if I am in a relationship with a woman I admire and greatly respect which is what I or any man would be in a relationship with you.

I am old fashioned too...but I am a responsible man too. You are right, I will be lonely for the rest of my life and I guess I will deal with it. I would love to be with an amazing girl like you...especially you...but you said one thing I never gave thought to....falling in love!! I, at no time, would think a woman would fall in love with me would care in a sincere way for us both in a world we could create forever us and only us.

Now I will be specific because I think you are wise and very understanding and I think telling you may add some insight. I care for my wife and will always take care of her. She gave me three beautiful children whom I love them so very proud of...she did that...gave me a wonderful home and raised my kids ....for that I owe her eternally. What has happened to her is entirely my fault....completely and totally and I accept that responsibility and will not abandon her. We have not be married in that way for 14 years. Most of that time was spent in de-tox, rehab units and away care all because she will not stop drinking and so an alcoholic and drug taker is her life now. !4 years ago she put the bottle to her head and pulled the trigger...leaving me alone, and wanting. Interventions...kids begging...my imploring...all ...will not change her. She will not stop...AA ...also helped but to no avail. Why did she start drinking because her husband worked all the time...traveled all the time, provided the best for her and my kids..I did it for them...and for me cause I liked the feel of success only I let it go too far, I did not see the empty nest syndrome coming...I did not see because I was not looking as I should have. My kids saw is and could not wait to go away to college..they did not tell me ... so I as resigned to being alone and not ever having that warmth again....maybe it's what I deserve and rightly so. But as you say ....would I want to hurt you? No ...never...I've hurt one woman and that's one too many in my lifetime.

Me to Match Man:

There is nothing worse than the suffering and anguish which you are experiencing. I can relate because we all have stories of personal anguish. It is courageous of you to explain your personal story w me. But I have to say that with all that happened as a result of you being an absentee father, I am saddened how you remain locked in your present state of pain.

Not wishing to be a therapist, however, I have found from my own experience that it is best to make the effort to put things to rest for one's own sanity! Right or wrong considering your past actions, you might consider making a break from your current state. Your so called "little bit of warmth, love, and to dance again" – the things you sorely seek will most likely never be. Then you can never be whole and realize that there is life after pain, suffering, and tragedy. It's all in you and the choices you make, and to be brave in making them happen.

Guilt is a terrible thing to be allowed to hold you back.

Match Man to me:

So, I will rethink what You have said...I have no right to be on here....maybe a girl could love me as you suggest ....then maybe not ...I don't know...you have given me pause...so I will say this - you are amazing and I admire you so much and can only say that the man who is worthy of you would be so very lucky indeed.... I wish it could be me...

Thank you Nancy....I will remember you always!....For the record I never would have made demands on you or your time...my hope was to have company of a woman like you once a month is all I wanted ...to feel alive again...to dance again...to feel your scent as we danced ...yes I am a hopeless romantic!!

Me to Match Man:

Again, a married man such as you – no matter how good and decent you are - would kill my spirit. Would that make you dance and be happy?

Match Man to me:

Well said..... with admiration... sincerely...

With that, my adventures with three romantic Match Men came to a closing.

Match Men Who Romance With Poetry

Throughout my two plus years on Match I was impressed by some of the many poems Match Men wrote to me. Here are some of the best:

You raise a spark in my awareness;
A beacon shining through an endless sea;
A mirror catching a pure ray of sunlight;
That shows you what things, that might be;

Another Match Man:
I found a flower opening today
it all happened in the most delightful way
and as it unfurled in all its glory
so was the beginning of a beautiful story
and as I lay my head down to sleep
my head is filled of thoughts so deep
and as I lay here with thoughts of you
I'm hoping in some way you are thinking of me too.
angles on your pillow :-) xo

Another Match Man:
This should hold you...

My roses have begun to bloom
And great each day with crimson red.
They trumpet in an early June
Upon whose sunlight they are fed.
As spring arrives we're born anew
And passions fill both heart and head
Renewing vows as lovers do.
To new adventures we are led.

Finally, this longer one:

*So weary grows the sailor searching, the constant rocking
yet no shore;*
*Though not with fear, and yet a yearning...but dreams of
what was had before;*
*To one's surprise and startle be; when a glimpse of
treasure, cross an endless sea;*
*Does show itself, to value thee, the ocean gone, so
seemingly;*
*To rub one's eyes, to wonder doubt, could such exist when
so far out;*
*My longing might it mocking me, might draw my eyes to
that not be;*
I stand my post and laughing when;
Did that; o might I see again;
*And now again I search near more, with such desire, and in
such chore;*
To beg, that my ears, might hear more;
*For sailors know, the chances be when so far friendly shore
from thee;*
*The chances not to find a soul; amid the wind and oceans
role;*
But like the fresh and morning air;
I'd know such verses, anywhere;
*I turn my ship, my ears might stare; in blunt amazement
finding there;*

And then there are Birthday Poems from Match Men:

Today is your birthday
So I've been told
Despite what some say
You're not really old.

So don't be depressed
Stay home and be lazy.
Go out with your friends
And do something crazy.

Another Match Man:
Happy belated BDay!
I enjoyed your profile on Match.
Hope your birthday was a smash.
I'm sorry I missed it,
but thought I would risk it
and send you a happy birthday email.

Your smile is like a radiant beam
that makes me dream,
if we were together
nothing could be better.

Your bikini in green
is the hottest swimsuit I've seen.
But it's more than the bikini that catches my eye.
Your pretty face and gorgeous, sexy figure make me want
to be your guy!
P.S. - ever make it to Atlanta. I like horses too (as you can
see from my profile).

Lastly, my favorite for making me sooo much younger!

Hey there! Happy 35th Birthday!...
Roses are red
Violets are blue
I met you on match
Happy birthday to you......Timothy

Unrequited Love

Clay was a well rounded man with good looks and charm to match. There was a quality about him that I adored—his special writing talent that brought words and thoughts to their highest meaning. His first emails to me sparked my interest. After just a month of dating this handsome architect from Atlanta, I was in somewhat of a dilemma over why my romantic interest in him was not as strong as his for me. He had the kind of background, manners and easy going personality that many women would consider royal in a man.

Looking back, the first problem was that he was falling for me too quickly. Not only was I suspect but I do not like any kind of pressure, and so I remained on the fence. Clay sensed my distance but he was reluctant to let me slip away. After a while I was beginning to sense that he really cared as opposed to the concept of the chase. Still I felt compelled to maintain my distance. A passionate animal lover, for now I could not imagine trading in my country lifestyle for a city one to be with him. Despite loving the city life with all it's cultural offerings, still, I had to take into account my ownership of two horses and an aging tiny doggie. The big dilemma was that it would be up to me to figure out how to re-locate my animals. The timing was such that I felt more inclined to try to find a mate with my own same passions. The six hours between us did not bode well either. My life here in North Central Florida was well established, and so driving to Atlanta was a choice I declined to make at this time.

Nonetheless, I thought I had given the relationship a fair shake. Initially, the two of us did agree upon taking turns making the six hour drive. The following exchanges from Clay represent the initial magic we have all experienced leading into a new relationship that rings out: *Can't wait to see you!*

Subject: Hello goodvibesonly, I keep coming back....

...to you! There's something about you..I'd love to know more. Although we are not neighbors, I do hope to hear from you soon..!

Subject: There's something tugging at me..

...I can see, we have that beautiful essential element, tugging away..!

And to know for now, it comes from just a few photos and a handful of words.

Thanks for all the good vibes I'm catching, and want to run with..!

Keep-on-keeping in touch,

Subject: I'm so looking forward

...forward to meeting you next week..! There's something so very special about you.

So watch as the moon gets brighter each night, feel free to enjoy the anticipation...wanting to know more about who I am, knowing I'll enjoy all that is you too..!!...want you to write to me too...Clay

Subject: What's in-between Ocala...

...and Atlanta?" she asked, wanting to meet me after Thanksgiving. I just wanted to write since I haven't heard from you in a few days. I know Nancy's book is taking precedent over writing to me and really, that's OK. I'm so impressed with her ! She is motivated and energized with all that and remember: I had promised to keep you in the loop..! So I think I know you well enough to reveal, I'm beginning to feel...what's in-between seems to be our hearts..!

Today I googled Ocala. That's where she is, and that's where I'm going...of course, after Thanksgiving. She likes the idea. I'm excited too, a little nervous yet so ready to explore.

The town has accumulated some pretty awesome nicknames like The Brick City, Kingdom of the Sun, and Horse Capital of the World. There is a place called Silver Springs..clear fresh water river. She wants to go swimming with me if it's warm enough..! I'll pack a swim-suit. Even now with sight-unseen, please wish us luck...OK?

Subject: Warm-Caribbean salt waters!

I'm so sorry I haven't responded until now. Thing is, I've-well..been talking to this wonderful girl the last few days. Nancy. She looks pretty gorgeous and I love hearing her voice. She had me on 'til 11:30 last night..!! I don't think she'll mind if I keep writing. You know I enjoy reading your notes to me, almost as much as talking to her..!! I really want to meet her too...so, stay tuned and I'll write again soon....promise!! Clay

So very talented...in so many ways..! Drinking plenty of water..?

I can hardly wait...? So nice it will be tomorrow... heading south on I-75, when I see Atlanta in the rear-view mirror...wee-hoo...!

After spending several weekends together getting to know one another (Clay loved hiking and cooking) his attraction for me kept on growing but mine did not. Then, when I thought I had met my soul mate in my same town, the next time Clay and I spoke I told him about that. Then there were the two factors making it easier to part ways— the chemistry wasn't strong enough and the distance in miles between us was too great.

In repeated efforts to woo me back, Clay continued text messaging me. Again, he had a special talent for putting words together with a playful twist. He never crossed over the line of good etiquette and he was a true gentleman. Unfortunately, his efforts were unsuccessful. I did feel sadness over this. In his final emails, Clay once again affirmed his love for me including ending his Match membership of more than a year:

There was the before we met. Now it's the after, and with that my perception of the Match women I've met before YOU has shifted...so much. Clay

The look of love, is in your eyes.
A look, your smile can't disguise.
you impress me in all the right ways! Xmas eve Clay

Subject: We met and…...we ascended to Love.

I won't be writing you anymore, I'm OFF-MATCH, and wanted to give you the news on Nancy and I.

Like I said before...I'm so impressed with her! She is motivated and energized, smart and sexy, so beautiful on Bella (I call her La-belle..!), so magnificent standing next to me (especially seeing us in the mirror...Nancy knows what I mean..!)....I feel love through her eyes, and she is strong too...in Mind, Body and Soul. Clay

I think I'm still on…
...this is my last chance. When I sign out I'll never get back on here again. I am the best for you...as you're the best for me, with time I love you more.

So maybe there's a place, somewhere near the end of a "best-seller", in the center of the town square under the brightness of a full moon, at midnight we'll embrace 2010 together..!! Clay

Hope......a beautiful new beginning for US...!!
Smiles, Clay

I'll sign out now......au revoir from here. I can't wait to see you Christmas night...a big present you'll want to unwrap..!! How's my Santa LaBelle...?
I LOVE YOU.......Clay

This IS the last note to you....I Love You..!!! Officially off Match now..!!

Looking back, I would say that my three month relationship with this handsome Match Man may have sprung more out of intrigue and a change of pace.

— CHAPTER ELEVEN —

Match Might Be Boring Without Him and The Hilarious Conch Master

I would never choose to go on a date with this Match Man but he certainly amused me enough to write about him. Using my own words, he came across as, *all blow and no show.* Donning a full-length black robe as his sole garb in his primary photo, Mr. Conch Master seemed to have seen and done it all—stewarding ships as a captain, traveling the world, setting sail from places heard and unheard of, and cleaning up oil spills. All the while he was collecting sea shells. So, who was this guy?

First, I did not find his black robe inviting. Hardly a Hugh Hefner comparable, a quick glance revealed that this man was enormous around the waist and rather scary looking in so much black material. Someone who dressed like that, I thought couldn't be serious about attracting a level-headed woman. Then there was his braggadocio. There had to be a purpose to this and when I received this Match Man's only email his agenda was obvious. Repeatedly referring to himself as the *Conch Master* his mission was in branding himself as some sort of shell king. Out of curiosity I visited his website which he conveniently included in his email. What I found was an entrepreneur trying to sell more varieties of beads and shells than I could ever have imagined. Who would buy such things? Alas, the women of Match.com! Mr. Conch Master had to have figured he had the largest potential female customer base in which to market his shell jewelry. Smart thinking on his part; once his membership fee is paid he has free advertising! I've often wondered how much money he made under the radar of Match.com

His email to me was so amusing that I kept it handy whenever I wanted to have a good laugh. Simply conjuring up an image of him up would accomplish the task. Here was his email to me:

I have lived and worked all over the world. I sailed an 85' Camper and Nicholson catch from Buenos Aires to Perth Australia and then through the Tasmanian straights and on to Sydney, Australia. I lived in Monaco for years and had a 20 meter Palmer and Johnson aluminum hood roller furling in to the mast itself yacht that I sailed all over the Mediterranean and the Baltic for years. I lived in St. Croix for 25 years and had numerous boats and airplanes down there as well.

You are an elegant person I would like to know more about. Please see my website and my Match bio to know more about me! I had an apartment in Monaco while I was working for the Bonaire Oil company in the Persian gulf as a ship's captain for 9 years between the two wars cleaning up all the oil that was dumped into the gulf by So Damn Insane. I worked for two months on and one month off so I had my boat to play with for years in European waters.

Now I have landed in Central Florida and I have started an internet website. Please send me a letter when you have a chance. Cheers and best wishes, Donald

I'm still wondering if he really did all the things he described: living and working all over the world, circling the globe in his boat, living abroad for years and listing various boats and airplanes he had owned. I will never know because, again, I chose not to pursue a date with him. This Conch Master did serve a purpose:

Match might have been boring without him!

— PART FIVE —
Sticky Issues

— CHAPTER TWELVE —

The Age Factor

Did your mother not tell you, it's not nice to lie regarding your age ? You SO beat anyone in their 30's .. :-)
— *A Match Man to me*

It's Just a Number, Guys
Biologically I am younger than all of you!

I used the above expression for my headliner during a period of disappointment and frustration with Match Men. Using my own standards, most of the Match Men I was viewing were less than acceptable to me. The daily evening grind of viewings seemed endless. Some of the ones I responded to and thought might be good prospects would vanish or drop off before making a date. Yet they were the ones who made the initial contact. Was it something I said? My friends would roll their eyes and reply, *That's men.* There were other factors, too, a major one being distance. After exchanging several emails with men from afar and realizing the impracticality of a long-distance relationship, I quickly gave up on them. I am sure many of them were of the same mind.

The age factor will always be a mystery to me. There are those who go after younger women, in particular, the post-45 men who might need an ego boost on a sexual level. Then there is the desire some men have for the older woman for the purpose of having a MILF (sexual) relationship. I have dated men in their mid-twenties and early thirties who are intrigued by a youthful beauty who is much older than they. I am convinced that this concept drives some men quite wild with fantasy especially since the talk on the subject of the cougars (older women looking for younger men) versus kittens (women dating older men) continues. The tide has changed and there are numerous older women who are physically fit, beautiful and sexy who are putting men their age and older to shame.

In the days following Michael Jackson's death, the media disclosed different facets of his life which were explored more in detail than when he was alive. One had to do with his close and rumored romantic interest in Diana Ross who was many years his senior. When the question about the age difference between the two arose during a publicly televised interview, Michael Jackson responded, *How old would you be if you didn't know how old you really are?*

His question spoke volumes in reference to a person's chronological age versus the number. Historically many of us think about age between the sexes this way—older men with younger women. Men have always had a double standard on the subject and they have always had the luxury of being entitled to the younger woman of their choosing. The reverse has not been true for women until fairly recently. Thanks to celebrity couples, particularly those with considerable years between them—most notably Diana Ross, Kim Catrell, Cher, and married for six years, Demi Moore and Ashton Kutscher (recently divorced), the cougar decade is here to stay. More and more it's becoming less an exception to the rule.

Call it what you will, but at various intervals I have changed both my headliner and written profile on Match to reflect my wishes. During one, I emphasized how much I desired youth and fitness in a potential mate, thereby tagging myself as a cougar:

He takes good care of his health and physically he is in line with my own youth and fitness.

I hoped to eliminate very overweight, unhealthy men who, for whatever reasons, paid no attention to their health and fitness. At the same time age became irrelevant to me. On the other side of the coin if an older man was in great shape and health I would have no prejudice in dating him.

Getting back to Michael Jackson's statement, there are many women today who look biologically younger than their true age. Then, why should we women be forced to stick with men closest to our age bracket when they are chronologically *so much older* than us? Then, why should we physically fit and attractive women be stuck with men with unsightly girths, erectile dysfunction, and a host of other health problems stemming from years of poor lifestyle choices? Today, statistics show that one in four men over 50 has ED (erectile dysfunction problems).

The dilemma for many Match women remains: What number should some of us list in our Match profiles if we look ten or more years younger than our real age? Many of both sexes on Match continue to lie on this subject. If you are a beginner to the internet dating scene, you will learn quickly that everyone is drawn like a magnet to the younger age. If they can get away with it (which everyone does), that younger number *will* be falsely listed in their profile.

Lying about one's age is the largest single issue in online dating. As one Match Man pointed out, the standard rationale goes like this:

Making your age younger allows you to be in a broader range of viewers who might wish to date you. Therefore, it is a benign lie for your own good... so we can meet, you know.

The largest disparity in what men put down as their age is in the 50-plus bracket. Men get themselves in trouble when they go too far and state their age more than five years younger. Match Men have told me that same about women they have dated. In the three different periods which I have subscribed to Match.com I have run the entire gamut—initially declaring my true age to listing myself up to five years younger. So, I stand guilty and proudly so in light of receiving numerous emails from Match Men who say:

Hi Goodvibesonly, It's hard to believe you are in your 40's! You look like you are 30 or YOUNGER.

I admit that by the time it comes down to a live date I come clean immediately about my real age. Either way (revealing it before you make a date or not) the age issue can be a potential killer for the start of a relationship. Indeed, it has gone both ways for me. Below are some positively interesting Match Men perspectives on the age subject.

I added you to my "hotlist" a bit ago because I wanted to e-mail you at some point when I had more time. But since you sent your inquiry about age, I'll go ahead and respond. I just figured I should normally write something of substance if I am going to initiate a conversation on here.

As far as looking for someone younger...I actually stated that I wanted someone similar to me...or, indeed, younger...this having the same affect. Lol.

Certainly, there are women who are older than me who have similar youthfulness and energy levels that are similar to mine...and also have the maturity that is often lacking in younger women...In either case...I am looking for the exception...young with maturity...or more seasoned with youthfulness. I guess simply put...someone with whom we are compatible.

_____

Nancy, I winked at you because I like what you wrote, and I think you are attractive. You are only a few years older than me. I have come to realize that women a bit older than me are more mature, focused and know what they want. I think you are a very attractive lady who seems to have a lot to offer.

_____

You have a really nice way of making the 40's look like the new 29...or at least 39! :-) It was fun reading your profile and admiring the beauty in your photos. You improved my day.

———

Subject: NO WAY!! :)

There is no way you are in your 40's!! You look amazing and about 33 years old in your bikinis :) would you like to chat sometime?

———

Subject: Your Age!!!!

There is no way in the world you are in your upper 40's! My name is Harold and I am a former Marine and currently a federal agent. You're one beautiful woman.

And finally:

Subject: *I think there is a mistake!*

Hi Calamity Jane,

I was answering some e-mails to the lost souls searching on Match and decided to do a quick search before I logged off.

I must say, I think they made a mistake and listed your age wrong...

Should be 35, give or take. Either that or they posted your daughter's pictures on your profile.

I always enjoy seeing a woman who takes care of herself physically, as well as mentally...It shows that they have a great deal of self respect.

I personally believe that "Confidence" is what truly makes a woman sexy. You seem to wear it like makeup. Your town is more than a buggy ride from mine.

What a shame. Stay true.

On the other side, there are some men who lose all sense of security with women over this subject. I've experienced it all. One Match Man cancelled a dinner date with me at the eleventh hour after we had talked on the phone a half-dozen times about our common interest in equines. During our final phone conversation, I came clean with him about my real age at two years his senior. Upon asking if he was okay with that, he responded, *No problem.* However after mulling it over for five days he had a change of heart. In a text message sent to me just two hours before we were to meet for dinner he canceled! His text went: *because you lied about your age I would never be able to trust you again and, therefore, cannot go on a date with you.*

Another age related disappointment was with a Match Man who called himself *HorsemanLarry.* By the third telephone conversation, I had already been invited to go horseback riding with him in the Ocala National Forest where he lived. He told me he owned three horses, two of which were rideable. There was one red flag, though—he chose to delay making a dinner date with me until later in the week and didn't offer a reason. My sense was that he might be interested in dating younger women. I was right. When we did finalize our dinner date later in the week this Match Man eventually revealled that he wanted to attend a church singles event. How odd to tell me now, I thought. The reason he eventually disclosed this information to me was because of his grave disappointment in not meeting his younger dream girl! It was then that he questioned my age because he had forgotten what I had listed. Upon disclosing my real age, I added that people always make a huge deal over it. Noting a twinge of discomfort in his voice our conversation began to turn cooler. In an attempt to relieve his uneasiness I asked him if he wished to keep his dinner date with me. By now, I was well prepared to end things.

He wanted to keep the date with his famous last words over the phone went: *I'll talk to you tomorrow.*

Tomorrow arrived and my instincts told me he would not call. They were correct. My cell phone beeped me in the late afternoon with the following tm: *Nancy, I thought about it and I think that we should cancel tonight. I can't get past the lying about the age. My thought is if you lie about that, what else is there? Good luck in your search.*

My first reaction was not to reply and I was relieved not to be spending any more time with someone who was making the age subject a bigger-than-life issue. At the last minute I changed my mind. Right or wrong, as many women do, I just had to get in the last word with this tm:
U appear to be the 1 who lied when you assured me you had no problem with my age. In canceling dinner at the 11th hour u don't have much character or class to say the least.

As a result of my experience with the above two Match Men I have come away with my own thoughts on two types of men who have distinctly different perspectives on the subject of age. The first are those who truly understand the nuances inherent in the age issue. To them age is just a number and chronological age speaks volumes. This one is my kind of man and I would imagine most of us, too! With all of the current anti-aging health, nutritional and cosmetic information available, it can be difficult to tell a person's real age. Then there are those of us who age more gracefully than the rest of the human population. Call it genetics. Add to the mix the subject of etiquette. Haven't women traditionally had the privilege of keeping their ages unpublished? My belief is that if the age a woman lists on Match seems reasonable, men should not make age an issue. Fortunately for women like me these type of men *do not* make it an issue. Then, when a woman admits to her true age on the first date (which she should), a Match Man can make his choice about whether to ask for a second date. End of story!

The second type of Match Man tends to view lying about one's age as a major breach of trust. For these men the age issue comes down to personal prerogative. Someone who is not truthful from the beginning downright scares them. As with the Match Men described above they are thinking, *What else is she lying about?* It makes you wonder about the degree of inflexibility in other areas of these Match Men's lives. Let's take lying. The latest research shows that men on the average tell up to four white lies a day, and on the average twice more than women. No matter how big or small a lie, men (as well as women) take lies one of three ways—as black or white issues or as grey matter. If men are more into the grey you would think that one's age might be a less poignant issue. From my own experiences on this subject men might quiz themselves on this. The skit below shows how age can create that sudden, deleterious effect between two. And, like lightening you both break apart from each other with less than good feelings.

After playing out the above two age dwellers I found myself blown away by the next Match Man who had an even bigger issue going on—little patience.

Impatience Is a Non-virtue!

It's like that daisy thing: Wants me; wants me not; wants me; wants me not...he wants me not!

The Match Man below was so incensed about my lying about my age that the effect (intentional or not), was deflating to my ego. In his communications to me there was only one direction in which he was headed with me: rejection and hurt. This Match Man seemed impatient to say the least. First, I didn't seem to respond to his emails fast enough because I was not on my computer every day. Just before his short fuse erupted, this Match Man suggested I call him after leaving his phone number with me. His email was written Friday during a weekend that I was out of town. Did this man assume that I would bring my computer to the beach? Did he assume I had a smart phone as well? When I opened up his final email to me on a Monday morning, I was stunned at his response. Here's how it all went down.

Match Man to me:

My name is Richard. I think we like some of the same things. We are fit and healthy. You look fantastic, very lovely smile. No kids, Yeah, me either. Would you like to have a conversation to see if we have any chemistry to meet? Thanks

Me to Match Man:

I have an age question. Would u ever go out w a woman who is older than u?

Match Man to me:

Yes I would, Why?
Thank You, Richard

Match Man to me:

Nanci, you never replied, I answered you question about age...Are you telling a fib about your age, lol??????? Richard

Me to Match Man:

If I say yes, would u tell me you can't trust me because I lied a little about my age?
I have been very busy these past 2 days – that's why I didn't get back to you

Match Man to me:
OK, so how old are you, my number is 123-456-7890
Thank You, Richard

Me to Match Man:
Please re-read the 1ˢᵗ part of my profile and see if u can come up w a poem for my birthday...and I'll give you an exact answer. I am a little older than u but biologically very young. By the way, my birthday is this coming Wednesday, Oct. 7. Tell ya what – please write me a birthday wish and you could be my best man! Lol.

Match Man to me:
Subject: Hello
Who do you think you are. First you have already lied about your age, and what you think your special...I don't think so, you have a problem lady

Me to Match Man:
You seem to be angry because I didn't get back to you or call you soon enough. Then you throw the age issue at me. Boo who to you, I say!

This Match Man's rage over my higher age along with his lack of humor may have been intensified by my playfulness. Might I have turned around his final response to me by responding apologetically? I'll never know because booing him came so naturally. Another guess is that I was toying with him during a case of bad timing. Whatever it was there was a definite personality clash. If I had to do it over, might I have taken the higher road in my communications with him? No.

This leads me to required lists men frequently have regarding woman.

— CHAPTER THIRTEEN —

Required Lists... She must have this, that, and that...

I think there are times when men's expectations of what they seek in women are as lofty as the stars. It's not like we can be newly unwrapped from a roll of cellophane to be this ideal woman about which many men fantasize.
— Author

If men might be a bit more lenient when it comes to their required criteria for women, I believe there would be less war between the sexes. For most though, I believe the following holds true: *The female as a potential mate must be near-perfect.* Yet that same criterion for perfection in men from a woman's perspective is more often than not, absent. For many Match Men it goes like this: At the minimum, she has to be a year or two younger than the man, slim but with curves, either with brains for conversation or without brains for less conversation. In many profiles where men list the age range of the women they desire, the number always seems to top out at one to three years short of the man. Further complicating matters, there is the double standard of men lying about their age as much as fifty percent of the time.

How does some of this strict criteria factor in when searching for a mate? It complicates matters to the point that if there *is* a connection between two people, the connection can get lost in some petty feud over some minor physical flaw. That was the case with me and my *Kitty Guy* Match Man who was chock full of judgments—that I was too thin. *Please!*

Let's face it, if someone hints around, or in my case outright tells you that you don't measure up to their required criteria, you're not going to jump up and down with joy and excitement. Instead, you will be thinking that you must come pre-packaged with all of the custom toppings. For a few Match Men, who the woman is *inside* doesn't always cut it.

Here are some interesting Match Men quotes:

She should have some brains, keeping in mind that 90 percent of all men surveyed stated that they would prefer to be more intelligent than their spouses.

Another Match Man:
I think as I get older I become more picky as to what that woman will be like.
I want to complement a woman and her to complement me.
I am looking for a special friend.

Finally, here is the other end of the spectrum from a Match Man who just might have had a string of bad luck in his past with women. The beginning of his profile reads:

Not Looking For Anything Special
Not looking for anything real special as long as you're not a liar or cheater or an alcoholic or a drug addict and not bi-polar or manic and have a job and your own car...And unlike most men I don't care how much money you make or what you do for a living as long as you're not a hooker, stripper, lawyer, politician or a car salesperson...I don't like to spend time in front of the TV except sometimes watching NASCAR...I would rather be working on my house or riding my Motorcycle...I have 3

sons 2 who are in the Army guard and one going Army active...I also have 4 grand kids and 2 cats.

Regarding those universal guy-truths that all women should understand, it might behoove us to pick up a men's magazine from time to time to read about the *50 Things Men Wish You Knew*. After all, men make attempts to understand the female sex, so why shouldn't we try to do the same? The male opinion below (written anonymously) is a great example for what men wish women knew about them.

One important criterion for us is that women should be caring and should have a lot of kindness. Men don't like being berated; it sets their testosterone going so they would see it as a challenge and fight it out. A small challenge is ok, but kicking a man when down is not done. Men love women who are happy and at peace with themselves and are assured about things in their life.

Here's my best story regarding Match Men and their required lists. One particular Match Man who named himself *Kitty guy* (he did not own any cats or profess any love for them) behaved nothing like a pussycat when it came down to the subject of my age and weight. Even though he thought I was a little agey for him (at five years his senior) and too thin, he continued to pursue me. Why? It took several dates with him for me to figure this out.

This Kitty Lover Dashed the Hopes of Blue Eyes and Me

The watercolor painting, *Blue Eyes*, was on display at the entrance of a well known restaurant in the downtown square of Ocala. It is a vibrantly colored painting of a brown horse with blue eyes and yellow mane. There is a handprint on the top of the rump of the horse suggesting a gentle physical connection between human and equine. In the background, the sun is shining with blue skies with five mountain peaks as a majestic backdrop. The artist is an eleven-year-old girl who is a survivor of sexual abuse, domestic violence and parental substance abuse. The exhibit read, *she is quiet, loves her family and cares for animals. When she grows up, she wants to be a policeman or veterinarian.* At the bottom a charitable fundraiser followed:

Our community working together to protect serve and advocate for abused children. Kimberly's Cottage, Thursday August 6, 7 to 10 P.M., Hilton Hotel. Donation $35.

My time with Kitty guy ended abruptly after I noticed this painting upon leaving the restaurant where we dined for lunch. I stopped to view the art. This Match Man gave the small exhibit an unwilling glance as I paused to read the credits. His impatience with my pause was discomforting. I could feel how much he wished the painting had not captured my attention. The behavior of this Match Man proved such a turn-off that I could not wait to get back to my vehicle to leave the square, hoping this would be my last contact with him. Here was a man whom I would eventually characterize as having *nitpicky criteria* for women. We began our date with his bewilderment over my more senior age and by the time the *Blue Eyes* exhibit appeared at the restaurant the following week, the date was in the graveyard.

His name was Carl and he was from Ocala. Carl regretted our fateful ending, professed repeatedly how sorry he was, and then proceeded to give one reason after another for continuing to see me again. He never really understood what went wrong. Not only had I given him all the hints in the world but also he had fatally alienated himself from me with his blasé disinterest in the *Blue Eyes* exhibit. The next part is how the rest of my story with Match Man Carl unfolded.

Chock Full of Judgments

Carl was a forty-six year old real estate broker who was searching for a woman between the ages of forty-five and fifty-two. Times were rough in the real estate market and as a result Carl was not the happiest camper. He was not earning any income and he did not have a lot of control over that. During the first two dates, I found him to be a bit of a crank and like so many others, he constantly whined about the lagging economy.

Searching me out he made the initial email contact. During this time I had listed myself as forty-seven. Carl was seeking a woman in the age range who topped my age by three years. It seemed I fit his criteria even though in truth I was actually a little older. I thought that if he had been on Match awhile, he must have known that both sexes are guilty of listing a younger age for themselves in their profiles. On our first date he brought up the subject of age and how he felt violated when it turned out that some of his past dates confessed to being five-plus years older than what they listed. I answered him agreeing that five-plus years might be a bit high, but noted it depended on the case. At the same time I explained the argument in favor of falsely stating one's age so as not to get bypassed in the search process. Following my statement, I owned up to being several years his senior. Carl responded that he would never have suspected that I was older; nonetheless, he tagged me as a *fibber*. Later, I learned that this fib would set the stage for him to use the age subject against me whenever he was the least bit displeased in the course of dating. As anyone would, I disliked this facet of Carl's temperament and told him so. Specifically, I told him that he made me uncomfortable by emphasizing my age and how I had fibbed about it. Upon announcing to him that perhaps we should end things he abruptly stopped his little tirade in the hope of continuing dating me.

The next thing on his list was my weight. Weighing in at one hundred and four pounds at five foot three inches tall, Carl seriously thought I needed to gain some weight. I was surprised that he shifted the subject to my weight and then having the nerve to tell me to beef up. Annoyed with him for the second time I verbalized my feelings to him. And once again, he immediately stopped passing judgment. His bad habit didn't stop there and on the next date he would start up again about something else. Prior to these episodes Carl became rather stoic. Each time I thought I might end our date (this was the second one), he apologized and made his plea to continue dating. It was clear now that there was an annoying dynamic at play. For obvious reasons I was curious to see how this would play out and in the process find out just where my tolerance threshold was!

The following week, Carl asked me out for a third date, a special visit to the Appleton Museum of Art to view an exhibit on weapons of war. The exhibit was in its last week, so we needed to go as soon as possible. Following the exhibit he invited me to lunch on the downtown square. This gesture seemed a genuine attempt to make up for any discomfort he had caused me earlier. I accepted, even though my expectations were low. However, this time I decided that his desire to make amends would no longer fly well with me. Alas, two hours at a museum would reveal the kind of person my instincts were flagging about Carl—rigid, judgmental, nitpicky and possibly a latent temper lurking. The last one I couldn't be sure about. Nevertheless, I had never been to this museum and I had heard it was very special. Therefore, I decided to go, and the plan was to meet there.

I enjoyed the museum exhibit, but my time with Carl was less enjoyable. He didn't go into any of those earlier described criticisms with me because he was preoccupied with the exhibit. However, there was a chilling moment during the viewings when I stood at one end of an exhibit room and observed him from a distance. My vision of him now, and in the future as an older man was scary. Several moments at different times, and in different halls of the museum, I felt that familiar ring of fear. So I decided to end things following our lunch on the square.

By the time we were finished at the museum it was already mid-afternoon and we were both quite hungry. I suggested dining at Harry's, a landmark restaurant with a New Orleans flavor. It's expensive, but good! Even though Carl invited me to lunch I suggested going Dutch. After all, I would not be seeing him anymore. Without the least bit of objection we entered the restaurant.

A hostess greeted us and led us to a dark table in the back. On the way we passed several empty booths with more light and I mentioned to Carl that I would rather sit in one of those. Just as I was ready to say something to the waitress that very moment he shouted to her in an angry tone, *No, we're not sitting there*, and proceeded to a table of his own choosing. Here was a man who could be flagrantly loud and rude when things were not to his liking. I spoke up and told him that I did not like his undiplomatic approach and was embarrassed. He became silent. I could see in his face that he knew he had erred. Old habits die hard and personalities are difficult to hide. Poor Carl, I thought. Nothing he can do with me seems to go well for him.

Blue Eyes and I Say Good-bye

My unjoyous lunch with Carl above was just the tip of the iceberg in ending our acquaintance. Along with his judgements and my own view of him from afar, it was the *Blue Eyes* charity exhibit which cast the final straw, thus ending our two week sojourn. The juxtaposition of the abused little girl's artwork alongside the lack of compassion Carl represented was unnerving. Still I was so taken by the joyful message of the little girl's artwork that I gestured to Carl once more to take another look. Again, he barely gave the exhibit a glimpse. At that moment I knew that following our departure I would never see him again. He called me one more time and when we spoke, he knew by my flat tone that our brief sojourn together was over.

The simple lesson I learned from my Kitty guy Match Man was that *misery does love company*. Who wants to be around that?

— CHAPTER FOURTEEN —

Rejection is No Fun

The world breaks everyone, and afterward, some are strong at the broken places.

— Ernest Hemingway

Online dating is similar to buying a used car: You don't want to get stuck with clunkers one after the other. In shopping for a vehicle, you view ads and decide which promotions look the best. Yet you can't really decide which car to buy until you go to the showroom and see the vehicle firsthand. Unless you get lucky, you continue passing on them until you find *the one!*

Rejection is not fun. I don't believe anyone in the world likes being passed up when it comes to love and romance. When you have arrived at the point of taking a serious look at a profile on Match and you are interested in a date, understanding each other's timeline is crucial. For instance, less patient Match Men sometimes require immediate action. From my own personal experience, it is wise not to dawdle with these men over the internet. Otherwise you shouldn't risk taking a bite. As they have done to me they will come back to bite you with harsh words. With so many others available to date, it's easy to find excuses to keep on surfing without stopping for a date break. And that can become a fierce habit. That's just the way it goes on internet dating when there are so many possibilities from which to choose.

Surfing and rejection go hand in hand in internet dating. Therefore, get used to it and don't take rejection personally. If you think about it rejection is just like being in sales—a numbers game. Here's what I found out about men and rejection: Few take it well, some take it quietly, and many take it personally. The ones who take it personally sometimes lash out in their emails as a sign of controlling behavior. At the first sign that they were not in control of securing a date right away, they would become verbally abusive. Here's what one stockbroker Match Man had to say following my reply that I didn't think we were all that compatible:

You're such a b...!

Then there was the Match Man who was pursuing me for an entire year. I was upfront with him that he wasn't my type. But typical of men captivated by the chase, he would come back with a different approach thinking that I didn't know what I was talking about and simply needed convincing. Call it the NO means YES thing. The impression he had of me was that of a confused woman who might not be in touch with herself. The first time we dated and I refused one of his physical advances. On the second date (only God knows why I went again!) he presented me with a self-help book. It contained four rules for getting along with people. It was amazing that, without knowing me, he assumed that I was not fulfilling those four written rules. His approach served to make me feel inadequate as a human being because I did not go along with his beliefs. That people can attempt to force their own individual perceptions onto others!

Another Match Man proved how sensitive he was to rejection. Here is his response to my earlier email.

Good to hear from you, Nancy. I didn't change my mind about wanting to meet you, but when you responded, you seemed a bit put out with me, so my enthusiasm was dampened a bit. I didn't want to start out by being on the defensive and trying to provide a lengthy explanation for why we hadn't yet met.

From another Match Man who had a lot of doubt:

This is really not working out. and I don't believe for a second that you are helping a friend. As you noticed I am quite a good judge of character and of people. You are quite obviously juggling men around. I've met your type before and I have wasted enough of my time with you.

There is no need to respond. There is no way you could convince me that you are an honest and trustworthy person.

Another, who did not get a timely reply from me:
Here's a birthday poem to you - Thanks for ignoring me, Nancy!

Finally, the next Match Man proves that there *is* such a thing as normal communication:

Hi Nancy, that sounds great to me. Sorry it took me so long to get back with you. I have been on work travel and away from the computer. I will write you more later. I am just getting home and have lots to do before turning in for the night.

— PART SIX —
Men Who Don't Understand Dating

— CHAPTER FIFTEEN —

Men Who Can't Commit to Live Dates

Who says marriage is a tough enough commitment?

The Fit and Fun Match Man

I am looking for someone that doesn't want to play games, and when contacted, they make it easy to meet, and get to know.

This Match Man was quite the contrary to what he stated. It proved a bit perplexing in sorting this out. In the end, I concluded that this Match Man wanted to kill one bird with two stones. The first had to do with his making a pit-stop halfway between Jacksonville and Clearwater late one night. I lived conveniently half-way in-between. The second one, *I think,* had to do with his wanting to spend a little time with an attractive woman. Many women have experienced *being used* for different reasons at one time or another and you never really know what's going on until you've had time to look back.

Looking at the brighter side, though, I noted that he did commit to a date. I also noted that he deliberately left out some important information so it might be less complicated for him. For instance, he did not commit to dinner that evening even though I had brought it up in earlier communications. It so happened that the timing of our date was exactly around dinnertime. Wouldn't it be natural to dine together if we were getting along and he was a man of convenience? His story went that he was on a return trip from a company headquarters meeting. He also mentioned that he would not have had dinner before our 7 P.M. date.

His name was Scott and on this rare occasion I picked him out. Average looking, we had emailed only briefly before giving him my number. He called right away upon viewing my profile and pictures. Leaving the subject of dinner open I asked if he had plans to have dinner in Ocala. He didn't say. So I knew he was guarded and maybe choosey about women. It turns out he was, and so much so that he would have a difficult time committing to a date. At the time, I was okay with this. We are all coming from strange places during these cyberdating times in our lives. In my usual fashion, though, I gave him the benefit of the doubt.

Then, as if a thunder storm had rolled into town, I almost had to cancel our date. My precious and aging pocket purse dog was not feeling well. This had been an ongoing issue for the past three weeks and I didn't want to leave her for even two hours. I did tell Scott over the phone that I had almost lost her twice during the past several months, and that I was a bit stressed over this. He seemed understanding so if I had to break our date it wasn't going to be a big deal. After all, he made this same trip once a month, so he could always meet me on his next drive through.

At his insistence, we met at a restaurant of my choosing. It made me wonder why it is that men frequently defer to women more often than not when it comes to making a decision on where to meet or what to do? Some men have told me they simply wish to be polite. I believe them. But there is also the other reason: not wanting to make a decision that might turn out badly. At any rate, I chose Mark's Prime Steak House, an upscale restaurant in the historic downtown square of my town. Most men like steak and Scott welcomed my recommendation. He also deferred to me in the selection of wine. I chose a New Zealand Pinot Noir which turned out badly. It had a decidedly sour taste so I asked him how he liked the wine.

He thought that it was sour too, proving he knew something about wine.

Little did I know that evening that Scott had made a pre-meditated decision to have one drink with me and drive home, regardless of how appealing I was. He never chose to mention anything about his plans until he was about to leave. I had been hoping to have dinner with him since we met at 7:00 p.m. and I was starving. When my subtle hint went nowhere I came right out questioning him why he didn't wish to dine together. His responded, *I have an appointment to meet a buddy of mine in Clearwater to look at used Jeep for sale for my daughter.* In wonderment, I asked, *at 10 p.m. at night?* He answered, *Yes, so I'll need to leave here by 8:15 at the latest.* And that was the reason for calling him my *Pit-stop Date.*

That wasn't the end, however. Scott emailed me the next day, perhaps out of guilt? I'll never really know.

Subject: How Was Dinner

Hi, Nancy—how was dinner? Wish I could have stayed for it. Did you have a better day today? Scott

I replied back:

Wasn't that great. I didn't have quite enough money for an entrée because I had switched to a smaller purse for our dinner date and didn't have my credit card with me. It was the tip I was concerned about. But I was really hungry so I had a crab cakes appetizer – way too much for one. Then the place suddenly filled up with couples so I left. Nancy

I did not expect Scott to reply to me after this and he didn't. He did continue to view me from time to time, though. My parting thoughts on this date were that no matter how disappointing, telling the truth is always best because of the consciousness it might raise in another.

The Yin and Yang Match Man Who Preferred Skyping

His headliner read, *If I were in a film, I would be an indie.* In the end, the only memory I had of this Match Man was a 52-year-old, never-married who said he *liked all his five senses equally.* The last part was pretty cool, but the part about not being able to commit to a single date over a long period of time wasn't.

I could not seem to shrug off this guy. Maybe it was his *Yin and Yang* screen name. In a cute fashion, I emailed him at the start that I could be his *yang.* As CEO of an import-export company, he lived and worked half of the year abroad, mostly in China. He told me he was a workaholic trying his best to reform. Placing too much belief in those words, I stuck with him for as long as he dangled the carrot so close. I simply liked what he wrote and was impressed by the brevity of his profile:

I'm appreciative of every day, and wish to spend my time in a meaningful way. I'm very bright, polished and fun. Musical, visual and practical, I like all my five senses equally. My career takes me all over the world, and I travel internationally often. Working and living abroad has taught me to see the world with global views. I prefer those that follow their own path and create their own happiness. Life should be full of pleasure.

This Match Man enlightened me on skyping later in 2008 when most people had never heard of it. Oprah had introduced it to the country on her show. At any rate, we began skyping back and forth between the United States and China. In getting to know him better, I noticed he lacked basic manners. For instance, when he skyped me and I wasn't available, it showed up that he had done so but he never messaged me to tell me when he *was* available. We connected on his terms and if we didn't connect, who knew when we'd connect the next time? My messages went unanswered for a week at a time and it was disappointing. The twelve-hour difference in time zones between us made matters more complicated, too.

In the end, the straw that broke the camel's back was this Match Man's long chain of breaking dates. Plans to visit me in Ocala on three different occasions only to break them at the last minute was discomforting enough, but when he got to three, it was near-death for me. It was going on six months and I was still patiently waiting for this man to commit to a real live date. He spoke about flying into my area three times and three times he dashed my hopes with his busy schedule. This Match Man would continue to go on with this behavior until one day I put a stop to it all. I all but read him the riot act in my final email to him.

You have broken three dates to meet and regarding two, you didn't even have the common courtesy to warn me in advance. And you say I should be patient. I think I have been very patient. Are my plans unimportant? I find your actions rude.

Before emailing that message, I had listed the pros and cons of possibly continuing with *Yin and Yang*. It was obvious that he had a commitment issue, but one of my friends also told me that I should be patient. Looking back, she was dead wrong with this one. I felt that *Ying and Yang* had turned me into a fool. Out of 14 questions below, rating the pros and cons, I found only six positives (if you include learning how to skype). They are represented by asterisks, and the rest negative.

The pros and cons list went like this:

Questions	Yin & Yang Match Man
Is he sensitive to treatment of others?	No, it's all about him
Does he have manners?	No, his work schedule breaks engagements
*Does he watch his diet?	Yes, he's says so and he's slim
*Does he have a nice voice?	Yes
Does he follow thru?	No, *I'll call u tonight.* He doesn't
Is he way too guarded & uncurious?	Yes, & *U ask a lot of personal questions*
Does he speak from the heart?	No, criteria-oriented
*Intelligent?	Yes
Playful?	No, very reserved
*Good conversationalist?	Yes, conversationalist about global stuff
*Well traveled?	Yes, spends ½ yr. abroad
Open-minded?	Open to good-looking women, period
Time for him to Smell the Roses?	Says he's a workaholic attempting to reform
*What did I learn?	How to skype well. LOL

The memory of my *Ying and Yang* Match Man was akin to a pen pal. Added to that, he was a long-termer (more than two years) in the world of cyberdating. His workaholic ways seemed to be his alibi for not keeping a date. From my experience with him I believe that the web was his zone of comfort, existing somewhere between real live dating and not being able to commit to a single date with a woman he claimed to be interested in. As for being pen pals I thought that hiding that desire from one was an *unkindly* thing to do.

The Far-Sighted Ophthalmologist

I have every intention of meeting you, he said more than once. This line went on for several months. This Match Man had more excuses for not getting to first base (defined as a live, in-person, conversational DATE!). His excuses amounted to having a very busy work schedule and residing in another state. Earlier in our communications, I instinctively felt something was *not* going to happen. Nevertheless, I decided, as I usually do, to give him the benefit of the doubt. Again, sorting out the interesteds for a date and those to leave behind is not always easy! Looking back, I believe it was my appealing photos that would reignite this man's interest in me every two weeks or so.

Upon emailing this cute hunk of an eye doctor and asking what his interest was (as someone from out of state), he replied, *I am going to take a quick flight from New Orleans to Orlando, and we can meet for dinner.* It sounded too good to be true, and it was when the weekend he planned didn't pan out. He was the head of his practice and he told me that things suddenly got *crazy-busy* and he was not able to take the weekend off. Then he proceeded to postpone his plans for another two weeks. I forgot about him and looked to other possible Match dates. But he would reappear in my inbox saying, *this time it really would happen.* When another weekend didn't pan out, I lost all interest in him. My friends would always tell me to be patient. Finally I told them that *they* were being stupid, responding, *if a man is interested in meeting a woman he will make the time!* Then I proceeded to tell my friends to quit trying to make me feel better in light of the cyberdating disappointments that were continually staring me in the face.

Busy with other Match Men, I soon forgot about this one. And one day when I found an old email of his (that I had forgotten to delete), as in a coincidence he emailed me again! Apologetically he messaged me with conviction that *it was not over for us. Us?* It may not be over for him, but it was certainly over for me. I deleted him from my contacts so that in a weak moment his cute photos would not tempt me to reconnect. Before doing so I emailed him not to contact me anymore. And he was gone for good.

The larger lesson I learned here is that sometimes patience is not just a virtue, it's a *greater* virtue—pain and suffering, the kind that builds character! LOL.

First, The Lights Must Come Back On

His name was Paul but he told me to call him Peter. Could he be my *Almond Joy* Match Man or more like *Puff, the Magic Dragon.* Although he looked good on paper and in his photos, Peter and Paul proved to be a POOF. Here's what he wrote in his profile:

SORRY I HAVE TO ADD THIS, BUT NO PICS, NO REPLY.

I'm 50 years young, I look 40 and feel 30. I think it's being from the Midwest that has kept me young. I'm very outgoing, spontaneous, with a great sense of humor. My cup is always half full. I have a ton of energy, so I hope you can keep up. I have no baggage and all of my ducks are in a row. Don't worry ladies if you can't cook I can and love to make you your favorite dinner. I'm also a master griller I make killer ribs. I have thousands of jokes and stories, so if you like to laugh I'm the one. I love doing anything outdoors from biking to swimming to sitting by the pool or going to the beach. I'm very much into sports, either watching or doing. I played Rugby for 20 years and retired seven years ago, I miss it very much it was my passion. I'm very loyal with class and high morals and I would expect the same from my partner. I'm also stil one of the only men left with old fashion values, I open doors, pull out chairs and I always pay. I also lov eto entertain. I just built a new house 7 years ago for that purpose. I would like to find someone who enjoys the outdoors, stay's in somewhat of good shape, likes sports, I do travel to watch my favorite teams play. I'm a diehard Cubs and Bears fan. I also hope she would like to travel. I would like someone who can dress up on Friday night for a business dinner and Saturday night put on jeans and a t-shirt and go out and eat wings, oyster's and beer and look great both nights. I get a lot of time off with my job and like to get away for weekends sometimes. I've made a great life for myself and looking to share it with someone. I also just discovered how much fun cruise's can be, I've been on two in the past year, but with a group of friends. So I would love to find someone who enjoys, cruise's also. P.S. extra points for knowledge of Rugby and can make great chocolate chip cookies. Great legs are a plus also.

For Fun: Anything outdoors, I love being outside either boating, sitting by my pool or Golfing. My favorite day is sitting by my pool with that someone special getting a nice tan then later cooking out followed by cuddling on the couch watching a good movie.

My Job: I'm a sales rep for a wholesale company, I love it very much. I've been with the same company for 19 years.

My ethnicity: I was born in Moline Illinois. I'm Italian and German.

Favorite hot spots: I'm not into the bar scene but I do like beach bars. My favorite place to eat is Flemmings in Winter Park (best steak in America). I love anywhere that has a beach. I also love Europe, I played Rugby there and would love to go back and see old friends.

Favorite things: I like sitting by my pool. Since I've retired from Rugby I'v etaken up Golf, it's a lot safer LOL. I love all sports, I'm a diehard Bears and Cubs fan. I also like dining out. I also love to take cruises.

Last read: Chicago Tribune. Read it every day.

Everything was looking good with this Match Man. We sailed smoothly through all of the preliminaries—initial emailing, talking on the phone, and finally setting a date to meet. He was in sales, and his travel covered a large span of territory in Florida and South Georgia. Every two weeks he came through my area. However when it came time to meet, I took a different approach and decided I would travel to his area first. I was overdue for an outing and always enjoyed visiting new places when I was in a place of my own comfort.

Paul loved the new house he had built and had been living in for the past seven years. A self-proclaimed grill master, he planned our first date where he would grill up some good barbeque on his spacious outdoor patio. We later would watch his favorite football team, the Chicago Bears, play in the playoffs. It sounded warm and cozy for a first date, and the word *gentleman* rang in the back of my mind. Everything was going to be cool. Romance was definitely in the air! The day before our date, we both agreed to meet at his house at 5 P.M. It was an hour's drive to get there and I would leave when the game ended.

The next day I called him at 3 P.M. to tell him I would be leaving in 45 minutes. Suddenly as fast as Jack descended down the bean stalk he said he had to cancel our date. (Would he have called me as I made my way out my door?) Before I could ask that question, he told me just why.

When he had arrived home the night before, he was unable to get some outdoor lights to work. He said he had a hard time sleeping because of trying to figure out what was wrong. He said he had been working all morning both inside and outside trying to fix the lights. No luck. In an attempt to be courteous, I agreed about how frustrating things can be when there is no logical explanation for something that doesn't work. I suggested he might want to take a break from that frustration and enjoy the rest of his day since it was Sunday and it would be difficult to get an electrician to come to his house to fix the lights before Monday.

To my amazement, he had already arranged for an electrician to make a call to his house in the next couple of hours. He couldn't bear to wait until Monday, despite the fact he would be home that day. The electrician was not a friend so I assumed Paul was paying an expensive rate for the call to his house. I asked him if he planned on calling me. He said he was just going to do that when I called him. How convenient was that!

It was amazing how this Match Man was so obsessed with his broken outdoor lights. I joked to him about how I thought his preoccupation with his lights was a bit on the stranger side. He answered to that along the lines of not being able to proceed with a date unless the lights worked. Here was another Match Man who looked so good on paper, calling himself a *gentleman* and one who had no apology for canceling our date. Instead his last communications were that we wouldn't be able to get together for another two weeks because he'd be traveling until then.

My final communication with him went:

I'm not sure I understand how not having a few of your lights working would cause the cancellation of our date. Wouldn't candlelight be much more romantic?

And he responded: *whatever.*

The lesson I learned was that flexibility and compromise in a potential relationship are important to have and if you don't see them early, beware!

Too Busy to Keep His Date

This next Match Man invited me to attend a live rock concert at the Hard Rock Hotel in Orlando. So excited I was by the lure of this invitation that I wasn't seeing the situation for what it really was. I do know that, in the end this salesman let me down royally.

Call it prejudicial, but I have this thing about salesmen. First you can't trust much of what they say. They work their pitch on you but after a while it wears off and you begin to see it for what it really is: just trying to sell you something you probably don't need or really want. Second, they do the same pitch thing on a personal level, only this time it is an attempt to generate major interest in them. This was the case with my next Match Man.

His name was Ted and he was a successful insurance salesman in a small Florida town. He had worked in the field most of his life. Over the years, Ted became involved in town government and politics. This combination added to his financial success in business. Another benefit of his involvement in politics was that Ted made many contacts which gave him high visibility within his town. A successful run for city councilman quickly put him inside the town's power base. However, Ted had another side interest—the world of rock and roll music where he produced and booked live concerts.

During our first few conversations, Ted told me he knew three members of the ACDC band who had a vacation spread near his town. He said his live-concert hobby eventually turned into a side business. I thought it was pretty neat to accept a date with an interesting guy like this. What made him more appealing was that we were both alumni from the same prep school but from different graduating classes. I felt an instant camaraderie with him and the trust level was equally comfortable.

The dilemma was in finding a way to meet. He lived four hours away and he had a busy schedule. Shortly after, I found out that he had another job making him even busier—working part-time as an arbitrator even though he did not have a law degree. Wearing four different hats, Ted still seemed determined to find a way for us to finally meet on a date. He mentioned he was looking for time off and had rented a beach house on the West coast of Florida for the entire month of July. Upon inviting me, he made it a point to tell me that there were separate rooms. It was early June when we first connected on Match and July was just two weeks away. Mention of the beach house was a tempting offer but certainly not for a first date. Ted must have sensed my caution, because suddenly out of the blue he came up with an exciting opportunity which would make it easier for us to meet: a VIP invitation to a live Warrant Band concert. The concert was just a week away. The band would be playing at the Hard Rock Hotel in Orlando at the end of June. I accepted the invitation whole heartedly and our concert date was a go. There was one said he was going out of town on business and asked if I would help by calling the hotel for room rate information. He did not say anything about staying in separate rooms and when I inquired he obliged to that. Our concert date was set and I was on cloud nine bragging to all of my friends. Ted was definitely the man of the moment. He was happy that I was so excited adding that we could go backstage and meet the band members after the concert was over.

I called the hotel and passed on the rates to Ted. There were no discounts at the time and the hotel rates were unusually high for summertime. I left the information on his voicemail Tuesday and eagerly waited for him to get back to me. The concert was Saturday night. He called me two days later to say that the rates were too high and that he would come up with another plan. I was feeling a bit discouraged because it took him two days to reply back to me which left two days before the concert. Nevertheless, I remained hopeful that I would be attending.

Late on Wednesday morning a voicemail was beeping on my cell. It was Ted:

Hey Nancy, it's Ted. It's about 11 o'clock on Wednesday. Sorry I haven't gotten back to you sooner but I've been running, running, and running, morn, noon, and night...just ducking from one meeting to another. I have had no time to look for anything now. So, I don't know what we're going to do about meeting or what because I've fallen behind in everything I have to do. I've been out of town and it looks like I'm not going to be able to get out of town now. It looks like Friday would be the best day because it looks like Saturday I have to go visit at a local hospital...a children's hospital and that's Saturday at noon....

So I think the best thing to do would be to meet on Friday. If you like, you could come all the way down here or I could meet you, uh, uh, halfway, maybe halfway up around Palm Beach, if you like. Call me...you can reach me on my cell, and so, if you don't get it it's because I'm going into a meeting. Thanks. Bye.

My disappointment over missing the concert was one thing, but my disappointment with Match Man Ted was all out disconcerting!

— CHAPTER SIXTEEN —

Men Who Are Hard to Communicate With and the Helpful Carpenter

From time to time, I would use my small circle of girlfriends to sound off with about the Match Men I was dating. I found it helpful to hear from them that all important perspective; especially since I was the involved participant. One thing I really appreciated about talking to the girls was that they always initially gave a man the benefit of the doubt. The friends that they were, though, they would come to my staunch defense upon hearing about any improprieties men presented. You can imagine the things these girls said when they were not impressed with some of the men I dated. My *Helpful Carpenter* Match Man was one of the unluckier men I reviewed with the group. One friend of mine penned him something that I would be too embarrassed to say. Another, knowing that this Match Man was just out for one thing, gave him the denigrating name, *the ignorant wrench twister*!

Men who lack communication skills leave women in doubt. We just don't know the *real reason* why he's not talking. This one was awkward and had difficulty being honest. Call it shyness, playing it close to the vest, being secretive, or simply not communicating well with people, this is a difficult one. Nonetheless, I found out quickly that this silent carpenter wanted one thing that he couldn't ask for on the first date, *sex*.

Here is what Mr. Carpenter emailed me:

Good Morning Nancy
Would you or do you have time to chat this morning?

Me to Match Man:
Yes. I am on my way out to some land I own to do fence repairs - don't laugh. Horse stuff.

Match Man to me:
Yes, I'm sure it would be a great pleasure to meet you, so anytime would be great.

Me to Match Man:
Hi, leave your no. and you just might hear from me.

His name was Murphy and he had a soft-spoken and pleasant tone to his voice that went well with his somewhat killer looks. *Too good to be true*, I thought. He looked ten years under 54, took good care of himself, was on a regular fitness program and still looked like a young hunk. Like many others before him, he insisted I make the decision where to meet. Sometimes I think men just don't want to make the simplest decisions. This had nothing to do with the subject of politeness. We met at a diner for breakfast and we both ordered pancakes. What a nice way to start the day, being in the mood for the same food. If things could get better, they did. We talked to each other fairly easily, and he elected to exchange information about himself in a way that made me comfortable right away. Little did I know, though, that following breakfast all informational exchanges would come to a halt and the games would begin. The process was gradual but deliberate.

Below is a capsule description of Murphy. One thing stood out in his written profile: He was retired and had time to do just about anything he wanted.

I'm not your average guy, in no way do I look or act like a man in his 50's. I stay active, doing too many things to list. Being retired gives me the opportunity to travel at anytime. I've built just about everything with these hands and still enjoy helping out on a project. My perfect match would also be active and enjoy at least some physical activities. For fun: Staying active is a must for me, anything from working out and bicycling to riding the Harleys and traveling. I've been fortunate to be able to retire early which enables me to do many things. I've been blessed with many talents.

At breakfast, Murphy told me he enjoyed being a builder. This was music to my ears because I was in the middle of a construction project myself: fixing horse fencing where my horse was pastured. Thinking he would appreciate a hands-on girl, I suggested we take a ride several miles up the road from the restaurant to see where my pastureland was located. He agreed. When we arrived, he looked around the run-in shed area, which provides shelter for horses and noticed that a corner beam was cracked and bent outward. The damage to the beam had just occurred in the past twenty four hours. Panicking, I asked him how much of a project it would be to fix. He said it wasn't that big of a deal and he quickly offered to fix it for me. I insisted on paying him, but he resisted and replied, *You can give me a good hug and a kiss.* And the games would begin. From that point on, he began talking in sexual overtones such as mention of how he enjoyed watching me run down the field to open a gate to another pasture where the horses were grazing. Deciding not to ask for his help we then parted.

The following morning, I became increasingly concerned about the broken beam thinking it might be structurally unsafe. The sooner it was fixed, the better. There were two options to consider: I could hire someone and wait my turn, or, I could call Murphy and find out whether he would be true to his word. If I waited there was the possibility that the building might begin to fall and suffer more damage. Instinctively, I knew Murphy would probably be true to his word to fix it. I was sure that he would continue to try to get closer to me, too. Disregarding the latter, I called him. He arrived at my land an hour later even though he had a scheduled job that afternoon. Talk about rescuing a damsel in distress when there's an agenda at hand!

When Murphy arrived he seemed like a different man. We drove together to get some supplies to fix the beam and the little he actually said were more of sexual overtones. For instance, if I asked him a question he'd reply with a wise-ass question. My responses to those silly questions were to ignore them which he did not appreciate in the least. By the time we arrived at my land to fix the beam, I had my helpful carpenter somewhat off guard. I think he might have been thinking he wished he had never volunteered to do the job in the first place. For one, he underestimated me for the cute little girl who could be had. And there was no possibility that he was going to get what he wanted—a roll in the hay. I must say that he did a great repair job on my shed's beam Friday morning. It was a team effort as he advised me how to hold the braces around the beam as he twisted them tighter and tighter to straighten out the crooked break. Here was a Match Man who could appreciate a woman breaking apart steel nails and handing them to him one by one to complete the project. When the project was over and I gave him the obligatory hug he requested, he moved to the kiss. If that wasn't enough after knowing this person for just 24 hours, he asked to go to my house so that he could watch me swim without a bathing suit in my swimming pool! I told him I was NOT willing to oblige. In response, this *looking to trade favors* Match Man was readying himself for a quick departure.

In the aftermath of this Match Man, I took another look at his written profile to see what I might have missed about him. There were no signs other than, he was a MAN.

As harmless and benign as he was I emailed Murphy one more time to see if he might confirm my belief about him:

After u left Sunday morning I read your profile again. Now that I know you a smudge better, I think I know what you were getting at when you said,
I've been blessed with many talents. Ask me about them. Lol

And Murphy responded:

And what do you think that might be?

For me, it was the corner beam of my shed. LOL.

— PART SEVEN —
Men Lol!

— CHAPTER SEVENTEEN —

Men Are Just Too Funny and My "Cheetah" Match Man

An example of comical tactics follows in the story of the Match Man I nicknamed Cheetah Man for his far-out behavior. He fabricated the story in the hope of getting a date with me. It turns out that his father used to hay the glorious thirty-acre field where, to this day, I conduct my walk/run meditation workouts in the quiet of nature. One morning I was out for my morning exercise and he pulled his car over on the only roadside end of the farm field where I was jogging. Even though I was clearly identifiable as a runner in my attire this Match Man waited for me to close in on him before attempting to initiate a conversation with me. Insistent in wanting to know that I was unharmed he asked if I was running from something. I replied, *No, I am jogging*. But that didn't stop him from attempting to carry on a conversation. In fact he made a cautioning comment—that I was unaware of, *THE THINGS* that went on in the field! I replied, *Other than a few coyotes that live in the woods, there are young kids who come during the wee hours of the morning to party and light firecrackers*. I also told him I had permission from the owners to jog here. He was amazed at my general knowledge of what was going on in the area.

If that wasn't the end of our small encounter, he added, *You should carry a pouch*. Thinking his idea was for me to carry a weapon for my own safety I asked what he thought the dangers were in the large field surrounded by wooded tree lines. He responded, *There are coyotes, bobcats...and even a cheetah once came out of the woods*. Before I could respond he rifled through a stack of what looked like one hundred business cards in an attempt to find one of his own to hand to me. As fast as he was writing his name and number on the back of someone else's card, he said he was in the security business and had just taken a test to get into the FBI. He added he had been on Match recently, too. So here I am reading between the lines with this ex-Match Man who seemed to have lost his head in the five minutes he had been parked on the side of the road. Had he not told me of his recently deceased father, I would have thought for sure that he just might be sociopathic. I sensed a deep loneliness about him, too. From that day, I would remember this Match Man as the *Cheetah Match Man* who interrupted my peaceful run in the Ocala countryside. In his rush to impress I often wondered if this man ever questioned the approach he took later.

When men do foolish things, many times they are taken to task for it by women. With my *Cheetah Match Man*, I chose not to become antagonistic with him because I would rather be happily laughing. I always maintain that some humans (both male and female), simply cannot get out of their own way. We have all heard those familiar comments men make about women when there is any kind of fallout between the sexes. *What did I do?* Or, *she became un-glued over nothing!* The misunderstanding between the sexes is never-ending and many times I toss it up to, *Men are just too funny*!

In the end, I'd have to credit the differences between the sexes to the English and Math thing: more men understand numbers better and more women understand English better. As for my Cheetah Man, the rush to impress was all that he understood and wished to accomplish.

My Cat and Mouse Match Man

There's a real bad, bad boy in there screaming to get out.

His name was Kenny and he was a deadly attractive bad boy who knew he possessed the power to attract numerous women. He made it his game to use his bad boy persona as the lure during his email communications. Might he have been the product of a gnarly divorce or some other baggage? It seems this Match Man was more about unloading his wrath in a teasingly subtle manner. For example, he would lead you on with the sweet purrings of a cat in Italian such as, *My bella amore, ciao*. His goal was in getting a sweet response back from me, and then proceed to come and go like a random ghost.

This good looking hunk featured his primary photo shown with his head lying down on a comfy pillow with the peak of a colorful southwestern blanket partially covering him. He was pictured smiling intently with a hint of mischief. His hands were positioned behind his head giving off the air, *I can get away with anything I want.* He exactly that—attempting to game around with me. For a short while I decided to go along with his playful antics ultimately to see where things would go. His profile read:

About My Life and What I'm Looking For

O.K. I gave up golf for tennis. Tennis is much more entertaining and I don't have to wait behind two hacks in a golf cart. I hope you enjoy my profile. I am a stable, emotionally mature autonomous man…looking for the right woman to sweep me off my feet. That being said, I have a full life.

For whatever reasons, Kenny searched me out for a game of cat and mouse. Perhaps my third headliner, *A man with a little bit of swagger, have it?* encouraged him. Before discovering that a game was in play, I admit that I found Kenny's bit of swagger somewhat attractive. Then, following several of his emails, gradually I discovered how enamored he was with HIMSELF! His game was pretending to be interested in a woman. From there, if he got *you* to email *him* back, his game consisted of not responding back until you emailed him a minimum of two times. I discovered this pattern after testing him several times over the course of a month.

Kenny's game got old quickly so I bade him good-bye. To my surprise, his reply was instantaneous. He seemed forlorn that a pretty babe had found him out! As he said good-bye, I asked myself what else it could be but a futile game? Sometimes assumption-making is good for the soul (at least I found it to be in the case of this Mr. Cat and Mouse).

Below are some of the sillier, out-of-the-way things men have emailed me.

The Things Men Say!

Hey I'm heading to mountains this weekend, be standing out by 1-75 and I'll pick you up!!!!!!

Hello. I read your profile and would like to get to know you. If you don't agree after reading mine I will have no choice but to go to the nearest curb and throw myself in front of a speeding BUG (mesquito type I'm not crazy! (LOL) Now you wouldn't want that would you????? :)))))

Frustrated at last; going nowhere? N'es ce pas? The last 2 months, more then 200 woman's contacted me but, Believe me, No one came forward , I never had any chance to met anyone of them ? talk about frustration.

We have a lot in common.

You're simply beautiful! ...and sexy! Come join me sailing and lets make Blue Skies. From, Funtimesarehere

OK, So what is the catch? If something sounds and looks too good to be true, it usually is. You're really a match plant, the black widow escaped mass murderer, you secretly do crossword puzzles at night by flashlight under the covers while eating crackers, or...?" :)

Looking forward to hearing your view and sharing a drink or 2 with you! Tim :)

Ocala—that's the boondocks –damn woman, why you so far away? Mature modeling huh? Do they need a guy? Maybe I could be your cabana boy in a photo shoot? :) Actually, I dated a model/actress—personality disordered though. Nice house, but no one was home. Does horseback riding provide a workout? Serious question thre. I don't think jockeys look too buff! Take it easy.

Hi, Thanks for the e-mail, I think? I thought we share a common interests because I interpreted the picture you painted of the hayfield, smells and views as you being a person at peace with yourself who enjoys and respects nature. Your traits blend well with mine as you can probably see from my profile.

Written profile and email of *Funtimeman* pictured beside the RV he lives in:
Yes I live full time in my recreational vehicle (rv), and have so for the last 7 years...it was my choice and only true women will listen as I explain. New to the area and looking for a good friend. I have a very good job and can support myself with plenty left over for fun. I am open to all kinds of fun. I want to buy a Harley in the fall.

His email: *I am ready...gather your family and friends...let's get married!*

Nice profile! You look great too. Most of the women on here look like they just got out of prison for murdering their husband while on crack...a French fry short of being a Happy Meal. Hope you are doing well. I started this ride wit the somewhat reserved hope that I might meet someone in Savannah. Then, I added 10 miles, then 25, 50, 100,...now 200. I am about to throw the towel in and bag it. However...my search mileage criteria has increased with the size of asses and deplorable women that respond on here. Why is it that all the good looking girls live a ways away and the lab rats seem to be closer. Just a thought. I wonder if it's the same for the girls, or is it a match.com scam that keeps you searching...and paying. My name is Allen

Subject: Avast me proud beauty
ARRGGHHH. How be ye this summer eve me fine young lass?

You are beautiful!!!!!!!!!!!!!!!!!

I am not online anymore and very choosy about who I write to and you are WOW!!!!!!!!!!!

Hi, my name is Rudy, How would you like to have a Starbucks coffee with The Italian Stallion?

Let me take you to Venice!

— CHAPTER EIGHTEEN —

Wild and Crazy, Handsome, Rich and Way Out of Line

Men use a wide range of expressions, from the typical to the obnoxious and the bizarre. My Match Man with the screen name, *rebelmillionaire* indeed was handsome, yet contradictory. For example, his profile description was entirely different from his emails and read:

True to life rebel with pirate DNA. Also a strong Romantic side that loves a beautiful lady to spoil. I love exotic travel and have and extreme lust for life. I workout regular running or free weights. Endless energy for fun. I'm also looking for a true soul mate for long term romance. I'm living a blessed life and I'm looking for my soul mate to share it with. If this is you get ready for the time of your life. Come on be my partner in crime.

Then there was his email which went:
It aint braggin if you can do it
You the one with the swagger, I can feel the heat
Ciao, Albertino

Hmmm…many times I asked myself whether it was the sagging economy that was making men behave so bizarrely. Of course I did *not* reply back!

Ron, the Incessant Sex Texter (I wished I had never given him my phone number!)
This Match Man was in search of a woman for the sole purpose of having phone sex. He used texting because he

didn't want his two daughters to know about his fetish for phone sex during their visitation. This California Match Man reminded me of a scene in the movie, *Valentine's Day* where actress Anne Hathaway takes a side job as a paid phone sex performer to earn extra cash. One key difference was that this guy was using the Match site to get this service at a more nominal monthly charge. Again, I wished I had been better prepared in picking up on him from the start, and more importantly never given him my phone number! With two replies telling him to stop immediately here is how his texts went before they finally *did end* as abruptly as they began:

Feb 1

12:37 pm I admit I am very attracted to you and want to make love to u

4:10 pm No, I want to flyu out and make love to us us out and make love to u all weekend or night! I am serious. I think we are going to have hugh chemistry! So do u want to make love to me then have sex after that

8:27 pm So do u like me as much as I like u

8:38 pm U are exactly the type of sexy woman I am looking for! Older mature and sexy!

8:41 pm Wish I was in a bath tub with u

8:49 pm I want to make love to u asap!!!

9:33 pm Wanna come see me next week

10:59 pm Going to the movies with my neighbor sleep tight and think about me

Feb 2

11:25 am Miss u honey

4:48 am Dreaming about us

Feb 3

11:43 pm Hi my love

1:38 am Love you babe

5:27 pm Do u miss me

Feb 4

2:20 am Falling for u

8:42 pm Miss u can u talk?? Think u will want to be my girlfriend

10:29 pm Sorry babe I have the kids tonight things get hectic at times with two teenage girls! Don't worry I am into big time! In fact I predict y will be my girlfriend soon.

Feb 5

12.18 am Hi babe can u talk now

Feb 6

1:28 am Hi I want u bad u are so hot and sexy and u will be my girlfriend

10:03 am hi babe dreamed about us

7:49 pm Love u

7:53 pm Not right now but later honey. Let's talk tonight or have phone sex

8:02 pm Why your sexy and I dig u cougar

8:49 pm Called u babe

Feb 7

4:46 pm Hope your doing better today

11:37 pm Hi babe

Upon telling this Match Man that I had enough text messages for this book, I received no further texts!

From the man who wouldn't be rejected for two years!
Eight ball????? Snake eyes?????
Patiently waiting

A year later the same Match Man wrote:
Time 4 a reunion
Wow…time has flown by…I've been in town for over 5 years now…how are you? Let's get together soon?
Smiles & Hugs

From the dit dit dit...Stockbroker

What is it about You.........................that I find interesting?

The words, now *and* imagine *in your profile in* caps..............may your dream be there *as I am* here...

I have the canals of Venice *in a beautiful colour painting which will blow you away......................did you* paint it?

In the end, my faith would be continually restored when I would stumble upon an email like this:

What's the matter with the men in your area, are they blind and dead?

What can I say except...again, some Match Men *are* just too funny!

— CHAPTER NINETEEN —

Most Annoying Date

Stone Man with a Boo to match!

My idea of the perfect date is sitting on lawn chairs next to the barn, sharing a nice glass of prune juice with a beautiful woman, and watching the grass grow, while listening to the harmonious sounds of my farm animals. We would neck and hold hands…

— *A Match Man*

He was my third date on Match and his screen name, *Stoneman2Boo.* He proved to be my most annoying date due to his refusal to take *no* for an answer over the course of a year on Match. That year rolled into a second year on Match. He had yet to stop contacting me after more than enough negative responses from me. At the same time, I chose not to block him just to see how far he might go regarding rejection. That is also why he probably persisted. His refusal to back off and go away quietly caused me to find the first paragraph of his profile a turn off rather than the cute humor that he obviously intended. I did go out on three dates with this Match Man. My instincts told me he was harmless. Why I dated him at all had more to do with my being new on the dating scene. Also he resided locally. His effect on me was annoying, like two gears that just don't mesh. He made your average Joe taste like butter cream icing even though this man was college educated and sometimes had a romantic way with words. However the more I got to know him, the less I liked about him. For instance, he didn't seem to have the best control over his lower apparatus. Another thing had to do with him getting testy when he did not get his way. Our acquaintance with one another began and ended rather quickly after three dates. Who *was* this Match Man chasing my tail?

StoneMan2boo (for the name it implies) happened to be a college graduate and he lived close by. He alleged targeting me for two reasons: that I resided locally and because I wasn't a redneck. He also added he didn't date outside of the area because he had neither the time nor the desire to travel. Regarding the redneck thing he said he thought most of the population in my town was just that. My reply, *By the way, I drive a pick-up!*

On our first dinner date, I was curious to know two things right away: the first was why he chose such a caveman screen name. Expecting an offbeat humorous story, I got one with no imagination—*StoneMan* managed a limestone mining quarry. I guess in some odd way that is creative, but hardly interesting! The second had to do with whether he experienced a similar occurrence involving plane travel during sleeping hours. Nearby where we both lived, Actor John Travolta would regularly fly in over our homes at two in the morning in his 707 jet. Without taking note of what I said, *StoneMan* seemed to have one particular preoccupation on this mind. In fact, he went right to verbalizing it—his vision of me—as *the sexiest, most sensual, romantic, and beautiful looking woman he had seen in a long time.* For a first meeting he was clearly overboard. It wasn't as though I was wearing one of those skimpy Brittany Spears pop star outfits. So I quickly concluded that this Match Man was bent on pulling out all the stops to try to get me into bed. His weaknesses, though, were in underestimating me and his inability to maintain control over the smaller of his two heads. He said he had been *doing the Match thing for more than two years.* Was he a match addict, too? I dated him two more times after which I decided to restrict our communications to phone conversations. I never felt he was dangerous and initially I found him interesting. He was just sooo persistent. Whenever he stepped up his pace for the so called chase, I told him to stop acting like a caveman. Again, here was a man who did not take *no* for an answer.

Another annoying tactic *StoneMan* used at our first dinner date was in trying very hard to impress me. A talkative date, he monopolized the conversation by sharing the wisdom he had gained over the last few years since being divorced. His conversation revolved around one particular book he had read, summarizing it as, *The mysteries of life.* He believed all of the answers to life and living were contained in this one book. He brought it to our first dinner date and insisted I take it home to read. He seemed to have this notion that everyone else needed to catch up to *his* level. Tiring of the subject and his long-winded conversation, I interrupted him with a new topic. It threw him off-guard when I asked him how he came to be divorced. He eventually told me his wife left him for another woman. At a loss for words, I politely took the book off the table and said I'd take it home for a look. Looking back, I could have killed myself for accepting that book and giving him the opportunity for another date with me!

During our next communication by phone this Match Man was quick to ask if I had read his book (I had looked it over but not read it). The book fell into the category of self-help and contained inspirational readings. I said I thought it was all good. As in an omen, my *StoneMan* was confident that reading the book would surely transform my life. I didn't really know what transformation he was expecting and he never defined it. I did mention to him that I was on my own spiritual path. He gave my comment as much credence as a passing thought. When he finished talking, I told him that one's interpretations and perception of things varies widely from person to person. More pointedly, I said that just because someone reads your book does not necessarily mean one will automatically become a different person. *StoneMan* seemed so wrapped up in his own world I'm not even sure he heard this! For a moment, I felt like shouting the word, *Boo!*...to break his self-preoccupied trance.

For all of the paradoxes represented by *StoneMan*—a college graduate who wrote an obnoxiously comical opening in his profile and naming himself stone man and then acting like one—his use of poetic prose in his emails revealed a sweeter side. I admit to some fascination with this Match Man. At times, he captured my attention when he emulated the words of a Shakespearean prince in a few of his emails to me. He loved signing off as *Prince Joseph of Florida,* although I think he really preferred king. What man wouldn't? In every one of his emails, he mentioned the princess waiting for his princely kiss that would wake her. Eventually tiring of this, my noticeable disinterest in him became his biggest frustration. His weakness and eventual downfall as a potential friend was impatience. Yet I will confess to my own particular weakness during this stage of dating— reveling in the attention from a man.

One day out of nowhere, *StoneMan* snapped and said nasty things in an email to me. He later regretted saying them and apologized. I forgave him and felt like a saint for doing so. The problem was that *StoneMan* was continually chomping at the bit to get me interested enough to go to bed with him. Perhaps being nice and not sounding off gave him the signal to pursue me romantically with added intensity. Stone Man began sending me email after email. Most of them were jokes which typically circulate around the web. I told him I didn't care to receive them, and reiterated repeatedly that I just wanted to be friends. I didn't hear from him for a period and then he'd be back in my inbox. I created a new hotmail address transferred my important contacts, and no longer checked into my old one. After six months, I did check into my old hotmail to see what was there. Surprisingly, I found nearly two hundred emails (primarily web material) from *StoneMan*! The next time he left a message for me on Match, I told him I was not *ever* going to be interested in him even as a friendly acquaintance. He stopped messaging me for almost a year. Lucky for me, by accident he had lost my phone number and could not contact me.

Every few months *StoneMan* would pop up in my Match inbox. He would leave a polite inquiry that never exceeded a sentence. This was a delicate balancing act he had going on I suspect for fear of being blocked. Annoyed that he hadn't gone away I emailed him once more to tell him to stop all communications. Then, after six months, once again Stone Man attempted to mend relations between us. Once he became so frustrated that he sent a second angry email. Calling him on his rudeness he humbly replied, *What a stupid man I am!* After a second year of sporadic communication from this man, his final email went, *What went wrong between us?*

This Match Man could no more figure out that what went wrong between us just as I was unable to tell him out right how obnoxious I found him.

— CHAPTER TWENTY —

What's Wrong With This Scenario?

The Pilot Who Claimed to Be a Profiler

Someone might ask, *What gives me the right to think I know what a man is thinking?* I don't have that right but I do have the right to put together my best thinking based on a series of communications that come right from the horse's mouth. Therefore, my scenario of what this pilot Match Man might be thinking goes like this:

I've taken her out to lunch twice and given her a ride on my Harley Road King all in one week...so, there's no two ways about it: If I can't have her, I'm just going to get all pissy on her. (And that, he did!)

Here is a series of email exchanges between this Match Man and me.

Me to Match Man:

We just met a week ago and you want to go out a third time before you leave for Europe. You mentioned being anxious that you could lose me by the time you get back. Well, I think we should wait until you return in a couple of weeks. I have been considering going to the beach on Sunday with my friend whose farm you visited at my invitation. Sunday is the only possible day considering her busy schedule. Have a nice trip and we can talk when you get back.

Match Man to me:

This is really not working out. And I don't believe for a second that you are going to the beach with your girlfriend.

As you noticed I am quite a good judge of character and of people. You are quite obviously juggling men around. I've met your type before and I have wasted enough of my time with you. There is no need to respond. There is no way you could convince me that you are an honest and trustworthy person.

Me to Match Man:

Not only have you erred in your profiling, but you are downright rude. Must I give you my friend's cell number so you can ask her about our Sunday plans? I would not have invited you to her farm to watch me work my friend's horse if I had no interest in you. What is my motivation for that?

Also, I take exception to your belief that I am juggling men around. I'm very offended at that. I did tell you that I went out a couple of times with another during our initial communications. I believe that is called honesty.

You will not get very far with a woman with your impatience. Perhaps you have a hidden agenda -- like getting into the sack fast. Or perhaps you have a temper. I believe I made the right choice to be with my friend on Sunday. The beach sure beats being with the likes of you. See ya...

Match Man to me:

The truth hurts, doesn't it? Especially when you get caught in multiple lies. And you did. You know it and I know it. You tried to run your game on me and it didn't work.

Now your acting pissed at me when you should be pissed at yourself for the way you acted. You're a game-player. Apparently since you have been hurt by a manipulator, now it's your turn to try and manipulate people. Guess what, it won't work on me.

You should just come clean and admit what you did. But you won't.

The only lesson I learned with this pilot Match Man is: *Everyone looks good on paper!*

— PART EIGHT —
Put Offs and Come Ons

— CHAPTER TWENTY-ONE —

You Decide

I'm Just an Ordinary Guy

Nobody special, just an ordinary guy, love to fish, play golf, spend time with my horses and cattle. Life is for the living and I've done my share. Looking for that magic that seems to be only for the special few.

— A Match Man

More often than you think, you'll come across men who write at the beginning of their profiles, *I'm just an ordinary guy*. That expression happens to be my biggest turn-off. It's like saying I'll settle for being a common cog in the wheel of life and be happy about it! Like millions of other women, I don't consider myself ordinary. So why then would a statement like that be appealing? Perhaps for those of us who *are* more *ordinary* like-minded, the statement might be better stated: *I'm an ordinary decent guy looking for the same in her.*

Read again at the beginning of the chapter what the Match Man really says. If he's just *nobody special* then how does he expect to find the love he says, *seems to be for the special few?*

On November 23, 2009, American Idol star Susan Boyle sang her favorite childhood song, *I Dreamed a Dream,* in Rockefeller Plaza, New York City. This was her Monday morning television debut where she rocked the hearts of all with her talented voice. As I watched her sing on national TV that morning, the tears were streaming down the faces of the crowd as her music sent chills down their spines. I was right there with all of them.

Before Susan Boyle rose to fame, she had the misfortune of appearing even *less* than ordinary to many. Then, when she showcased her signature voice, instantly she became extraordinary. The question remains, was Susan Boyle ever really ordinary? No. She chose to follow her *passion* and *dream* to become a singing sensation. What set her apart from ordinary others was her courage and tenacity to show the world that she could achieve her dream through her gifted voice. She transformed herself into an extra-ordinary person. As a result of her success she has become more confident and more physically attractive. And, as she has said on national television, *more of a lady*! She proved extraordinary not only for realizing her dreams but also as an inspiration to the millions of Americans watching her singing debut on the plaza that Monday morning.

Using Susan Boyle's example perhaps we (as unique individuals) all might stand back every so often and realize the special attributes we possess and just go for it.

As to my own definition of ordinary:

Choosing not to take on challenges or follow your passion in life, and never attempting to make a difference.

As for extra-ordinary there is a quote I like to live my life by:

One person with passion is greater than ninety-nine who only have an interest.

Out of State Match Men

Hi, just want you to know you're a very sexy and pretty. Lady, we are too far from each other, but sometimes you just need to tell someone they're a 10.

— *A Match Man*

How far away from each other is too far? For some, distance is a deal-breaker when it comes to meeting in person. For others, it represents an opportunity to plan an overnight trip. I have had several Match Men tell me they would be passing through my city and could meet for coffee or lunch. They would email me on such short notice that some of them had already passed through by the time I got t my inbox. Are they trying to kill two birds with one stone similar to, *The Fit and Fun Match Man* in Chapter 15? Yes. This one shot approach is most unappealing because of the ultimatum it confers. Can some of you guys who have taken this approach appreciate what I'm saying here?

However, if the destination is a fun place like Orlando, New Orleans, or Las Vegas, distance *can* potentially turn into a deal maker! One time, I chose to pick up a date at the Orlando International Airport. I was excited at the prospect of spending the afternoon at Universal Studios with one who wished to do the same with me. To my dismay, things did not turn out that way and the date turned deal-breaker! The Match Man was a workaholic who spent much of his time on his cell! I found it both annoying and rude that he never stopped working on our date! When I had had enough of this, I inquired about who it was that he was having such a lengthy conversation with. He responded that it was a buddy of his who lived in Orlando and someone he was trying set up a meeting with. Unfortunately for him, he said it wasn't looking good for later today. Then I turned to the lack of conversation between us, and with guilt he replied, *I'm not that good at relationships.* He didn't make up for his bad manners by reforming on the spot, either. Increasingly curious to know what this Match Man's agenda was we began looking for a place to sit down to talk and eat. One thing had become apparent: his agenda had nothing to do with a sexual nature and he was flying back the same evening.

After fifteen minutes of walking around, we found just one possibility, a place that served only appetizers (it was between lunch and dinner time). We ordered three different appetizers to satisfy our palates. My date was so hungry he realized his favorite one right away and wolfed it all down before I could grab a taste for myself. Wow! Following this date, I added this caveat to my search criteria in my profile: *He must have good manners.*

In parting our separate ways the mind dwelling thought was: I hoped never to hear from him again. I was certain that he sensed my disappointment in him in my telltale expressions. But I did hear from him just a week later. He texted me about a new internet dating website he was creating with a business friend. (The one he had trouble arranging a meeting with that day!) He said, *with your attractive looks we'd like you to submit your profile and photos for the new site and in exchange, we'll give you a free membership.* So much for an agenda! That this Match Man flew to Orlando to meet with his business friend and at the same time solicit me for my personal profile for his new site was indeed a surprise. Feeling used I did not give this Match Man the dignity of a response. My conclusion to this is: the grass is *not* necessarily greener from *out of* state.

Regarding men from out of state—a few expressed a desire to fly me to them (quite the go-getters). Of course, they all fell short of their plans because I just don't know who you really are and I'd like to stay alive!

Just Too Lazy from In-state

During email communications with a Match Man from South Florida, we both discovered we had a mutual friend. I thought this might provide to be an interesting connection. We never did meet because this Match Man (as much as he continued expressing an interest to meet) was just *too lazy* to make the effort. He wanted me to make the four hour drive to South Florida. I was planning a business visit there in three months, but waiting that long seemed ridiculous. We did exchange several emails, and his last went:

Hi, Nancy,

I'd love to meet, probably the best way is when you're in Wellington for a show. That will make it easy for both of us.

As for why I'm on Match, I'm looking for a partner/ companion to live the rest of my life with. I assume that's what we are all looking for, right?

I think as I get older I become more picky as to what that woman will be like, but then again, I know I'm capable of being swept off my feet. So I guess I just have to see what happens. Here's my number: 123-456-7890.

We talked once by phone and it turned out we didn't have much in common. Once again, he reiterated waiting three months to meet, and ditto plus, I chose not to make any such plans.

I concluded that it doesn't make much difference if I dated a Match Man from my own state or one from an adjourning state. What really matters is the eagerness with which each of us has to go on a live date.

— CHAPTER TWENTY-TWO —

Best Come Ons...or Compliments (?)

Entertaining Match Men Quotes

How can u just swan in on here looking like that? A *British Match Man*

Please choose me. I am sweet and cuddly. Gary

Was that you shopping at Sweet Bay store Saturday/

Can you please tell me if my first e-mail was complete. I am curious if it was cut short of print. Kindly, Dan

My cell is 123-4567 call me. I promise I don't bite, unless asked to

You coming to play in the snow with me for the winter???

Good morning gorgeous,
Would you meet me for lunch today? I am in your town

Subject: Meet Bill for coffee today
I meant to tell you that you are gorgeous.

I am contacting you to say good evening. Denny

I've been through the Suez Canal also, and I would love to spend an evening with you, making you laugh, dancing the night away, and kissing you like you have never been kissed before!!!

You're so charming and beautiful, and you resonate femininity. You're adorability factor is off the charts, and your smile, is brighter than the North Star!!! You are a work of wonderment.

You have a look that would for sure "launch a thousand ships."

Contact me, I so want to know you!!!

Drop dead sexy smile!

Hi cutie, I'm in Florida, as we speak, I'm at The Villages, not too far from you, drove my mom down here, and I'm house shopping, send me a text, so we can get together and have some fun. I love flirty beautiful women, and you are beautiful. Let's see if your fun!!

You are beautiful!!!!!!!!!!!!!!!!!!!!!!!!!!!!!!!!

I am not online anymore and very choosy about who I write to and you are WOW!!

Someone got your age wrong, not one day over 35!

You are so pretty...the rain would stop for you

Love to hear from you hope so

Subject: Your attention please Ma'am
I have written you a couple of short notes, but to no avail. I am sure you are attracting thousands of suitors...you are so very pretty :-). Nonetheless, that is certainly no excuse for missing the best one out here. You need to pay attention here Ma'am. I am worthy of you. I will make your heart pound. You will feel safe in my

powerful arms. You will run to me. I am your Lancelot! Kiss—

Okay I agree. You can certainly turn heads. You would certainly turn mine. Regards, James

I just wanted to give you a compliment...you have by far the best body and looks of anyone I have seen that is your very young...How in the world do you do it?? I know I live too far away but I just could not resist sending you this compliment. VERY NICE!!! Best wishes...

The kiss I desire is the one I see in your eyes for me not yet given

*I am a easy going native Floridian. I treat people with respect and dignity. I am considered very thoughtful but can also be forgetful at times. I am looking for a nice woman for friendship, dating and good times. **I am not into heavy intelligent conversation as I deal with that during the work day.** I am interested in someone light and breezy and not looking for a long term commitment at this time.*

*I am looking for a fun, fit, and cute woman. **I do not want to work at a relationship...I simply want a relationship that works naturally.** I am looking for the girl-next-door type.*

Hello, I just got this durn thing to work a little, no picture yet but will figure out shortly. I am 51 also but you are way prettier than I am. I was wondering if you had lived here long as I went to h.s. until 11 grade then had to move to orphanage but moved back long time ago. I also like to dance to roc k mostly but did learnsome 2 step in ark when I went to college a long time ago. I don't know how this site works so I will just send you this and see if we could chatalittle until then or if never again stay pretty and happy……Thomas

— CHAPTER TWENTY-THREE —

My Two Oh Wells—

A Fly by Night Pilot

Based on this story, I wondered if the sagging economy and rising fuel prices might have had something to do with the fewer hours pilots were logging? Lol

My next Match Man was a pilot from Clearwater. Two months had gone by and the dating game was beginning to get mundane. It was time for a change, and a plane ride might just be the antidote for the case of the doldrums.

Lots of pilots hail from Clearwater, Florida. It has been said that some are strange from here. Yet the screen name of this Match Man, *funforalltobehad* was too compelling to resist. Add some excitement to the mix: high flying actor, John Travolta lives two miles up the road from me. His two planes, a Gulfstream and 707 are regulars in the otherwise quiet Ocala skies and the actor routinely flies to Clearwater in the early evenings to attend Scientology.

My Clearwater pilot would make the same route to fly into Ocala for a date with me. I was all set for some flying fun. The thing was, he moved fast, suggesting we take a fly as early as the next day. We had just met on-line two days before!

Pilot Mike's first email to me:
We were matched and i liked your profile and wanted to say hi, Hope you have a great week, Hugs, Mike

<u>Me to Pilot Mike</u>

I am wondering why all of the pilots on match come from Clearwater? I've had a weird experience from one already, and was cautioned by friends to beware. Lol.

Did you know that John Travolta commutes to your town regularly for Scientology?

Would you like to fly into Greystone airport on the first Sunday of next month for a fly-in brunch at Jumbolair where he lives? There are fly-in's the first of every month for brunch, and they are wonderful!.

<u>Pilot Mike to me:</u>

Love to meet you and I am originally from Illinois so you can't judge me for living in Clearwater. Thanks for writing back and giving me a chance. I could rent a small plane, we can talk about it. Hugs Mike

The plan was that Mike would fly in to Ocala International Airport to take me out to lunch. Again, this was fast: after talking with him on the phone just once. He said he would call back in a couple of hours to get organized. During our twenty minute phone conversation I mentioned my two sibling ex-pilots, therefore I was aware of the required list of things before taking off—checking the weather and filing a flight plan. Waiting to hear back from him following our late morning telephone conversation, that time never came. When I called him back his son answered and said his father was outside and he would give him my message. Again, I never heard back!

What happened to this flier Match Man? The weather for flying was picture perfect with blue skies and few clouds high up. Regardless of that, might I have scared him off in my conversation by knowing a little something about flying? Perhaps it was a big fantasy of his to fly into town and scoop me up for a mile high experience. When push came to shove, it seems he didn't have the guts to come clean about something—that perhaps he wasn't pilot at all. I'll never know! No more guessing here.

I got some good laughs for the soul from my friends who raved: *You got stood up high in the sky!* The following day I sent an email to my *funforalltobehad* Match Man and not expecting a reply. An interesting note—by accident I had not removed his picture and screen name from my *Connections* page on the Match site. I discovered later on that he changed his screen name to another catchy phrase and viewed my profile several times over the course of the next few months. What can I say but: *there's such a thing as phantom fun with pilots!*

My next *Oh Well* was even a kinder sort. (Lol)

A Wink from the "kind" Man

I woke up this morning to find a wink from Scott, a Bond man who writes in his profile that he is looking for *a kind person with both shared and new interests*. He wasn't my favorite type of Bond man (you know like my favorite Roger Moore with that wry humor). Instead, he was into paper bonds you never actually see. I'd like to think of a man who works in the bond business as shrewd, savvy, and a bit hard-edged. ...And it is no wonder that he checks off the *$150,000-and-over* income category.

Kind (as a characteristic) doesn't really work for me in the business world of high stakes financial trading. He might be looking for that quality in a woman but what about him? I decided to find out whether he might be equally kind. Like most I must admit the income factor did have a bit of a pull on me. More important, though, this fifty year-old Match Man had a slender athletic body. His primary photo featured him on the beach without his shirt. Some men just love to show off what they've got and he did it rather tastefully. He happened to have a nice chest, great body tone, and just the right amount of hair on his body. I think the hair on his head was a little long, but let's face it: He *did* have hair at age 50! Finally, as much as his photo was a bit fuzzy, he's cute looking.

I emailed him to thank him for the wink. For a moment, I didn't have that squirmy feeling about getting a wink. Here's what I wrote.

Thanks for the wink. I used to think they were corny but I'm beginning to get used to them. I live over 50 miles from Sarasota. Your specs don't go beyond that...hmmm.
But I liked your written profile especially your point about the importance of one's accomplishments in life and what you do with yourself. It seemed genuine. You impress me as someone open to learning from others. I, too, believe that we can never stop learning about ourselves and the world. That's what makes life interesting and challenging, don't you think?

I love the simple country life, having grown up in a rural part of Connecticut. Yet I have traveled some of the world and consider myself fairly sophisticated.

One of my strong traits is honesty. Many have told me that I look 37 but did not think twice about submitting my true age. It's nice to see the same of yourself.

Tell me a little more about your interest in me.
Cheers,
Nancy

He responded.

Hi. Thanks so much for writing; I'm actually much closer than you think. (I have a beach house not far from you.) I have just returned to the States after living and working in Europe for the past 5 years. I returned to structure a bond that will have me commuting between London, Bermuda and Florida for the next few years. You're cute and I'll bet we would find each other kind, interesting and fun. Steven

This Match Man's last sentence repeating his use of the word, *kind* had me thinking again. Was I overanalyzing things, or was it my gut?

My next email asking for some personal information became the demise for further communication between us. I have written similar letters to other men and they have, without hesitation, answered my questions. So what was really going on here? The answer came to me upon reading his last sentence for its literal meaning: *you're cute and I'll bet we would find each other kind, interesting and fun. We are closer than you think.*

Looking back this Match Man's quick reference to his beach house and personal description as *kind* led me to the obvious conclusion that he was looking for sex. He proved it after suddenly dropping off from me after I questioned him further about his specific interest in me. Another *Oh-well-Match Man.* I have heard the expression, *never look a gift horse in the mouth.* Substitute *kind* for *gift,* and that's exactly how this Match Man left me feeling about him—questionable.

Following two *Oh-Wells* in a row, my interest turned to hanging out with a younger group of Match Men. Refreshing and un-jaded by life's long list of baggage some of these younger men can pep you right up. In many respects, they come off as more intelligent, refreshing and fun to be with. Many of them, too, appreciate beauty at any age. How wonderful is that? So I dallied with some of these young hunks via email as a needed boost to my ego. At the same time I was visiting a couple of highly reputable restaurants in my area for happy hour where some of those non-online hunks frequented. While I admit to a short stint of socializing (as opposed to pen paling) on Match it sure felt good during this part of my journey.

There was one thing I did learn about a common thread between the olders and youngers on Match—they both have the equal goal of sex. For example, just as the younger woman, older men syndrome exists so does the cougar one play out with younger men. Here's my experience: I received a wink from a younger, attractive Match Man from Gainesville. George was 37 and he was eager to meet me at his substantial junior age. New to town he said he was looking to meet and make new friends. He was in the process of changing careers and going back to school to become a lawyer. This all made sense except for one thing. How is it that one has a difficult time meeting new people in a university town streaming with young people? Was this guy shy, into the cougar thing, or, simply looking to validate his existence with the likes of ME? Maybe *all of the above.* After noting my only cool response back, he dropped off. I was expecting that… *it was all good to me.*

— PART NINE —
Unmatched Adventures!

— CHAPTER TWENTY-FOUR —

The Player

Getting Down to Sex

No matter how much he was attracted to a woman or how many times he went out with her, he refused to use the words *dating* and *relationship!*

By the time I had met my *player* I had logged into Match for a year and a half. It was time to take a break from cyberdating as I was getting frustrated with the quality of Match Men on the site. There appeared to be many serious prospects but they just weren't for me. Ironically, the more men I dated the more confused I became about what my type was and who was good or bad for me. So, I changed up my approach and decided to go with the flow instead of taking things as seriously as I did in the past. I was beginning to let my instincts down, too. For most of my life, people told me I *was* too serious about the stuff of life, so here was my chance to explore unchartered territory with a new attitude of having some fun. First I would take three months off from Match and pursue traditional routes for meeting men. Following that period I would resume my journey back on the dating site for six more. Then, I would end this most time-consuming online habit whether or not I found my soul mate. I had put in much effort and time with Match Men amounting to many lessons learned from the savory to the unsavory experiences. For now I would let my fate rest with the stars. What would be the meaning to all of this toward the end of my journey? In opting for a more relaxed approach to dating, my next date (not on Match) turned out to be a type we have all experienced at one time or another—*the player.*

If some players of the world knew how much of a

turn-off they represent to women, they just might change their ways. But they don't because their consideration does not extend beyond themselves, and there are enough women to go around who are tolerant of them. At first glance, the scenario of a player is similar to the ending scene in *Gone with the Wind* when Rhett Butler uses harsh words to Scarlett saying that he no longer gives a damn. The difference here is that Rhett *did* care for a very long time because he was so love. It makes you wonder at times just how much women are to blame or men in the fallout of a romance. In the case of my player, he was nothing like Rhett Butler. He wasn't looking for love but he *was* looking for casual sex.

Women are the player's catch and the player is all about the take. Therefore not only do these players sometimes make a bad name for the male sex but I have found that they fall generally into what are commonly named categories: bad boys, users, man whores, self-absorbed, and emotional loners. My player could best be described as the latter. As benign as he was I thought we might become friends due to our mutual interest in horses. Soon after dating him, though, I realized the difficulty of that. Typical of most women my emotions are intertwined with the sexual act, and predicting friendship with this type of man would be like the roll of the dice. A friend means many different things to different people. To the player, I discovered that an integral part of being one means someone to have casual sex with.

In beginning of my relationship with this player, I attempted lowering my expectations more than usual so that I might learn quickly how this player was going to handle me as a prospective candidate. After all, he *was* very interested in me and I began bumping into him frequently in the bar areas of two well established restaurants in my town.

I agreed to meet my player man after my new Russian girlfriend, Sanya encouraged me to go out with him and proceeded to set up a dinner date between the three of us. We met over two dinners and drinks over the course of a month. In that short time I found him to be quite the oddball. The good news, though, was that he posed no danger to a woman because we had mutual acquaintances in town.

His name was Carlo. Strange as it may seem, while he was hot on my trail, Carlo seemed to speak in contradictions. For example, he told me over dinner that he never used the words *date* or *relationship* with a woman. Hmmm...my mind pondered this in struggling to find other substitute words to put to him such as meeting, rendezvous, dalliance, or get together. Of course I came up blank. At the same time he said he relished being genuine friends with women. I had never met anyone like this and my mind began churning with the questions: Is he telling me what I think? And, if all he wanted was sex, why couldn't he just say so? Curious to know more, on the second date this player intimated that he preferred a woman to always make the telephone call (contrary to tradition). Again how strange! Without knowing each other much beyond these two live dates and learning that there were certain words he wasn't fond of in the dictionary Carlo presented an interesting challenge for a girl who was curious to know more.

This ex-jockey turned thoroughbred pin hooker was of Italian descent, and well mannered and with good looks. In the thoroughbred racing business, the definition of pin hooker is one who purchases a young race horse prospect at a sales auction cheaply, later hoping to sell it at a big margin profit. An example of this kind of success is one who buys a horse for $10,000 and has the good fortunate to sell it for upwards of half a million a year later. Done repeatedly, this kind of success puts a one on the map instantly as a top agent in the business. Not everyone can do this, but Carlo did. Like many endeavors in life, timing and luck also play a role. Now in his early 50's, this attractive, wealthy, and taller than an average jockey was a desirable catch…and don't well positioned players know that?

Carlo trained racehorses for his customers with as much success, too. Just how had Carlos become so successful? It turns out he had some help in the beginning involving a female mentor who was already at the top of her game as a bloodstock agent. Attractive and married at the time, she was well established in business. But on a personal level she was suffering some bumps… and voila, she became Carlo's partner teaching him key secrets of the trade in more ways than one! Regarding Carlo's past, fast forward through two marriages, two daughters, and girlfriends in between, to present day. Carlo was now single and intent on remaining so. Without a girl in his life at this particular moment he would attempt to play me as his next conquest. One evening, staring intently into my eyes he said, *I only go out with attractive, confident and hot beauties,* and I was one of them!

Before my second date with Carlo I decided to get references about him from some local people who were the best handicappers regarding *Whose Who* in the horse business. Isn't that what a smart girl does in today's dating world? It turned out his stats were just as I had expected— it depended upon who you talked to. Then there were several women who knew friends of mine that didn't have a positive read. I did keep in mind that some of the information I received was dated, and that people do change. Was Carlo one of them? As I habitually do I decided to give this player man the benefit of the doubt. At the same time, I remained conscious of his strange notion that the word *dinner date* was missing from the dictionary. On our first dinner date I asked Carlo, *What do you call it when a man treats a girl to dinner?* His reply went, *we are out to dinner.* Nonetheless, I decided to have dinner with him again. To some I might be considered playing with sure disappointment. Not me. I was in it both for the challenge and the attraction. Remember, I would take this time in my life to go with the flow and live with the predictable consequences.

Going back to my initial dinner with Carlo, he initially impressed me as a bit cocky and self-righteous. The good news was that the information he so freely volunteered about himself provided the most direct self-disclosure. It's difficult to fault receiving that kind of personal information in this day and age! So, there was Carlos who talked on and on about himself and his seemingly well packaged life as if he knew the answers to most everything. In a nutshell he noted how much he liked living alone (proving himself the emotional loner), and that he didn't want to be in a relationship because of the pressures implied by it. Most important to him were his two daughters who were in their early twenties. His sound bytes about them made him appear responsible and loving as a father. That was more good news. Then Sonya and I found ourselves becoming bored as Carlos continued on about himself without the common courtesy of showing any interest in us. But he was paying our dinner bill so we patiently listened. Perhaps he had gone through a lonely spell lately and needed to talk.

Annoyed by the lack of a two way dinner conversation, the following day I took Sonya to task for introducing me to him. She replied, *It's a free dinner.* So, I knew what her game was with Carlo and I also knew a bit more. He had been interested in her for quite some time, and to the contrary she had no interest in him other than as a friend. Then I shared the rest of my opinion of Carlos as one of arrogance in response to my question, *I think you might like me quite a bit.* His response: *Of course you're hot or you wouldn't be sitting here next to me.* If that were not the end, my friend's response was, *You are not going to marry him so use him for exercise and free dinners.* Stunned by that I was beginning to realize how times had changed since my divorce from a man I had been with for fifteen years.

So what was my plan with Carlo? There didn't seem to be one because we were both in entirely different leagues for sure. My feelings traveled the gamut of not having any interest in going out with Carlo, to eventually going to dinner with him two months later. Unlike my girlfriend, though, I wasn't playing the free dinner card, instead, it was the lonely for companionship one. Like all of us, I'm sure Carlo had his lonely periods, too. Since he wasn't seeing anyone at the time the next question was: would *this* girl end up sleeping with him? It turned out yes, and I had no regrets. It also turned out that on the outside Carlo was everyone's perceived impression of a player. On the inside though, I found him to be more of a loner in need of solitude. Nothing too far out of the ordinary I thought. Therefore, I chose to see Carlo when the opportunity arose. The following journal entries are an account of my three month (call it rendezvous) with Carlo, the player.

Journal Entries

We met at Carrabba's restaurant for a third time, but for the first time without my girlfriend. I had to call her to get his number because remember, Carlo had made it clear that he preferred the woman to call him. At dinner, Carlo was in bewilderment about my more favorable stance toward him. In return he was more attentive to my feelings, and apologized for coming across earlier as cocky and self centered. Our missions were accomplished!

The more closely acquainted Carlo and I became I could tell that he was trying to downplay his attraction to me. At the same time his voice was pleasantly soft spoken and we enjoyed each other's company as well. This change in style reflected a change in my own personal opinion of him. I was mindful that he was probably playing my hand but I didn't seem to care (remember, my instincts were on the back burner). In high spirits from good food, wine and yes, his good company, we finished dinner and proceeded to say our goodbyes outside the restaurant. Without saying anything, Carlo could not hide his romantic interest in me and hinted subtle cues to follow him home. Leaving the ultimate decision to me, I asked Carlo if he wanted me to go home with him. His answer was an obvious yes and so I followed behind in my vehicle to his house. This was the first for me to engage in sex without intimate feelings and with a player no less! How did it leave me? The next day it left me feeling empty without the reciprocal feeling of emotional intimacy. The feeling had more to do with what Carlo said to me upon leaving his house—how much he *enjoyed me!* What an expression which proved to me that he considered his own enjoyment over mine. I asked myself, *could I eventually learn to enjoy this kind of sex?* That was an unquestionable, *No.* Still, the only other option I imagined for myself during this period was living in solitary mode. At the time this was something deeply troublesome if not painful for me.

Reflecting back to this experience, it was clear that I had not yet evolved in becoming a person who cherished aloneness, or learned how to live *with* myself (as opposed to *by* myself). But I had made an important discovery in the aftermath of my experience of having sex without the emotional intimacy—my player helped me to discover what would never be acceptable for me, thus marking the potential for my personal change and spiritual growth. Little did I know that Carlo, the player, had an important purpose in crossing paths with me—that one day I might possibly come to cherish being on my own, not always with a man, and happily so.

I had not heard from Carlo in over a week and then one evening I ran into him as a regular again at Carrabba's. He came into the bar after I had eaten with another friend and with the friendliest of greetings invited me for an after-dinner drink. He happily reiterated how much he enjoyed my company and offered up a surprising proposition: teaching me how to become a successful pin hooker (just like him) in the horse business. Could this proposition have anything to do with having more of a relationship with me? As much as his offer was genuine I was having trouble with our confusing relationship. Remember, according to Carlo there was no romantic relationship and his proposition felt more like a casual partnership in which he called all the shots. Hoping to hear some clarification from him about his plan, it was not forthcoming. As I was about to get up from my seat and leave for home, he offered to buy me another drink. Normally I would not, but on this cool evening the bartender was mixing up some old fashioned Brandy Alexander's for some guests. Appealing as they were, the brandy would be a decidedly sweet ending to an evening with Carlo regardless of anything he said that wasn't in line with my own personal values.

In my own effort to learn more about this man I took the lead in initiating a discussion on the subject of values and morals. Our differing opinions suddenly sparked more of an attraction to our still undefined relationship. Carlo emphasized his honesty with people. To the contrary, I told him for the first time that upon meeting him he came across as a player. He was offended by the bad boy label. Nonetheless, he was enjoying himself tremendously to the point of encouraging me to have another drink. He ordered one before I could refuse, and then made a genuine apology to me after telling him I was not up to more than two drinks ever in one evening. Upon ending the evening, I wondered whether or not I could imagine myself sleeping with him again. I had a definite condition for that—he would have to agree to have more of an interest in my experience!

Ten days went by without a word from him. I still wasn't used to his requirement that I would be the one to initiate the call. I knew that he was away on horse related business for several days and he had told me he'd be back the next week. He surprised me by calling early one evening to see how I was doing. I told him that not hearing from him for so long gave me an uneasy feeling. Then he made an obscure comment about why he hadn't called earlier and then jumped to his plan that evening with the interest of watching a home movie. Did he happen to leave out, *with me?* Again, that was Carlo's way of suggesting my invite to his house. I reminded myself of his preference for the woman taking the lead, and shrugged off how much nicer it would be if he extended the invitation for once. I wasn't used to Carlo's eccentric ways, but I knew the drill and I asked him if he wanted my company this evening to watch the movie together. Of course he replied, *Yes.*

When I arrived at Carlo's house, several things were out of order. The water pressure was down to nothing. I learned that the problem was fire ants which were causing a blockage in some moving parts of his well (a common occurrence in Florida). Then there was the smoke alarm chirping away. I asked him about the annoying sound which he didn't seem to hear or have a clue about it. Then there was a problem getting his TV and DVD player to operate and he was not able to fix it. With the electrical malfunction movie night was off. Having recently moved to his new digs Carlo was not as disappointed as I was and shrugged it off as, *This would happen the first night you come over to watch a movie.* Then he told me that all sorts of problems had been mounting for several months. Sounding off my own disappointment in the evening I responded, *Welcome to being a home owner.* Suddenly the annoying sound of a second alarm chirp broke the silence with such a breach that Carlo turned on the stereo to muffle the noise. It was obvious that Carlo was anything but handy. Without as much as owning a screwdriver, my offer to help was null and void. Then he noted that the electrician was coming the next day. I stayed for a little while and then made a decision to sleep over. Again, there was no pressure from Carlo. Whether it was a night out to dinner, having a romp at his house or dinner out, he preferred that the woman initiate the activity. My newly formed description of him became: *a gentleman, an oddball and a player.*

At the end of the evening, Carlo once again reiterated how comfortable he was living by himself. It was his panacea for having to deal with so many people every day during business hours. Perhaps he was telling the truth but I felt a sense that he might also be reaffirming his desire for bachelorhood so that I would keep my emotions at bay. Finally, he said he'd like to take me to some special restaurants, specifically a Spanish one he thought I would enjoy. At this moment I concluded that he may like me more than he was letting on whether he was in favor of the idea or not.

Following our date a week went by and I did not hear back from Carlo. Once again, I knew the drill. I called him and asked about the status of our relationship in knowing each other. Were we on, or off? He told me how much he enjoyed the evening with me and not much more. His communication skills regarding personal relations were at times as difficult as pulling teeth from a comb. Yet he was very good at talking about other subjects. Was there insecurity lurking on the personal level? Yes. Having known him a while longer, I began expressing myself with him more freely and let him know that a girl likes to hear from time to time that she is appreciated. To my disappointment he criticized that concept. Specifically, he said he thought that women shouldn't need validation. Then without being overly offensive he accused me of being judgmental on this subject. Right or wrong, it seemed Carlo didn't like hearing about things he disagreed with and labeled them as judgmental remarks. How ironic it was that he didn't realize just how judgmental he was!

Oddly enough, I got the sense that Carlo believed everything he said. Likewise, I believe he spoke with honesty about himself and his beliefs. But something about him was lacking in human emotion, and in having consideration for others. The reality was that his outward persona was strictly dominated by his own needs and desires. At the end of the evening, I threw out a challenge to him to call *me* the next time we would meet. After computing that information for just a moment he turned to me and said he would be away on business for three days. A pause followed, I didn't say a word, and my guess was that he wasn't going for my suggestion. Despite the possibility that I might be annoying Carlo by tinkering with his terms I remained certain he wanted to see me again. So, I left things open to see if he would call upon his return.

Monday came and went and I had not heard from him. I patiently waited to see what would happen. By Friday, still nothing. So I texted him and he called me back within a few minutes. Without looking to be suspicious, still, I felt like I was on some sort of list. He had told me more than once that there were no other girls and that he had gone for months without having sex. I saw no reason not to believe him as I came to learn more about his reclusive ways. Then, he texted that he would be leaving for Miami and returning Tuesday. I asked him if he still wanted to see me. He answered in the affirmative and offered an invitation to have dinner with him the night he returned home. That was a first and I happily accepted. Tuesday night arrived. By 6 P.M. there was still no word from him. I texted, *Hey*. He called to say he was really tired and postponed to the following day. I complied with his wish.

The next evening, I had not received a call or text from him. I called him and he replied that he had been with his daughter and lost track of time. Sensing my growing frustration over the past two invitations that went nowhere, he said he had a call but insisted on call me right back. He did, but then he received another call and said there was a horse race he needed to watch and that he would call me back again. Instead, I told him *not* to call me back. If his evening schedule was getting too busy I didn't appreciate feeling like a pot of rice cooking on the burner. But Carlo did return my call fifteen minutes later. I accused him of rudeness. As if to apologize he called himself an *airhead* over the phone, saying he had lost track of time again. Sensing that he might be losing me over this series of events, he suggested that I invite him over to my house for a movie and added, *to have wild sex!* No, I don't think so, I said in a tone that could never be reversed. *Oh, come on,* he replied. Again, I said, *No, you're a turn off, period, and I am not interested.* He responded, *Well, let me know if you are not interested in me because you sound upset.* My response followed, *Yes I am upset because of how you handled things tonite.* It seems Carlo did not like the word *turnoff* one bit as if suddenly becoming testy. I don't remember his exact comments in my haste to get off the phone before hanging up. His parting words were that he didn't take anything I said seriously. With that I said good-bye and my jaunt with my oddball player had come to its own ending.

Despite the disrespect players have in their agendas with women I take full responsibility for my willingness to be a participant with Carlo. In making this point, I have to credit Carlo for two things: from the start, he *was* upfront in communicating a no-strings relationship. His deliberate omission of the words *dating* and *relationship* was an obvious indication of that. His manner of communication though, left something to be desired when it was necessary to read between the lines upon challenging his unilateral terms. But then, many men do just that, they pause or conveniently sidetrack a question when they don't wish to communicate. Second, Carlo *was* interested in being friends with women beyond taking them to bed. After two marriages and two divorces it seems that not even an acknowledged relationship with a beautiful woman would be in the cards for this man. Perhaps in another time this player might come out of his fold. And maybe not ever!

It was time now for me to recharge my batteries and get back to cyberdating for the last leg of my journey on Match.

— CHAPTER TWENTY-FIVE —

The Surgeon Who Fell Hard for Love

Does he move along too slow or too fast for you? Is he old-fashioned, modern, self-righteous, or just set in his ways? That his wife was clearly not his type was evident from a trip to Bed Bath and Beyond. He called their trip there the culmination of their marriage. In the parking lot he showed her a mistake on the receipt and right then and there the marriage was over for both!

After going on numerous dates with Match Men, among other things, I discovered that men have the same overly abundant imaginations that women do. For example, every time I meet one whom I believe is a great prospect and head over heels for me (you might call it love at first sight), ninety nine percent of the time it ends up *just not real*. Why? Let's start with the first date. My best description of the first date between two is similar to actors on a stage. The date starts out great because the actors are great. Such is the case when a man makes it known to me from the start that I am the woman of his dreams. (Oh, please!) From there all bets are on that he'll try his best to make me believe it as much as he does—that I am beautiful, sensual, sexy, and on it goes. Then, swiftly he concocts the notion that we have total compatibility with each other, too. Haven't we heard that overused expression many male cyberdaters use in their emails to women: *We have a lot of things in common.* Or, *we are very much alike.* Come on, as human beings we all possess similar universal attributes.

The second week into dating I discover how different my Match Man was from what I thought initially. Mix in the sex card (you know, the dog in the human suit thing), add a few others, stir the pot and things can unravel and become *not real* in a short period of time. Then we all return to being single.

How do things sometimes fall apart as quickly as they do in beginning relationships? A Match Man quote earlier in this this book jumped to mind: *Didn't you know that all men are imposters for the first two weeks of a relationship?* Most of us *are* guilty of being on our best behavior during the early stages of dating. Later on we discover many truths (likeable and unlikeable) about a person which eventually makes or breaks continuity between two. In the beginning, though, the prevailing rule of law is that past baggage is off-limits. Let's face it, none of us wish to compromise the start of a relationship by dredging up the negatives of the past. For me, the good behavior phase generally lasts one to two weeks, tops. For that duration here's what I am thinking: I don't really know the person beyond their written profile, and my initial impressions upon meeting for the first time are limited to physical appearance, personality, and that little dance of chemistry. The next item on the list is the subject of sex. Could I see myself doing it with him? I have asked men about this and many have informed me that they do not wish to risk the potential of missing out on having good sex with a woman. So they will keep the imposter thing going for as long as possible. Finally, I ask myself, is there a possibility that this man could be bad in bed? Yes, in the same way some women are, and men, you are lying if you say no.

Following the first week of dating here is the method I use to decipher *what's real* and *what's not* about a man. Using more grace than grit I become like a persistent terrier to pry out the information that I am seeking. I will take a situation he gives me about something that happened in his life involving key choices or decisions. Under those circumstances, what would I have done? I get my answers from the way he tells the story, the kind of decision he's made, and the tone of his voice. He might not realize how much scrutiny I am putting him under because he is so focused on telling his story in a way that makes him *look* good. That takes some concentration. Sometimes, I get a sense that he is still reeling from the memories of his divorce or if he's been single all of his life, still unsure of *why now?* I dig further and get more. In the end, I really *can* find out who he is and who he isn't. There's also the possibility that he's so scared of me that he might have run by now, too.

My date with Keith, a retired surgeon, illustrates all of the points above. By the time our relationship ended after two months, things were so off kilter that he might have well been standing on his head. Me, too. In his first email to me Keith gave an unusually lengthy account of himself including a few words about how he might treat a woman:

Hello goodvibesonly,

I live about 30 miles north of you. Let's see—how to sound impressive and worth knowing without being cocky or ridiculous. First, let me address your headline—having swagger. I can tell you without hesitation that I am a man of quality and high ethics/moral standards developed as a result of my southern upbringing and my years as a practicing physician. I believe I have good taste though I have no airs, and being raised by a strict Alabama father, I can assure you I have manners.

I am a general surgeon who practiced in a place of high tastes for 17 years before retiring from clinical practice 3 years ago and moving here to volunteer teach and be closer to family. I've gone from insane 100 hr work weeks to having time to pursue my many interests and in the past several years I have earned 2 personal trainer certificates, a commercial pilot and flight instructors certificates, and learned to play a little guitar. So, I don't think I am lazy nor do I think I am overly gifted, but I am self-motivated and willing to devote myself fully to the task at hand—I guess that gives me a little swagger. I have been divorced from my sons' mother for over 12 years (she remarried 9 years ago to a good guy and we all get along, i.e., I am stable and have my act together) and while I have met many women, I have not been able to find that all-evasive, vague, wonderful chemistry that most of us seek. It's just that I am not willing to have a relationship without it. So, here I am.

I have many interests as outlined in my profile, but there is much more to me than a few paragraphs.

From your particular perspective, I am a fitness fanatic—I work out 6 days a week and I believe I can hold my own with any other 52 yr olds I see at the gym and probably with those significantly younger. I was raised in a rural setting and love all animals, particularly dogs and horses. Haven't met anyone who has or rides a horse for some time, so I haven't rode for years, but I would like to. Having been around a while, I know how to treat people and how to make a woman feel like she is uber-important and special. Being a surgeon I was forced to learn to stay calm in crises and that has carried over into my everyday life—it takes a lot to push my buttons. I have no control issues, but I do believe in commitment and monogamy. I am biased, but my sons are great. They live with their mother and step-father and even when with me, they like to hang out with friends. They are always giving me both grief and pointers about women and as teenagers who now understand my situation, there is nothing they would like better for me than to see me happy with someone. Anyway, I have babbled enough—I think you get the idea. I think we have some things we could offer each other—I can say this, if the right woman does come along I don't think she'll be disappointed in me or in how she is respected and treated by me.

Look me over and let me know what you think. Would really like to hear from you.

(PS You are obviously in great shape and so I don't think you'll mind me telling you that I was voted best butt in my OR for 13 years in a row by the OR and Recovery Room nurses—a dubious honor to be sure but I am giving you my best shot here)—Take care!

Me to Match Man:

The length of your email certainly deserves a reply.

While I have yet to determine what it will take for someone to capture my heart and soul, I am open to dating a select few—call me choosey.

I'm open to meeting you based on what you say. If you would like to call I will be available after the weekend.

Match Man to me:

Thanks for your reply. I am very pleased that you are willing to talk with me and I look forward to our conversation. I will call you after the weekend. My number is 123-456-7890 so that you may recognize it when I call. I hope the weekend is good to you!

Me to Match Man:

Enjoyed our online chat and look forward to your call.

Match Man to me:

I was halfway through a text message to you telling you how much I enjoyed talking to you last night online when my blackberry displayed your message. A nice surprise! Have a great evening and I will call you tomorrow.

There were several things in Keith's profile which I felt were not matching well for me but I was willing to let them go because they were not overly significant. First, he was a very tall six feet three inches. Standing at a petite five foot three I preferred men not over six feet. Second, he did not come off even close to this girl's dream—an exciting, fun, modern day Errol-Flynn type. As a girl with lots of personality I was hoping he would not be boring. Third, in his profile he never described anything about the kind of woman he was seeking, not even a hint about her physical attributes. Don't we all have some visual of our potential mate? Fourth, he said he loved dogs and horses (after knowing I owned them) yet he could not claim personal responsibility for any animals in his entire life. That could pose a problem because of the serious role of responsibility I take on for my animals. From my experience I have found that people who are not animal lovers are generally not that understanding of those who are. Would he be? Finally, he claimed to work out in the gym six days a week and added to that, swam laps most days. A physical fitness buff myself, that amount of exercise and regimen seemed off the charts for a retired doctor. In determining if all of this was true I decided to give this Match Man a fair shot and accepted a date with him.

Upon meeting him for dinner, my first impressions zeroed in on his conservative values and soft spoken voice. In describing himself, he used *honorable* more than once. I found his laid back personality interesting for someone who had experienced a lifetime of adrenaline rushes saving lives as a surgeon. But I learned later, that is normal for surgeons. Then there was his gentlemanly way of telling me how beautiful I was when I least expected it. It was all good. So, why at the end of my first dinner date did I feel not much as a stirring inside? It seems Keith lacked charisma, a trait I happen to relish in men. Still, there were too many good things to like about this self-proclaimed *southern gentleman* so I was willing to forgo the enticement that comes with being a charmer.

Following our first date, we never exchanged emails on Match again and went right to seeing each other for our next date. Keith emphasized that he was trying to get off of Match ASAP, likening it to some kind of drug addiction while he remained single. In his haste to land a woman, I felt I was looking too good to him too soon. During one of our conversations he related some terrible experiences he had with Match Women. The big one for him had to do with a Match date physically weighing substantially heavier than that shown in her Match photo (the other one is money scamming). In comparing stories I related the same back about men. When I asked for an example, he replied that having sex too early in the dating process was detrimental to forging a real relationship. Were those the kinds of women he was meeting previous to me? In maintaining his guard this doctor resisted elaborating on any of his recent experiences with Match Women.

For fifteen years this surgeon spent one hundred hour work weeks saving lives. He said his marriage suffered irreparably for those around-the-clock hours. One day at age thirty-six his wife asked him for a divorce. Devastated over the breakup of his family he said he eventually came to shoulder the blame for being absent for all of those years. Two years following his divorce, he told me that his ex-wife happily remarried a man seventeen years her senior. By the tone of his voice it was easy to tell how devastated Keith remained to this day over the divorce. Several times on our dates he mentioned how happily re-married his wife was and that he was having trouble coming to terms with remaining single for the past twelve years. As he talked on I concluded that Keith was the southern version of a gentleman that many southern women might just find appealing. As a New Englander, I wasn't quite sure about all of this. But he was kind, seemed to have respect for women and appeared the *honorable* man he called himself. So why wasn't I excited over this Match

Man? More important, what was the other side of the story behind the failure of his marriage? I had to know.

With continued persistence I began asking more questions until he made reference to a story involving a Bed, Bath and Beyond store located where he lived. I had the feeling that there was something about this story which had to do with his divorce. Wishing to sidetrack the story, Keith jumped to what was his one and only important conclusion about the demise of his marriage, saying: *We were just two different people who never got along.* I asked, *if you knew that then why do you think you got married in the first place?* Just as others do not recognize the incompatibilities in their marriages for years, I surmised that Keith was one of those who realized it too late. Finally, as if to put my question to rest he came out with the full version of this unusual story which summarized it all:

We went to Bed Bath and Beyond to buy a bunch of things for the house. After paying for the items we left the store. Outside in the parking lot, my wife looked at the receipt and said, Ah ha! We didn't get charged for one of the shoe racks. We've been cheated on so many things in the past that it's time we got something back. Keith said he responded, *we have to go back in there and tell them about this mistake for three reasons: First, because we agreed on a price for the items we purchased, second, we got these things for such a discounted price, and third, it's the right thing to do.*

Against his wife's wishes he went back into the store, alone with receipt in hand and told the manager that the cashier had made a mistake. He said the manager was so taken aback that a customer would come back to make good on a mistake that he gave him a fifteen dollar gift certificate for a future purchase.

I asked Keith what the sale price was of the uncharged shoe rack. He said it was twenty five dollars but the receipt showed twenty. I thought, *just five dollars!...can this be real?* Visualizing the two of them fiercely fighting in a hot Florida parking lot over the pettiness of a five dollar mistake, it was easy for me to side with his wife on this.

What really bothered me about this obsessively minded Match Man was that he wrongly assumed that I was on exactly the same page he was. When I told him of my disappointment for not considering my opinion he suddenly realized his folly of making a false assumption about me. Still without a clue, he finally asked me where I stood on the matter. I replied, *Somewhere in the middle, and if I were already half way home there's no way I would have turned around and driven back to the store.* I added, *The price of the shoe rack was too petty to go back for, even if I was still in the parking lot.* Upon hearing this there was the pause of silence. Meanwhile, I was thinking about how a small mistake made by a store could signal the ending of a marriage. Obviously, there were other problems in Keith's marriage that had led up to this final straw. Then I offered my own opinion that he might have behaved self-righteously knowing where his wife stood and how alienated she would become. Knowing full well that my opinion might not be the diplomatic thing to say, I really couldn't help myself on this one. However, Keith appeared to take what I said in good stead and we moved beyond the *Bed, Bath and Beyond* matter and continued dating. His show of respect for my opinions was important to me and I took that as a sign of listening in the attempt to understand one. A short time later Keith told me, *I want to learn more about you because you are so important to me.* I liked that but I was unaware of an impending road bump related to his brother's wedding. I was hoping to be invited as his guest but Keith said he would be going solo.

I knew about the wedding from the first day I met Keith because he talked about it with much frequency. Without saying anything I wondered why he didn't wish to extend an invitation to me. A month later, when our relationship had become more intimate, I decided to ask him if I would be able to accompany him. He stood his ground with his initial decision even though he poked fun about it. I didn't joke back because it felt odd that he had been telling me how much he wanted me to meet his sons. Also, I made it known to Keith that I liked dressing up on occasion and hoped he might change his mind. Finally, I asked him directly what the big deal was. Was it a hang-up of his? He said it wasn't but offered no further comment other than it was a small family wedding with few guests. Could *not* going to his brother's wedding be the demise of our relationship? Better yet was this our relationship's version of Act 11 of Bed, Bath and Beyond? For the time being I made a decision to leave the issue alone. Whatever Keith's reason was for not inviting me to his brother's wedding was a bit of a mystery. The question I was asking myself was: *How is it that men have such difficulty connecting the dots on a line when it comes to the opposite sex?* If things were starting to get uncomfortable there was a third act to come—the Hepatitis B scare which by anyone's standards would prove to be the sure demise of our relationship.

The Hepatitis B Scare
Don't Complain; Never Explain!

That expression was embroidered into a small, rectangular needlepoint pillow which lay on a side couch in my grandmother's living room. It seemed eons ago during which time the needlepoint craze took off in millions of American homes. As a young child, that pillow stared me in the face when I visited her at her house. I asked myself what it meant. For the life of me, I could never figure it out. It bothered me that every time I visited and saw the pillow, my child's mind came up empty. I was too shy to ask because there was something about the expression that seemed bigger than life and it intimidated me. Each time I saw it I would tell myself, *Next time I'll get it...next time.* Yet all of the *next times* passed by. My grandmother eventually passed away, and the pillow disappeared along with her. Never did I realize that decades later, on one nerve-wracking day, *thinking that I might be infected with a lifelong liver disease*, would the words of that pillow rise out of the recesses of my childhood memories to haunt me. So suddenly their meaning would come to life. And it was this retired surgeon Match Man who would raise those words out of my subconscious.

The meaning of, *Don't complain, Never explain!* dawned on me in the aftermath of a three-day debacle in which I thought Keith had infected me with hepatitis B. I had just come home from a wonderful weekend swimming in the ocean at Daytona Beach with my girlfriend. On Monday, after comparing notes, both my girlfriend and I were feeling under the weather. We concluded that it was either a bug we were fending off, or a simple case of dehydration. I decided to call my doctor friend but was unsuccessful in reachng him. Then, he returned my call very late that evening—well after 10 PM. By that time, I was really feeling under the weather and not much on telephone conversation. What I didn't know was that he called to inform me that his own doctors thought he might be infected with the hepatitis B virus. The news hit like a bomb! Immediately, I bombarded him with questions about the virus. He answered, *You are at no risk and you cannot get it from me.* He assured me I could not get it from unprotected sex which I had had with him on three occasions. Yet the tone of his voice had a ring of fear to it. What was I to think?

Keith also used the word *mortified* as if he might already have the disease. As panic set in, what was I to think but the worst case scenario. I asked him if and when I should get tested and instead of answering the question he sidetracked telling me that I was at no risk. I asked again and received the same non-answer. Already in a confused state I became more anxious with his refusal to say anything beyond this one-liner. This made me feel like a person who was complaining for lack of an appropriate explanation. It was several days later that the intended definition of the inscription on my grandmother's pillow, *Don't complain, Never explain* became crystal clear. Reminiscent of her generation the words glared out at me with such a commanding tone: *don't complain to me because I refuse to explain!* None of the facts had been appropriately *explained* to me and now the doctor was *complaining* to me about my lack of trust in him. Yet he kept repeating to me that my life was the most important thing to him. Continuing to ask the same question over and over again Keith realized I would not let up and informed me that I could get tested after two weeks, the time it takes for the virus to show up in testing (he was wrong about that). My next question was why he would give such catastrophic news to me just before bedtime. He replied that he had an obligation to do so right away. I thought to myself, WOW, what horrible people skills this doctor possessed. Refusing to give me any facts about the disease, I began thinking that Keith might not know much about the disease because he was a surgeon, not a practicing physician. Yet he had spoken to his doctors and surely they would have given him the facts. After parting on the phone, I googled *hepatitis B* virus to learn more. To my surprise I found out that Keith's comments conflicted with information I had just read on the internet. There were two things in particular that every one of the sites I researched said: *you can contract the virus from kissing and sexual relations and you must wait six weeks* (not two!) *before getting tested.*

What worried me most about the information I gathered was the misinformation Keith attempted to pass on to me. When I read to him the statement, he stood his ground with the response, *you cannot contract the disease from me and you can't believe everything you read on the internet.* All the while he was reeling over the effects of his disease on his own life and how *mortified* he said he was that his life would change forever. How could I *not* think that the virus had not been passed on to me? Knowing that his comments had not added up, my worst fears were taking hold so I called him back a few minutes later. Upon further questioning, I received the same response he had given me earlier. In total frustration I began questioning his legitimacy as a doctor. My only conclusion was that he was *strictly* a surgeon with knowledge limited to surgical procedures. Keith continued to staunchly defend his original claim, period. The more he strong armed me back with his inexcusable defense tactics the more alienated and mistrusting I became of him. This led to total chaos in my mind!

The next day a close friend of mine telephoned Keith to let him know the emotional and mental trauma he was causing by not listening to or answering my questions appropriately. According to my friend, it took much explaining and time, and patience to get him to listen to her. By the time she had finished (over the course of two days), all the facts were in from his doctor. Keith called me to inform me that he had been vaccinated against hepatitis B the year he had retired from practice for recent elective back surgery. He added that he didn't remember being vaccinated. I found that odd especially since he was a surgeon who came into contact with other people's blood regularly. Just twenty four hours before there was no record that he had been vaccinated. Suddenly, there was good news that the record had been found in the computer! The explanation for the virus antibody showing up in his blood was the result of a vaccination titer. What a relief if all was true. Wanting proof of this, I requested that Keith send me a copy of that record (previously he refused) which he did via mail. Total relief came only after I waited six weeks and was tested for the virus. The test was negative and I was relieved to know that my life was no longer in danger from a life threatening disease.

s in the Bed, Bath and Beyond story described earlier, my hepatitis B scare contained a similar problem—when one person takes a singlehanded approach it frequently leads to mounting resentment. In the aftermath of my saga, Keith admitted to handling things poorly. In his unwillingness to acknowledge my fears and doubts this led to a deep distrust of him. Likewise, in my own panic I am aware that I most likely cut sharply into the core of his ego with some of my questioning. Yes, I used the word *stupid* when he constantly interrupted and talked over me. But here I found myself fighting for my life and bruising this doctor's super-ego had no relevancy in such a frightening situation. Through the aid of a friend, acting as an intermediary perhaps this doctor came to realize that his lack of consideration for the feelings of another (during a crisis he caused) only makes things worse.

One of the best things about this story is that my grandmother's pillow gave me this insight:

_Do_ *complain when an explanation is in order because right or wrong everyone is deserving of one.*

— CHAPTER TWENTY-SIX —

The Persistent Tiki Bar Owner and What Currently Separateds Have to Say!

What about 5 years separated waiting on final divorce never wanted to give up. Been apart 5 years never really dated anyone else married 20 years. Don't hold that against me, be a friend that's all I want to start and the worst thing that happens you'll have a good friend. Not looking to add notches in my head board for fun. I am currently at my house in Costa Rica swimming biking surfing and hiking.

— A Match Man

You are certainly very attractive. I had to tell you so. I have good vibes, but I cannot control what others do. **I am currently separated,** *but it is not typical. My wife and daughter do not live in the US. I recognize that rules me out in your criteria, but I wanted to say "hi" nonetheless. I drove through Central Florida recently on a wonderful road trip to New Orleans. At least drop me a line. Good Luck.*

— Another Match Man

I wasn't that interested in the Tiki Bar Match Man who, from the start was persistent in landing a date with me. For one thing he listed his status as *currently separated.* He was cute, though and had a harmless air about him. Instead of passing him by and using one of the standard rejection replies offered by Match, I gave in to his invitation for dinner in my town (he was from Gainesville, a forty minute drive north).

I had just come out of taking a small break from online dating and was not quite ready to jump into the live dating scene on all four. Once again, socializing from behind my computer screen sufficed. That is problematic when you're searching for a soul mate! But like a fox hound with a nose for a scent, this guy seemed to know what he was looking for. Early on, and in a tasteful manner this Tiki bar Match Man told me that I was pretty hot looking. Well, given compliments, they always seem to do wonders for a woman. Instantly, I was out of the doldrums. All the while, though, I had been giving him back neutral vibes that were not of the same kind of excitement he had for me. Was this about the chase? It seems so, but my laid back attitude was not deliberate, but rather a sign of caution.

From the beginning, I definitely had my Tiki Match Man off guard. Likewise, his aggressive romancing distracted me from noticing little red flags about him. It all started out with an innocent online wink which oddly enough would eventually turn into a small wink of contention. Here was our first tiny disagreement: he claimed that I was the initial winker. I refuted saying that I never used the wink button on Match because I found it, *corny*. He probably had me confused with someone else and I told him flat out. He believed me but only because I stood my ground without doubt. He shrugged off some other innocent accusations by romancing me with several fancy dinners and hand-picked wines. After discovering my personal preference for reds, he showed off his knowledge about them. After all, he was a Tiki bar owner.

In retrospect, here was one of those people who seemed to conveniently forget about how things actually happened and contrived his own scenario in an effort to be right (men are just like women!) Whether or not this was true, subconsciously I felt the negative pull of this little dance. And as he drew me in (with enough chemistry), I felt that once again this Match Man was trying to make it seem that I was the one who initiated contact with him. Whatever his motive or plan was anyone's guess. Perhaps it had something to do with dreams of having an attractive woman under his magic spell in his otherwise ordinary life.

Below is how the relationship unfolded:

Tiki man to me:

Good morning how are you? what a great profile! I would love to chat sometime! David

I did not respond following several more messages.

Tiki man to me:

Yeah, did you give up on me?

I emailed a brief hello.

Tiki man to me:

Hi Nancy thanks for the response. Hid my profile because of all the people I am not interested in always seem to find me, and then I spend most of my time sending emails back thanking them for their interest. I have no idea how you women keep up? I left my profile open for you!

Me to Tiki man:

Well, u are still married, and I can't imagine starting a relationship that way with someone I don't know or trust.

Tiki man to me:

Thanks for your honesty, I filed yesterday, hopefully I'll be single again soon!

Me to Tiki man:

That's a good thing!

<u>Tiki man to me:</u>
Since you are located fairly close do u want to talk?
123-456-7890

A week passes.

<u>Tiki man to me:</u>
I would still love to talk, can I this afternoon?

<u>Me to Tiki man:</u>
Sure, why not.

From there David and I ended up on our first date at Carrabba's restaurant. The next day he emailed:

Thanks for the evening, I enjoyed talking to you and dinner was great! I hope we can get together again! I will call you tomorrow if that's ok!
Ps You looked really HOT with your glasses on! :) kisses

Not yet sold on continuing to date David, he sensed this. Over dinner, I believe he used the lure of the Tiki bar he built two years earlier to interest me. He said he created the bar for his ex-wife to keep her busy. While relating his story I detected a note of embarrassment. Now that he was getting divorced it was obvious things had not worked out as planned. At any rate, his bravery in disclosing the Tiki bar story (as much as it failed the marriage) had an endearing effect on me. There was a vulnerable quality about this man. He emphasized how many friends he had where he lived was a way to impress upon me that he was a legitimate prospect to date. In discussing his Tiki bar, though, he did leave out key elements that revolved around his wife leaving him. It was still too early to ask him about that kind of personal information.

David's version of the Tiki bar went like this: He had a side business in construction. All of his work came from the large country club development where he lived. There were approximately 1100 homes in this golfing community. His wife was his partner and handled the accounts payable. In order to keep her happy, he built the Tiki bar around the swimming pool of the country club. He said, *It would be her own thing to run.* Upon asking how he built the hut he said, *All from scratch, and the roof was built frawn by frawn from neighboring palm trees.* David's Tiki bar served as the pulse of the country club and that was how he became well known in the community by so many.

Excited over the sound of a genuine Tiki hut I was taken over by visions of girls and guys dressed in island prints drinking tropical drinks and meeting and socializing with one another. The next thing I knew, I was commenting to him that I just might come up and see his creation firsthand. Of course that was exactly what David was wishing for. A second date was planned. So my original plan to go on one date with a *currently separated man* turned into having drinks and a refreshing swim at an unusual Tiki bar.

Several days later, I drove an hour to see David at his Tiki bar. It was everything I had envisioned. It loomed large over the grand-size swimming pool and there were men, women, guys and girls, professionals and non-professionals everywhere drinking and socializing. The men had a major game of darts going on and all were welcome to play. Behind the bar and five steps down at the end of the pool decking a giant grill with chicken cooking permeated the air with the heavy scent of BQ. The enticing smell set my taste buds popping. A large buffet table loaded with pot luck side dishes brought in by the community's residents awaited an impending feast. What an exciting surprise! The atmosphere was made to order, too, with lighted palm trees and streams of colorful lights along the pool area. This was definitely going to be a festive evening, so much so, that I didn't arrive home until the next morning!

At the Tiki bar social (lasting into the late evening hours) one of the girls I partied with was nice enough to lend me a movie for David and I to watch after dinner. I chose a favorite comedy, *the Wedding Crashers.* With David standing by my side I asked him if he had seen the movie. He had not and looked forward to watching it. As I looked around I noticed that many of David's friends and acquaintances were overly delighted that he had found a woman like me to date. No one knew me, but as long as David seemed happy, they all liked me the same.

David was eager to show me his home so we left the Tiki bar in his golf cart to go to there. The moment I entered the house the thick smell of cigarette smoke was evident. What a bummer! Commenting about this and my intense dislike for the smell of cigarette smoke, he admitted to his wife was a chain smoker and smoking in the house! I had no reason to believe he smoked because not once had I seen him light up a cigarette in the time I was with him. Also, in his Match profile David checked off the *No Way* box for smoking. But that was not the case. As we sat down in his screened in sunroom for a chat suddenly a pack of cigarettes emerged from his shirt pocket and there he was light up. When I confronted him with this he gave me the common line many smokers give, *I'm in the process of quitting* (a lie from him was now on the table). I wasn't marrying this guy so I let it go. David continued with his conversation emphasizing once again how much he was liked in the community to the great friends he had made from his business ties (he did all of the construction work for the development). It was interesting to me how David reiterated how much his friends here supported him and how much they liked me since my arrival two hours earlier. Thinking David was trying too hard with me I politely suggested that he be himself. With that, we both had an enjoyable evening watching the funny movie. Too tired to drive home after the movie, I made the decision to stay overnight with David. The next morning we found ourselves girlfriend and boyfriend.

David was already making plans to take me out for a nice dinner that evening. As smitten as he was, he was making every effort to treat me in ways expected of a man—kind, gentle and respectful. Yet his cigarette smoking remained a problem for me. Having been married to a smoker I vowed that I would not ever be involved with one again. Here I was breaking that vow, yet when I looked around it seemed like more than half the population was smoking. Not wanting to consider the subject any further, my attention suddenly turned to the bareness of the house. After David's wife walked out on him a month earlier, the only things remaining were several pieces of furniture. All of the wall shelves in the living room were empty and the walls were bare. What I could not see in the darkness of the night before was now staring me in the face. No one had cleaned the house in a while. In the guest bathroom a couple of large dead cockroaches lay in the corner of an open linen closet. Upon seeing them, I asked him when his house was last cleaned. He acknowledged that it was a mess but said he had more important things to take care of such as his business. I asked him why he did not hire a maid to do house cleaning. He replied that he had thought of that initially but added he was planning to have the interior of his home repainted and the carpets cleaned to get rid of the smoke smell. With that, I shrugged off his messy house due to his being newly separated. Also, I was developing a soft spot for this Tiki Bar Match Man who had an endearing vulnerable trait.

It seems that David had free time to wine and dine a girl yet he was at an impasse to accomplish the simplest of things (like cleaning up his dirty home). I went to get some water out of his kitchen faucet and discovered that the handle was broken making it nearly impossible to turn off the water. The process involved using the palm of one hand while beating down on the base of the handle with a hammer-like motion with the other hand to turn it off! He had lived with the broken faucet now for a month. Over time, I learned more: one month before, his wife walked out on him and she was living out of state with a new boyfriend. Since there was a child involved (no his) David told me that she recently contacted him over the internet to inform him where she was staying! Hearing such depressing news, things were looking different. In touring the house I noticed that one of the bathrooms was decorated in a princess theme for his 10-year-old stepchild. A towel was hanging in such a way as if the bathroom had just been in use. Walking back out into the main living area, David looked up at me and out of my mouth came the question: *What would cause a woman to be so unhappy that she would just walk out of your life when you didn't have a clue there was anything wrong before that?* Without hesitation David offered up a best-friend story: his newly separated wife was married to David's best friend for three years. Eventually David took an interest in her, she got divorced, and then David began dating her. David's best friend story wasn't as bad as those best friend messes. The two men were civil to one another and both lived in the community.

As my mind logged the news I was logging, too, that things might well be headed south. One day, while visiting David, I decided to have a swim at the country club pool with his step-daughter in a careful attempt to find out her side of things. She expressed that her mother *was always stressed out* and it seems it had to do with always having to clean the house. I found that strange but figured she hated doing housework and perhaps dreamed of having a maid for the rest of her life (who doesn't?) Stress over house cleaning was one thing, but in my observation of this young child it was apparent that she was eating herself to obesity. Outside the pool she was making trip after trip to the dessert area using sugar to alleviate her own anxiety (you could see it on her face). Later that evening I expressed my concern to David that his stepdaughter needed help. He responded, *She lives with her biological father here in the community and he has full custody.* I looked up from where I was sitting in the open bar area and suddenly black clouds were forming in the sky. The beginning sounds of thunder and lightning signaled a fierce impending downpour. Immediately, everyone was scattering to take shelter.

In evaluating whether David was the good guy in his marriage I gathered one more piece of information which led to the eventual demise of the relationship. After creating the Tiki Bar for his wife, David said she got bored with the bar a short time later. Spending long hours around alcohol that flowed freely, she began drinking. Along with her drinking she began smoking more heavily. There was no question how unhappy this woman was. While David's story unfolded I could feel a fear of a man who for some time had been living his life as if everything in it was functioning normally. There was also his divorce which supposedly was in the works. During a short ride in his truck from his house to the country club, I noticed three huge express mail packets on his dashboard.

What are those? I asked. *They're the divorce filings for the court*, he replied. I asked, *Why are there three of them?* He responded, *What happened was that the divorce package is really long—300 pages. I got to page 46 and realized it was the wrong package. So I had to go to the court and get the right package.*

It was interesting to note that during our first dinner date David said he had already filed for a divorce. Now I learned that this wasn't true. In an attempt to diffuse what he had just said David commented that the amount of present business he had going was just enough to make ends meet. At once a favorite expression that I used all versions of my written profile on Match came to mind: *I am looking for a man who is ahead of the eight ball.* I'm sure David read this, but then why would he think he would qualify for a date with the likes of me?

As I was ready to leave for my house David was telling me how much already he missed me. At the same time my plan was to politely say goodbye over the phone the next day. That evening I checked in on my mailbox on Match. I had not been online for a week. Before signing off I chose to take another look at David's written profile to see what I might have missed. Of course it was another case of *everyone-looks-good-on-paper.* But there was something else which caught my attention: like me he had been active on Match within an hour. I felt a rush of emotion. Was I having a moment of jealousy and doubt with the thought, *I've had sex with this man and now I am being tinkered with?* Without as much as a good-bye phone call instead I requested he meet me at an exit somewhere between his house and mine to return some of my belongings. In my haste to judgment about David's questionable integrity with women he did meet me with my personal belongings and before parting said this: *You are so wrong about everything!* From the expression on his face I think I might have wounded his heart. I decided he was too far behind the eight ball at this time in his life.

Two weeks later, I glanced at his profile again. He had changed from *currently separated* to *divorced.* Also, he changed his headliner from, *Is there just one good woman out there?* to, *Hi There.* If that was the ending a month later I found an email sitting in my inbox. David wanted another chance with me and wrote:

How are you? How's your book coming along? Have you finished my chapter, I know I'm in it! anyway your pics are looking good! And I hope you are doing well. Take care of yourself....

Me to Tiki Man:

I'm doing fine. I hope you are getting back on track now that you are newly divorced. After thinking about things I realize I may have hurt you. I just want you to know that if I did I am sorry. I think there are just too many loose ends in your life right now for me. I hope you find the girl of your dreams one day.

Tiki Man to me:

I am doing well, I hope you had a great weekend! Its back to work for me... I can't wait to read your book, I think it will go over well. Well just wanted to say hello, maybe we can chat sometime.

And that was the sweeter and more forgiving ending with David, my Tiki Bar Match Man.

CHAPTER TWENTY-SEVEN

Locked Up Like Fort Knox... While I Remained a Cool Rose Under the Sheets

I tried, but sometimes you just can't escape when it's a steel gate that won't open for exit. I tried thinking about squeezing through the vertical bars or climbing over the top. In the dark of night it just wasn't possible. Tell me if there is an upside to this downside.

One of my good friends insists that I date people involved in equestrian pursuits. This an attempt to find those who share the same love that I have for horses. I told her that it would indeed be my greatest joy to find someone with a similar passion. It's easy for someone to make a great recommendation, but making it happen is not.

As each date with men of dissimilar interests continued to end in disappointment, my friend would come back to her steadfast recommendation that I needed to find a man with a love of horses. Finally, I decided to tell her about the horse associated Match date that might have had all of the tell tale signs of success. It was my most hidden of secrets because of the bizarre and traumatic experience it caused me.

Ed was a semi-retired thoroughbred race horse trainer. He was ten years my senior. No longer actively training horses, even better, he managed and lived on one of the large horse farms in my area. The farm consisted of 1,100 acres of infinite beauty, equipped with two beautiful training tracks, two large ponds fully stocked with koi, numerous well-kept barns and living quarters, and miles of private roadways winding through the magnificent live oak trees and verdant pasturelands. Beautiful horses abounded everywhere. Moreover, the farm loomed so large that there were five different electric gates strategically placed around the property. Ed lived in the manager's house, which was a spacious 4,000 square-foot designer-appointed home. As the top dog employee of the farm, reporting personally to the owner, he had the kind of position that comes once in a lifetime.

I hooked up with this Match Man for a date through a round-about way during a visit to the Arabian horse farm where my girlfriend, Sonya trains Arabian horses. During an earlier visit to the farm, I had met a young woman, Bria, who worked under Sonya. She spoke of an attractive guy ten years her junior who was anxious to date her. He happened to be Ed's son. During a brief interlude of girl talk, Bria told me that she was a divorced single woman raising her young daughter and looking to meet an eligible guy. She was resistant to the idea of dating the highly attractive man because he was so much younger than she was. She also thought she might have to show him the so-called ropes. In the end, though, she did decide to go on a dinner date with him but asked if I might come along on a double date with his dad. We set up a double date for the following evening, Friday.

When I arrived at the restaurant, everyone was already seated. To my surprise, Ed appeared much older than I had envisioned. He was sixty-two and even though I wasn't normally interested in older men, I wasn't against the idea, either. I decided to take everything in stride. As we ordered drinks, the subject of women's hair came up. I mentioned that just two weeks earlier my locks were much longer. Ed immediately said he preferred longer hair on a woman. *Such a nice compliment,* I thought to myself. And as many of us do, I shrugged off the petty insult and went into a kind of denial mode. I pretended I didn't hear it because I didn't want to be disappointed on this Friday evening. The last part of the disappointment would have been to abort the date and go home. So I chose to reply, *Hair does grow back, you know.*

A small measure of this man was already on the table. Was I thinking in a petty fashion? I decided not. He seemed clueless about the effect of his comment, not only on me, but for any woman who might be seated opposite him. The rest of the dinner was going as well as expected, until a second measure of the man came up. The subject was about how difficult it was to find the right person for a relationship. His reply was, *You'll always run into someone. How indiscriminating a comment,* I thought. Was he really a take it or leave it kind of man? I thought that at his age he could not afford to be. What I did not know, though, was how intrinsically arrogant and self-centered this man would ultimately turn out. Perhaps the word self-entitlement was a more appropriate term. Some Match Men seem to think they are entitled to the best in women, whether or not they act in a way to deserve them.

Since he took on the air that he was the all-important one in a pending relationship, my coming to visit him on the farm was a one-way street. At this time, I didn't care because I was not interested having him come to visit me at my home. In not caring perhaps my subconscious was whispering that he was not the man for me. At any rate, I enjoyed hanging out at his house for all of the exciting amenities there. The views from the house were grandiose, looking out onto hundreds of beautiful equine acres. As time went by, things began to get better and he turned out to be nicer than I initially imagined. Perhaps he was nicer because he might have sensed that he wasn't the one for me and wasn't able to figure out whether I was having a better time enjoying the views or being with him.

After a month of visiting Ed on the farm and eating out at nice restaurants, the restaurant thing was getting old. I wanted to do other things. He suggested going scalloping on a boat or going for a horse ride on the sprawling farm. However, nothing ended up going beyond the talk.

The last time we dined out together was at an upscale steakhouse in the Ocala downtown square. I knew something was troubling me about this Match Man. It happened at the end of dinner as we were parting to go to our separate homes. I had driven my own vehicle to dinner since the restaurant was so close to where I lived. As we walked out of the romantic outdoor café setting, he suddenly turned to me and invited me to walk with him. He seemed so entranced by the dress I wore and commented how sexy I looked in my beautiful heels. I asked where we were going and he said, *You'll see.* A nice surprise, I thought. He took me to a spot on the square where his vehicle was parked. It was the car belonging to the owner of the horse farm (Ed's boss)—a BMW 425i sports car with really cool gull-wing doors and thumb ignition start. He wanted to take me for a ride in it. As he helped me down into this high-end vehicle, onlookers began to congregate around us in the downtown square. Were they just looking at the car, or might they also be wondering whether we might be VIPs that they could talk about with their friends?

In no time at all we were in motion just outside of the square and my date dug down on the gas pedal and we were flying at a speed I could hardly believe. Not for a moment did I relish the experience. The word *immature* rang loudly in my head. This man didn't have a care about getting a speeding ticket during a time when tickets were being doled out like candy to trick-or-treaters. He wanted to do it again, but I pleaded with him to not repeat the maneuver. What was he doing driving his employer's car with reckless abandon? Since his boss was in town only two or three times a year, my date had the luxury of using the car for weekly outings as if it were his own. This would be my last dinner-out memory with Ed.

After a month of dating him, I was invited to spend Easter at his house, along with his son and the girlfriend, Bria. I wanted to contribute a dish, and being the dessert specialist that I am the holiday was a great excuse for me to whip up a special dessert. The recipe was a first-time try and I was committed to making it a success. Taken from the *New York Times,* the dessert *Berry Pavlova* was named for the legendary Russian ballet dancer Anna Pavlova. It consisted of a homemade baked meringue shell which deliberately collapsed in the center upon cooling. Four types of fresh berries marinated in white balsamic syrup (raspberries, blackberries, blueberries and strawberries) were abundantly spooned into the center. A final topping of freshly whipped cream finished it off. Ed liked fresh berries because they fit perfectly in his dietary requirements for low cholesterol (minus the whipped cream, of course).

About this time, there were two things that stood out about this Match Man. First, he was always using the restroom much more frequently than normal. Second, he mentioned his high blood pressure on several occasions. There was no immediate connection in my mind regarding these two things; however, they had registered. I didn't ask any questions because I thought they were too personal.

Easter dinner went well on our second double date. Bria and her boyfriend seemed in lust compared to the more tempered friendship that my date and I had. It was dessert time and I was ready to serve my creation. Looking back, Pavlova's dream dessert was way too elegant and overwhelming for this crowd. I had gone all out, yet I received less than appreciative reactions. Ed suggested we have dessert later on in the evening, after shooting a couple of rounds of pool. Shortly afterward, I found out that the designated dessert of the evening was to be roasted marshmallows outside on the deck. No one had mentioned any of this to me beforehand. It also seemed no one really wanted a fresh, succulent, creamy berry dessert. Another disappointment with only me to blame, I thought.

It was getting late and Bria and her boyfriend retired together privately leaving the two of us in the main room at night's end. At that point, Ed and I made a mutual decision for me to stay overnight with him.

It's no fun when a man chooses *not* to discuss any sexual problems he might have with a woman with whom is planning to have sex. Added to that, my own lack of knowledge about high blood pressure, medications treating that condition and frequent goings to the bathroom should have alerted me to the pending disaster. Ed wanted to have sex in the worst way and, in the worst way, he did. When nothing worked properly (literally), he told me to *stay aroused* while he went into the bathroom to get his penis pump. I held myself together like a cool rose under the sheets. When he came back and that still didn't work, all I could think about was how I was falling off a bed that had a 45-degree slope because the mattress hadn't been rotated in a hundred years. I asked him how he could sleep on such a mattress and he mumbled something inaudible. I thought to myself, *Men!*

I had the urgent needed to leave. Without commenting on the disaster at hand, it was a given how catastrophic the night had turned out. Little did my date realize that the root of the problem stemmed from the fact that he chose not talk to me about his erectile dysfunction. As he began to doze off, I asked him which electrified gate to use to exit the farm. He said it would be easier to go through the main access gate located at the opposite end of the farm. My reply was that it might be difficult to locate in the dark so I would use the side road entrance closer to his house. He was already snoring before I could finish the sentence. Finding it difficult to change clothes in the dark, I left dressed in nothing more than a scanty slipover.

I headed out to the side gate located a short distance from the house. The night was pitch dark and the clock in my truck read 10:45 P.M. So many emotions were rushing from within, but the one that screamed out loud was, *I've got to get out of here! I've just got to get out of here!* It was an admission of disbelief over what had just happened. I thought, *Who cares that I am not wearing undies under my cute little navy slipover shirt?* As I approached the gate, just for a second I thought of putting on more clothes in the event there was an accident on the road, or worse, I got stopped by a cop. But no, I decided. The urgent need to exit the farm for the fifteen-minute ride home was the sure touchdown. Disgust and repulsion came over me more than disappointment and anger. Quickly I was at the gate. It failed to swing open as I got close with my vehicle. Earlier in the day, I had seen the wires hanging out loose on the call box located on the other side. But there was no genuine call box with numbers to punch on the exit side. I moved closer but there was still no arm action. I got out of my vehicle and started tugging at the arm of the gate thinking there was a temporary malfunction that I could fix through manhandling. Again, nothing. I looked at the gate and the vertical steel bars. They were too tall to climb. The arrows on top reminded me of the weapons used to impale the enemy in the final battle led by Mel Gibson in *Brave Heart.* Climbing over the gate would do no good anyway, since I couldn't get my vehicle to the other side. So I continued to drive on the winding roads in pitch dark for five long minutes down to one of the two main gates. Of the two main access gates, I chose the one which did not open. Strike two!

Ten minutes had gone by since leaving the house and I had no choice but to go back up the hill and wake up the *slumbering Ed.* As I approached the house a moving truck drew near. It was Ed, in a white bathrobe. With his window rolled down he said, *I had a bad feeling you would not be able to find your way out.* I responded, *How could I? You didn't tell me the gates wouldn't open!* And he led me down to the one gate that was not locked down like the four others. The purring sound of the opening gate was music to my ears, and off I went on my nearly-naked drive home.

The next day he called to tell me what a disaster the night was for both of us. I thought, *both* of us? He was leaving for Kentucky for a week and humbly asked if he could call me upon his return. In a gesture of politeness I answered with a weak *okay*. I was still in disbelief. With an experience like that, I couldn't say whether I'd ever want to see this man again. So I decided to rest on it. I'd talk to my closest girlfriend about Ed's problem since she had been married to a doctor and maybe I could learn more and, hopefully, keep myself from getting more depressed.

The following week Ed returned home and invited me over for that tour of the farm he had initially promised me but had never given me. Upon viewing the new offices, a slow churn tugged at my gut. The churn did not diminish upon seeing the training tracks where the young racehorses trained at the crack of dawn. My relationship with this Match Man was at a stoic standstill. Did he think we could somehow forget about what had happened and continue on? I suggested we go to dinner and from there I put all those questions to him that he should have answered before getting into the sack with me.

His sexual problem may have forced him back into reality somewhat, but not without the braggadocio of a self-centered man. For example, during a tour of his new offices, he bragged nonstop for a time about all of his laurels from earlier days as well as the numerous possessions he had accumulated over a lifetime. They were all there—from the paintings, trophies and accolades around us on the walls and tabletops for his feats as a young racehorse jockey to his recent accolades as a well placed farm manager/trainer. They were admirable but I was not interested in living through his possessions in such an audible fashion.

Looking back, I question whether I might have been used as a guinea pig in an attempt to fix the man's erectile dysfunction problem. Am I assuming the worst here? I will never really know because I didn't have the nerve to ask. I toss this up to naivety—this was my first experience of this kind and hopefully my last. Either way there didn't appear to be much form or substance in our relationship. And so it ended. The lesson I learned: *Sometimes the best way out of a bad situation is to go through it.*

— CHAPTER TWENTY-EIGHT —

60 Years Old, But Really 75 +

Sadly, He Was a Sad Sack

His gifts upon parting were two bruised apples and a tiny container of smoked oysters. When I arrived home my horse got a doubly sweet treat and the oysters...well they went into the kitchen pantry where they remain today.

Why is it that some people are so good at setting themselves up for such dismal failure? Sadly enough, this Match Man was one of them. He was a man who lived in the past. Most of the things he bragged about in his profile were from bygone days—his proactive sports lifestyle, his weight, and the number of his girlfriends. Yet he continued to live as though his most relished past was still going on at this very moment. I chose to go on a date with him because once more I wanted to try out the 60-and-over age range. I could not imagine this Match date to be any more out of range than my experience with Ed had been. I must have been in another one of my *Curious George* modes.

My first date with Gil was Sunday, the day after Halloween. He drove a little farther than I did to get to our destination of *The Villages,* a premier active adult retirement community located in Central Florida. A forty-five minute drive from my home, I had never visited this dream community for the retired, and thought it would be an interesting outing even if the date wasn't. Gil and I met at Walgreen's pharmacy at 1 pm. I came up with where to meet because, as do most men on Match, Gil insisted on leaving that decision to me. I was sure I was going to have a major hand in where to eat and how to spend the date, too. What the heck, these things were becoming common practice in the dating world. The following was Gil's summary of himself.

The pictures on the Bahaman beach were taken this past October 29th. I am fit, intelligent, industrious, active, kind, thoughtful, and easy to be with. I don't want to spend excessive time exchanging emails. If you are interested in me, we should speak on the telephone, exchange as many pictures and additional information as you like, talk about a happy place *and go there!!! I am a builder/developer, lacrosse player, pilot, skier, scuba diver. I work out* regularly, *don't smoke, rarely drink, love to read, roller blade, fish, sail, travel, and fly my airplanes to exciting places. I have a great sense of humor, am non-judgmental, a think-outside-the-box kinda guy, a creative thinker, assertive, honest with a real sweet streak and I love adventure!!! My ideal match would be a girl who enjoys good conversation, candlelight dinners, watching a sunset (or sunrise), slow dancing, snuggling, reading, warm hugs and kisses, has a great sense of humor, is easy to get along with, exercises regularly, has a fabulous figure, weighs between 105-125 pounds, is between 4'2" – 5'8", loves BEACHES, is adventurous, affectionate and a great kisser.*

More than any other profile, I thought that this one was worthy of going through play by play. Regarding the fifteen-plus photos, there were two of Gil standing on the ocean beach. Standing alongside a younger sexy woman whom I had guessed he might have grabbed for the shoot, he sported a colorfully trendy bathing suit. He claimed these photos were taken in the fall of 2008. The resolution on both photos, though, was similar to viewing a fuzz ball. In addition, he was pictured taking a deep breath, standing tall, abdomen tucked inward, and shoulders high. I could not help wondering how old this man really was. If you looked at some of the other photos such as one in a sail boat, his age appeared significantly different—like decades younger! Added to that, he was always pictured alongside a much younger sexy girl paired with a young hunk.

Then there was the question of the posted photos. Upon further scrutiny, the yellowish tone of the photos stood out. Unless one employed sophisticated photo retouching software, the tattered look of his pictures told of their antique age. Moving on to this Match Man's professed superman athletic side, I learned that the sports he played and the gym he regularly worked out in appeared impressive. Then there was rollerblading. Isn't that a crash and bang sport for kids with the physical ability to bounce back? Gil had injected a youthful spin into his alleged active sports lifestyle.

After reading through three quarters of his profile the thought flashed through my mind: *I can't wait to meet such an energetic man!* As I read more the volume of excitement heightened. He owned and flew two planes. Then I connected back to his headliner, *Bahama Bound.* With a profile like that, this Match Man seemed to have the endless energy of a young super dude. There were planes, boats, and great places to travel to. There was a tone that rang out, *when can you leave!* This older man in his 60s either appeared to have it all, or he was good at self-aggrandizement. Moving along to his stats, I noted he had checked the $150,000+ level for his income. Being the highest possible income category one might guess that Gil had a lot of girls of all ages gravitating to him.

Finally, what kind of woman had this Match Man specified he was seeking? In so many words, Gil wanted all the ideal traits a woman could possibly have in one package; a slender woman with *a fabulous figure, and weighs between 105-125 pounds.* No tolerance here for voluptuous women.

The Live Date

I arrived at Walgreen's in *The Villages*. The green Grand Jeep Cherokee that Gil drove was already parked. From a distance it had a kind of special gleam to it, but as I moved closer to the empty vehicle, it turned out to be a much older model than I first thought. Perhaps so old it was a classic. Then Gil emerged from under the overhang of Walgreen's as I pulled in next to his Jeep. Upon seeing him for the first time I was neither shocked nor disappointed because what I thought was too good to be true turned out to be just that. There's always that split second, too when one thinks that maybe it's somebody else. But he approached my car with a wave of confirmation. What I saw was this: the look of an unshaven elderly man wearing tattered shorts, an old tee shirt and well worn sneakers. Along with that was an un-gamely expression on his face. This Match Man was more like 75, not 60! Who knew? We quickly said our hellos in the blazing sun of the parking lot. Noting how hot it was, I mentioned a place for lunch as I turned toward the shade of my vehicle. Ignoring what I had just said, Gil responded that he had a special surprise for me. Similar to a child opening up a Christmas present he opened the hatchback of his Jeep and delved into an old cooler. Gil pulled out two red delicious apples that appeared to have gone the distance. Noting the visible bruise on the first, I had already imagined the plight of the second one. He presented them both to me as, *a healthy snack for you.* Was this Adam and Eve thing the surprise? I was already feeling antsy over the production, but maintained my cool to see where things might go from here.

Having grown up with the best of manners I was well aware that the apples he presented were given in good faith. So I thanked him and quickly moved to the topic of lunch. There would be no lunch just yet because there was another surprise. Knowing of my passion for horses Gil said he want to take me on a short drive from where we were parked. He asked politely if I would accompany him in his vehicle. Without hesitation I did because I felt *I* was more of a danger to this Match Man than he could ever be to me. I believed I could easily overpower him if he posed a physical threat. His weak walk alone revealed that he had age related joint pain going. Along with that he had the extra belly weight, and from the way he moved he was clearly out of shape. He did take notice of my body, and in turn I sensed some anxiety he was having about his own condition. For example, several times during our five-minute drive to our surprise destination he mentioned about how he *must* get back into the gym to work out.

We continued driving on *The Villages* road which winds around the many neighborhoods and mini strip malls brimming with fresh produce stores and other interesting shops. Gil was a pedal-pusher, both on the brakes and the gas, and sometimes both simultaneously. This didn't help my lifelong condition of motion sickness as a passenger. Finally, we arrived at a sports field where a women's polo tournament was in session. This was the surprise he had planned for me. As I thought about the effort he had made to romance me, we slowly rolled into an area where security personnel quickly greeted us. The polo game was in session, and we were the only vehicle roving in an undesignated parking area. We stuck out like a sore thumb. My date had thought he could pull off getting free ringside viewing while he congratulated himself for thinking up such a romantic surprise. Within a few seconds of watching the game, we were told to leave unless we paid the ten-dollar spectator fee. Gil had no intention of paying. Instead he attempted to talk his way into staying. I felt like I was in a movie scene where the young pretty date is used as privileged justification. Security wasn't buying his line, so we were forced to leave the game as quickly as we had arrived. Gil had nothing further to say so I turned the attention to lunch. At two-thirty in the afternoon and well past lunch time, I was starving. I reminded him that we agreed to keep the date under two hours. So we wound our way back to where my vehicle was parked. The Olive Garden was nearby and, alas, that was where we ended up. While Gil was parking at the restaurant, out of nowhere he told me that he had eaten *Egg Beaters*^{TM} earlier and was not that hungry. What a funny thing to say to a date! I thought to myself that going without something to eat wasn't going to be an option, otherwise our date was over. Instead of getting cranky with him over my grumbling stomach, I calmed his anxiety about lunch by suggesting we share a salad and dessert. He liked that and we entered the restaurant without further hesitation. I decided to be kind to this older soul and see how the rest of our date would play out.

During lunch, I learned that Gil was a small-time options trader who spent most of our lunch date talking about the trade. Sitting across from me he said, *You're lovely looking and smart and I am on a diet.* He didn't order a thing from the menu yet pressed on getting dessert later just for me. Imagine that this man was ready to buy a $114,000 motor boat to sail to the Bahamas with a much younger dream-girl mate? He loved coming back to *The Villages* where he had played lacrosse on the polo field decades earlier. Decades? Yes, it had to be. He was attentive to the black mesh tote bag with papers inside which he brought into the restaurant. (What did he have in there?) He never stopped talking and the time dragged on for what seemed like eternity in telling me of his life's stories.

The time for truth dawned on me. I interrupted him and asked about the girls he had dated. He paused...and paused. He told me he had an incredible twelve-hour phone conversation with a recent date. Taken by surprise, I responded that it was not normal to do something like that.

In fact, I told him, it was totally bizarre. He looked at me with an off-guard and please-don't-harm-me gaze and I realized how I had hurt his most sensitive feelings. It seemed that the lengthy phone date had been the most attention he had experienced in a very long time. I could see in his eyes how I had dashed his fantasy of attention from an attractive woman. Without pause, I asked him about other women he had dated. He said he went out with a nice, pretty woman whom he didn't connect with because she was slightly overweight. Extremely sensitive but *wanting* it all, this Match Man represented that last ditch effort to *get* it all.

Then there was the obvious Gil. As he spoke endlessly about his stories of the Bahamas and of women, the salad in the bowl wasn't getting any smaller. I was finished and was intent on dessert. So I interrupted him and asked him what kind of dessert he liked. He wouldn't tell me so I ordered lemon crème cake, something I personally relished. He was happy and I guessed it was because he wanted dessert more than I did. He ate most of it and then it was time to go. If I hadn't made the move to leave we might still be at *The Villages!*

When we arrived back at my vehicle, I couldn't help but notice the produce store, *The Fresh Market,* within walking distance. I told my date I had to visit the market before leaving *The Villages.* Not having these markets where I lived, the fresh shipment of honey crisp apples staring me in the face at the entrance proved too tempting. I entered the store not knowing whether Gil would follow. He did. I bought a few items to take back with me and he eventually found something that interested him (smoked oysters). As we perused the shelves of the canned goods aisle, the oysters continued to pop out at Gil. He wanted to know if I liked them and I responded that only recently did I try raw oysters during a visit to the small fishing village of Cedar Key, Florida. I told him that the oysters had been freshly shucked within two hours of eating them and were the best. Gil went back to the shelf location of the canned oysters. I noticed they were 20% off. He insisted I try the canned ones and at once grabbed a container. Off we went to the cashier. I paid $15 for my few items and he put the 60 cent can of oysters he bought just for me on his credit card. It was odd to note that he didn't like any of the items I bought—not even coffee. Nor did he eat out in restaurants except once in a blue moon (such as a Match date). But he did tell me that he had been known to eat a brick of cheese all at one sitting. I found him oddly amusing, but at least he was honest.

We walked out to our vehicles from The Fresh Market. I really thought I was leaving and began unlocking my vehicle. But Gil had one last thing to share with me. He seemed desperate for on last piece of time with me. In the big picture of things I thought, *What's another 15 minutes?* After all, he was a genuinely kind soul with a good heart. There was no reason to leave this human being feeling more ashamed for pulling out all the harmless stops in his attempt to romance a younger woman. Perhaps he could learn a lesson from our crossing paths.

The last item on his agenda was the mysterious black mesh bag. Out it came from the hatchback of his jeep. Inside it were at least a hundred photos of his time spent in the Bahamas. He spent those years with a group of lacrosse players. The photos were so ancient looking that I had to ask about their date. Feeling more comfortable that I would not pounce on him for all of the untruths about his age and other, Gil responded, *Really old.* He said it with a sigh of relief. I could see that he was in his mid-thirties when the pictures were taken. His friends, unlike him were much younger and coupled with mates. Was Gil always the lone man out? The photos indicated so. Then I found it heartwarming that this Match Man who relished living in the past mentioned his only son several times with love.

As we parted two hours over the time limit, Gil gave me a symbolic gift—two apples out of the back of his trunk. Perhaps he was fantasizing about dining on smoked oysters and red delicious apples with one sexy, dark-haired, petite woman aboard his boat, riding the high seas of the Atlantic Ocean, and bound for the Bahamas!

Many women would have bailed out of this date within a few minutes of meeting Gil. Why didn't I? Call it *good karma*—being kind to one who has good intentions of living exclusively in his past.

— PART TEN —
My Last Match Man

— CHAPTER TWENTY-NINE —

As Toxic as They Come

I scrape myself up off of the ground as he walks away knowing nothing of my injuries. For a fleeting moment he turns his head for a quick glance at me. My right eye is punched red, the inside of my lip bleeding. I feel a strange sensation in the front of my mouth and hold my hand over the left side. Seconds before, I paralyzed by fear, I watched as the other one smashed my phone to the floor leaving me in a more heightened trauma with no communication. When you're down on the ground, broken, you ask yourself,

WHO ARE THESE VIOLENTMONSTERS? ... the one who claimed I was the most important thing in his life? How do I get into my truck located thirty yards away and drive home? At 20 mph, I struggle to stay in the center of the road, my head crouched low over the steering wheel, totally dazed. The four mile drive is surreal and I must make a stop. Finally home I crawl inside and collapse into an immobile position on a couch. Consumed by white noise my heart beats fast and hard...so hard I'm afraid.. I don't ever want to come out of my house...I am ashamed and I haven't seen myself.

— The author

On our first date, smiling broadly, he said, *You wouldn't know Mr. Right if he stared you right in the face.* I thought he was crazy to say such a thing to a woman on a first date. My courteous but subdued reply was, *Time will tell.* In the first month of our relationship he repeated this several more times, and I back to him with the same answer. But this Match Man persisted saying it was *déjà vu* for him from the moment we met. Still, his offbeat pronouncement remained in the back of my mind. As curious as I was, I wanted to know what made this particular Match Man tick. His blue eyes dazzled as he talked a good line. Yet I refused to yield free rein to him. A straight shooter, I cautioned him not to underestimate me with the confidence he displayed and his attempt at schmoozing me. I'd seen it all. What I did *not* say to him was that his statement struck me with an air of undeniable arrogance. At the same time there was instant chemistry between us, something which I had not experienced in a very long time. Who knew if this Match Man might just turn out to be my Mr. Right?

On and off for two years I had struggled through so many ups and downs with Match Men. They continuously disappointed me. For the life of me, I couldn't tell a good one from a bad one. I couldn't trust my own judgment, either. I was beginning to question all that I had learned from dating over the past two years on Match. For many months, I had been in the ultimate testing mode. Now I was in disengagement mode and somewhat off-guard. For now, I was happier to be on my own, perhaps for the rest of my life if that was my final destiny. The last two Match Men I dated claimed to love me, but I just wasn't in love with them. Then, as if an omen was calling out to me, one in particular had recently texted:

It's midnight, many times this Earth has spun since we talked...and something still rings true with you...please tell me you are ok!...

For a moment a peculiar feeling came over me. *Please tell me you are ok,* was to be a prophecy of what was to come with My Last Match Man.

In as much as the last two Match Men were better prospects than all those whom had come before, romantically speaking, I was simply *over* men. Along with that, I found that my personal fight with cynicism was beginning to fail. Always the ultimate optimist, I didn't ever wish to become all those people in life who wore those rugged expressions on their faces. I would never give up on the human race no matter how many countless times people would disappoint me. I simply liked some of the more interesting challenges of life. There was also the word, hope. For all of my life, *hope* dwelled within my soul. Call it my personal trademark. Now, I was starting to lose some hope regarding ever finding my soul mate.

January 6, 2010. My Match membership would expire in two days. Unlike several times before, this time I would end my Match habit for good. I had a new career on the horizon and would be out of town undergoing three days of intensive training in my new health and wellness field. Lucky for me the second day of my training fell on my last day on Match. At midnight, January 8th, online dating would be over. I was sad and excited at the same time. Overall, I was relieved that the time and effort that Match.com required was coming to an end. This difficult-to-drop habit seemed like a timeless journey through cyberspace. I was worn down by the process and tired of men in general. Trying to find the right match was never-ending!

On the same evening that I instructed Match to terminate my membership, I decided to take one last glance at my emails. There were several new ones. Instead of passing them off lightly, I read through each one carefully as if stretching out my final goodbye to online dating. Looking back, I could always make the claim that I made the effort every inch of the way. The difference on this evening, though, was that I was really going through these last few Match profiles out of sheer curiosity rather than any serious romance seeking. Out of three new Match Men who emailed me, there was a little spark about one. He was convenient, too, living in the same town where I lived. Instead of looking at this potential date as a *why bother?* I saw it as a, *why not?*

His screen name was *CmeRomanceU*. I replied to his short email that evening, saying that I would be out of town and that my membership was expiring at midnight the next night. I gave him the option of leaving his number and if there was enough time I planned to check my inbox late the next evening. In a short take-it or leave-it style message to him, the ball was in his court. Desperate for this one, I was *not*. If he did not leave his number, I would be gone forever.

The next night, I signed into Match just to see how soon this Match Man might leave his phone number for me. I was confident it would be there waiting. Upon opening my inbox, there it was staring back at me and so soon! He was to be my last Match date. His profile was three short sentences. After two years of reading hundreds of profiles there was something appealing about brevity. Tired of the process I had come to the conclusion that profiles were all of the same cloth because they all looked great. So I ignored his mention of *not wanting to date women who want to be rescued*. It sounded like a pressure point.

His name was Jack. He came to Florida-horse country from California at the request of his long-time friend and former business partner to build a prototype composter for composting horse manure and other kinds of waste. He bragged proudly that his newly designed machine was positioned to transform the horse industry. In an area where the underground aquifer was said to be in danger of being polluted by equine waste runoff, his idea sounded appealing. At the same time his idea was based on a concept which already had been in practice for decades. But the ramifications for a newly designed machine that could accomplish this feat were enormous in terms of protecting the precious water resources of Silver Springs, Florida, home to the largest underground artesian well in the world. What a good cause, I thought; And the man behind the good cause must be equally good.

We decided to meet for our first date right away, Sunday, January 10th. New to town, he recommended the only restaurant he knew how to get to, *Bonefish*. On this off-night, it happened to be oddly packed. Upon entering the restaurant, I made my way to the bar area where there was barely standing room. In the blink of an eye, there stood Jack looking me with the most intent gaze. He had identified me instantly. A serendipitous moment followed as two seats opened up for us at the end of a bar table. This Match Man's first words to me were that he was taken aback from the first moment he saw me. He followed that by uttering the French expression *déjà vu*. Assuming he might be referring to love at first sight, I was a little nervous. And so, I remained little Ms. Cautious (as petite as I am).

Without going into every detail of our romance, the first several months seemed like a whirlwind. Jack had the kind of humor that made one laugh so hard that my stomach doubled in pain. He seemed smart, creative and sensitive, and most important he impressed me as being in *front* of the eight ball. What I especially liked was that he didn't seem to mind one of my more noticeable habits of sometimes talking too much when I was nervous.

Still, I thought things were moving a bit fast. I wasn't sure about returning his first call the next day. I did return it the next day. I had been a single woman living alone, and I was coming from a different place than him; He had two daughters and I had no kids. Although his were not living with him, one he said was a lively nine-year-old. Siding with caution, I didn't want to face potential pressures that young children often represent. Yet in all of this underlying romantic excitement, I felt as if this romancer of a Match Man was daring me to get out of my comfort zone and into a potential new life.

Following month two, my relationship with Jack began to take on the, *we* factor. His constant romancing turned into a fully blown romance. Things were not perfect, though. There was a bizarre fight that this Match Man began and I was left hurt. I found it noteworthy because the incident occurred during our first week of dating and involved unusual jealousy on his part. I did not understand it. Thanks to an enormous apology (he came to my house and apologized for ten minutes!), I let it go.

Over the next several months, there were special outings on weekends to escape the stresses of work and everyday life. I appreciated that these outings were not the kind of things which cost a lot of money. Instead, they were creative exploits. One was an island night for two on the beach that this Match Man dreamed up as a special surprise. He scheduled it during a cold winter week in our area. He transformed his living room into a magical tropical island beach using creative props (which he ordered online) and served an island dinner with tropical drinks. Looking back, the special festivities of that night became somewhat blurred due to the visible stresses on Jack's face that evening. For five long minutes Jack had brought those stresses to the fore asking me some highly personal questions to which he wanted specific answers. He became incensed over my hesitation to open up more than I wished about my personal life. I thought it was too early in the relationship to be asking these things. Because of my unwillingness to tell all, the night ended on a poor note. I didn't quite understand the extent of this but made a conscious decision to get over the matter as if it was minor. My focus was on the good times with Jack rather than the odd bumps that would arise. Our chemistry seemed strong. If there was anything that I could wish for in the near future, I wanted each of us to learn to understand each other better. Having our own separate residences, though, Jack and I did not see each other that much during the week. He was preoccupied with a multitude of things that were both work and personal related.

The good times we enjoyed together continued to stand out above the bumps. We were in the beginning stages of falling in love, and Jack reminded me what a *smitten kitten* he was. So how could I imagine our relationship as anything other than good? One special memory early in our relationship was Valentine's Day. If I was ever deprived in my life during a day reserved for romance it was February 14th. I had never been treated to a special day on Valentine's Day until I met Jack. In telling him all of this he knew celebrating that day with the one I loved would mean the world to me. He also had a good idea about the box of chocolates dilemma which many men have: *Will she miss receiving a box or will she think it will make her fat?* Jack seemed to know that a box of chocolates was not a requirement of mine. During such moments we seemed to be on a familiar plane; having an unspoken awareness of each other's needs. I was beginning to understand why he chose the screen name, CmeRomanceU. He was definitely a star at romancing.

Another fond memory early on in the relationship was his creativeness in writing and singing a song for me on his electric organ. The memory of him singing to me at the piano bar at Mark's Prime Steak House in Ocala in front of everyone seemed special. It was as brave a showing as he seemed genuine. That night, while receiving a standing ovation from restaurant customers Jack had touched my heart. That was my *wow!* A more powerful chemistry rang between us and we both seemed to be falling more deeply in love with each other. I know I was.

For the most part, the Match Man I described above seemed to have all of the makings of the kind of man many women dream about. It was recommended to me that I close the chapter here in order to have a storybook ending for you, my readers. I *could not* and *would not*. If there is such a thing as breaking any implied rules of the trade I am giving it my best shot in giving YOU, my readers the actual events which transpired from this point on with My Last Match Man. As a memoir, self-disclosure about my relationship with Jack *is* the successful ending for me and my readers. The facts are: this relationship was marked by the kind of emotional and physical abuse that many women suffer from every day (it goes without saying for men too!); the abuse occurred gradually over time; and the relationship sputtered between the highs and lows of a Match Man who was on the verge of a boiling point for many years.

That Jack had all of the makings of the kind of man women dream about would soon have me gasping, *So I thought!* I wanted to believe in this relationship so much that I became as blind-sighted as the deer that jumps across a dark road into an oncoming vehicle. For a split second, time freezes and your gut speaks to you. Unfortunately, I denied that instinct, and I was too far beyond the red flags even to note them. For the first time in my life I chose to wear the *idiot hat*. Similar to Bill Murray waking up to daily reruns in *Ground Hog Day*, I would awaken to the same kinds of turmoil that I would revisit over and over again with Jack.

There is the adage, *something is too good to be true,* which cautions us to our true instincts. Unfortunately, they were buried deeply in the recesses of my mind. Call it denial at a time that I was riding high on romance. What I did not know was that this Match Man *was* living out his own *abnormal* highs in my presence—highs which at the snap of a finger turned into dreadful lows. Many times he retreated into both his computer room and bedroom for days! The highs and lows gradually came to light and they worsened over time. The truth was that Jack was hiding an array of personal vices from me. At age fifty five, he was regularly consuming alcohol, candy bars (three specific brands from the era he grew up in), daily marijuana, cigarettes, tons of coffee and Nestle's chocolate milk. Could there be other things? Again, we were not living under the same roof, therefore, I was not privy to his lifestyle. However, the signs of moodiness and anger were making their presence to the surface with increasing frequency.

A particular discovery was startling to me. One morning, while we were out on the deck of his house Jack lit up a cigarette. Without a care in the world, I looked over to him and he said nothing. In bewilderment I said, *I thought you told me you were not a smoker and you know how I feel about smoking.* (Jack had checked off NO WAY under smoking in his Match profile!) Uneasy with my comment, he responded that he wasn't really a smoker but that the stresses of his business had become a contributing factor. I conveyed to him my worry that it might be difficult for him to quit since his partner was a chain smoker who also was diabetic. What I did *not* know was that Jack had been smoking on the sly since we met, and he deliberately hid this fact from me. His partner would shift outside to the deck of the house to smoke during several of my morning coffee visits. I made the decision to accept Jack's habit temporarily but let him know, in no uncertain terms, that I would not tolerate a long term relationship with a smoker—that it makes me physically ill, and nothing smells worse to me than clothes and a house smelling of smoke. Jack agreed that he *had* to quit as he had done several years before. He never did stop smoking despite two attempts using hypnosis.

It was clear to anyone but me that I had set the stage for a relationship with a man who now knew the following: that he could deceive me, he could point the blame finger at me for manipulative purposes, and he could get away with angry outbursts. Add to that, as one who gives people the benefit of the doubt and wanting to be helpful, the stage was set for lowering my standards! What I did not recognize was that my own self-esteem (not exactly stellar during this period) would be further eroded over the course of the relationship. This was another contributing factor in my falling victim to a man like Jack. Whenever I did stand up for myself, a fall out resulted and I would break off the relationship. After a few days, Jack would apologize, initially by email followed by cell short of begging to be allowed back into my life. Stupidly, I gave him so many chances that a hope chest could have been filled twice over!

The abuses I suffered under *CmeRomanceU* are difficult to write about. The passage of time, hopefully, will help dim these memories. Again, as a responsibility to be true to myself and to help others who have suffered under the abuses of men, I came to the decision to make this painful self-disclosure. I have chosen four incidents to describe the dynamics of the abuse. There were other events which occurred and which could be described as senseless to a normal person. The ones I have chosen best portray the story of a man whose cunning ways, manipulations, and charm succeeded in captivating a woman to the point of spell-binding her. Call it smoke and mirrors, a sport that I later discovered Jack relished using in business and on a personal level. He was a man who claimed to love his girlfriend to eternity and told her many times that she was *the most important thing in my life*. But his love was conceptual, his behavior at times bizarre, and his thinking an odd combination of the irrational, normal, delusional and cruel. So, why did I stay in such an abusive relationship for so long? In my best attempt to answer this there was an assortment of factors involved: I did not understand the tactics of a clever abuser such as Jack, and the progression of his abuse was both gradual and subtle. As confusing as it may sound, I found myself sublimating my own thinking as a way to adapt to the relationship. Also, Jack made the case for and emphasized how much time he had invested in us (already a year). He was convincing in his desire to maintain a committed and permanent relationship with me. All the while, he attempted to convince me that our conflicts were always of my making. Blame was his ally which he used conveniently against me, others, and the world. Working things out together was never an option because it takes two to do that! For example, when I wanted to have a discussion with him about personal matters, Jack would always defer to the next day which never came. His tactics extended to isolation, too. Continuing to believe he loved me, I remained confused until the entire picture of his use of spin tactics had become more apparent. And where exactly were my instincts in all of this? Sadly I had lost them *without even knowing!*

At the flip of a switch, handsome, charming Jack could turn into an ill-tempered angry man. During a discussion at the Hilton Hotel (just before my final break from him), Jack admitted to having a *vile* temper under stress. For years, layers and layers of what he called, *fear, anxiety* and *anger* had accumulated from all that had gone wrong in his past. His major unresolved issues were bitterness toward his two ex-wives, not having custody of his two daughters, and his repeated failings in business as an entrepreneur. He internalized those things for so long until it all came boiling out like the sudden burst of an erupting volcano. I broke away from him many times only to be masterfully drawn back into his life for continuous rounds that went like this: angry rants, blaming, manipulations, verbal contradiction, and back to the honeymoon stage. As much as Jack's emails might sound normal to a person who didn't know him, in the context of our relationship I found many of them confusing:

*I miss ya, love ya, I never broke up with you, you did
with me, I think you are extraordinary.*

*When are you going to come to your senses? I care
about you. It would be nice to know you are ok - if you dont
want to talk or see me I understand. I texted you twice - no
reply. I called you twice - no answer. To say my day was
not complete would be an understatement. Yes, I thought I
would hear from you today - am sad I didnt.*
Regardless of everything - I would like to know you are ok -
    I care about you.
    Perhaps a text saying whatever ....
    Love, Jack

For the very first time in my life, I became a willing
participant to a boyfriend's emotional and eventually,
physical abuse. Many times during tenuous moments I
asked myself the same two questions: *how could this be,*
and *God, what have I done to myself?*

Each of the four incidents below represents various
pieces of what I would later learn represent classic
characteristics of an abusive man. They show five major
dynamics at play: emotional and mental manipulation,
control, and physical abuse. The fifth dynamic—*using*
people to get what he wanted—became the most painful
truth. An example of this was when I had enlisted the help
of one of my closest friends for Jack to make a key
business contact during a time when he was going through
desperate times in his business. Later, he showed no
appreciation for those who helped him. The domestic
violence incident—incident four which follows at the end
of the next chapter—involved broken promises of a pre-
planned trip together to Puerto Rico (made possible through
my best friend and I). It represents the culmination of
betrayal when Jack physically abused me just before
leaving for the island for a second business trip there. The

emerging reality was, Jack loved my shell but had no regard for the inside of me, or any person for that matter.

When many pieces of the puzzle did take form, it became crystal clear, once and for all, why I must stop the on and off dynamics of the relationship. Toward the end one key factor was the support and guidance of a police officer who went to great lengths in educating me about men who abuse. He cautioned that my life was in danger and urged me to *get out while I was still alive*. Other factors were close friends and Google searches on abusive men. All combined these factors helped me come to my *real senses*. However, my decision to remain my own prisoner for a year cost me in physical and mental health. This was at a time when my life revolved around taking special care of a fragile health condition. One day, I began questioning what role the dynamics of my childhood might be playing. In my entire life, I had never experienced physical violence, but most of us, at one time or another, have experienced the painful emotional kind. I had for years. Still, the dynamics of this relationship were different because of Jack's substance abuse. That was unfamiliar territory to me. Putting such toxic things into one's body regularly was a scary concept to me but with persistence I chose to try to help him.

My last Match Man, *CMeRomanceU*, was the most difficult part of my journey but it was the key to my self-transformation; I had sunk to the lowest levels of human spirit making it possible for me to eventually restore my dignity and find wholeness. The best words describing what I had allowed myself to endure are: *manipulated, controlled, brow beaten, talked down to, spoken to like a child, and isolated from friends.* One day a close friend said to me, *you are not the person I once knew.* It was then that I knew that I had lost contact with who I was. One example of how Jack manipulated me was in using reverse tactics following a fall-out between us. He would initiate a text message such as this:

Hmmm, it's 11 p.m. and still no response from you. I've texted you and emailed you several times and still nothing. I want to apologize for everything. I fully understand if you never wish to have anything to do with me. I wish you all the best.

When I did not respond he would then progress to a more desperate stage:

I miss you, I love you and I don't want to fight. I am trying to fight for you the only way you have left me - in an email. I hope you will give me a call and we can get together and work this out If not - o well. I tried.

I hope you will not reinforce abandonment issues in me. We have been through alot and I hope it has not all been for nothing. I believe you are worth fighting for. If you don't believe I am - there is nothing more to be said.

Love, Jack

Eventually I would respond back with a call. The longest time I did not respond back lasted three weeks. When I did, you could toss it up to a combination of compassion for a boyfriend severely disturbed by his troubles, my own confusion about where we stood, and the lack of companionship which eventually allowed me to cave and go back to Jack. As far as his resistance to working things out, I had come to understand it as an incapability of his rather than the reality that it was his MO.

— CHAPTER THIRTY —

Four Incidents

Incident 1
A Big Red Flag of a Fight

Our first date was Sunday, January 10, 2010. Today is February 12, 2010. We had broken the one month barrier, with the exception of *a bizarre fight* which occurred during our first week of dating. The fight represented a beginning cycle of dynamics which held me hard and fast to a relationship doomed from the beginning. It occurred outside on the deck of Jack's rental house during a brief introduction to his business partner, Mike. There were no loud words exchanged and it had to do with jealousy on Jack's part.

It went like this: Jack's partner was a smoker so I made an assumption that smoking was not allowed in the house. Remember, Jack had me believe that he wasn't a smoker since I had listed that requirement on my Match profile. It turned out (a full month later) that Jack *was* a smoker and short of a chain one. Outside on the decking bench seats while the three of us were having morning coffee Jack was off on his own twitching around deep in thought. In an audible tone of voice I told them both that I needed to move closer to the overhang where Mike was seated to avoid the rising intensity of the Florida sun on my face. Sitting just six feet away from Jack it wasn't conceivable for anyone to think that Jack did not hear what I had said. A short time later, and as we were saying our goodbyes, suddenly I became aware that Jack was barely acknowledging my existence. In fact, he looked mentally stressed. I wondered, *What could be the problem?* As I headed out to leave, independently he headed to his vehicle. Without a word, he opened his door as if he had to be somewhere. I asked him if everything was all right and he replied that he needed to take a drive. My immediate, *What's wrong?*...was met by silence. With that he left but I decided to call him after lunch. When I did call, I received the most unexpected verbal lashing in which I was accused of making designs on his partner! When there was no reasoning with him, I told him he was *insane* and, that I wanted nothing more to do with him. I later called his partner Mike to tell him what had happened. Mike's scarce response was equally bizarre, indicating no concern over my distress. It seems I was guilty by two men who hung tightly—one who behaved crazy, and the other who didn't give a damn, yet knew the truth. I wondered who were these people?

Later that afternoon, there was a knock on my door and there was Jack standing outside asking to enter my house to talk. Refusing his request, a huge apology from him followed. Jack spent ten minutes apologizing for *his* mistake saying he never heard me announce that I was moving out of the sun and closer to where his partner was seated. Sensing my continued reluctance to have anything more to do with him he added that his partner, Mike told him to *get a grip*. His admission (made through his partner's words) that he had made a mistake got my attention and I listened to what he had to say. Over and over Jack told me he assumed the worst about my introduction with Mike. During the apology process, Jack wore me down and changed my mind about having a dialogue with him. Looking back, might this have been a test to see just how firm and how long I would continue to stand my ground? It seems he decided he wasn't going to lose me as a potential girlfriend. Call it effective spin tactics from a man under pressure, they worked! The following day, I decided to give Jack another chance. Unknown to me at the time, this bizarre fight was the mark of an abusive man who exhibited the signs of excessive jealousy and possessiveness. Also, subconsciously there was something about our relationship which felt familiar to me, perhaps going back to my childhood. At this juncture I wasn't able to make a connection.

Following our first fight during the first week of the relationship instead of things getting better a few more conflicts arose. I had never experienced the kinds of fights I had with Jack. His were filled with noticeable anger. The fact that there were no buyers for his composters, despite all of the contacts and meetings I helped set up, had a further impact on his anger, too. Conflicts between us progressed to one every month. What set him off was his possessive jealousy when I was socializing with people. Something as small as responding to a man's comment at the cream and sugar station at Star Bucks on Ocala's downtown square would launch Jack into an ugly mood for the rest of the day. I wasn't always aware of this because the majority of times he internalized his feelings and made them invisible to me. I discovered at a much later date that his anger had everything to do with things unrelated to me. Yet I was the trigger for his outbursts. As the only friend in his life I would instantly become a scapegoat when his anger exceeded the boiling point. After three months, I had initiated several break ups. Again and again Jack made up and reeled me back in. It was interesting to note that following our conflicts, a period of time would lapse and Jack would point the blame back to me. Without a definitive description he would say I provoked him. It was similar to his refusing to be human, foibles and all. Again, I questioned how I could get caught up in such an on and off again relationship where my boyfriend's moods could get out of control so fast. I doubted myself and asked, *Was I doing something I wasn't aware of to cause Jack's outbursts?*

As it turned out, the composter project was all about money, money, and more money for these two men. They wished to conquer the recycling of waste on a global scale. The money for the partner was purely greed. I remember the words spoken from Mike one evening at a dinner out at Carrabba's restaurant: *I'm in it all for the money, the money, and just the money.* As for Jack, initially I thought his motive was more tempered from the greed of his partner. He told me his was about making 54 million dollars in five years so that he could win the heart of a very young Turkish girl, Selena, whom he later confessed he had fallen in love with a year before meeting me. He told me she had broken his heart telling him he wasn't rich enough for her. The truth (I learned later) was that she all out rejected him (the 20 plus age difference might have been a factor, too). Why fifty four million? I learned it represented one million more than the amount of money Jack's deceased father had sold his New England billboard advertising company for. Having lofty financial goals was one thing but Jack's diehard requirement in attaining his goal was another. Once I overheard him say, *I will die before I give up making 54 million dollars.*

Worthy Mentions

Jack had invited two electrical engineers to reside in his house with him for six months during the construction of his prototype composter. One, whose name was Tony was Jack's ex-brother in law. They had not been in touch for over a decade but they had been college roommates. During several fall outs with Jack, Tony would encourage me to give him another chance. I debated him over this and Tony would reveal how desperate Jack was in not losing me. More specifically, Tony would tell me how much he *hoped a woman such as me could change his friend for the better because Jack was really a good man.* As I became more acquainted with Tony I believed what he had to say and *did* give Jack those extra chances. The community support for Jack represented by Tony was another factor which contributed to my own self-doubt. Then, when Tony's friendship with Jack suffered a total breakdown, Tony was sorry for the pain he caused me in encouraging me to stay with Jack. Once again, I disregarded my instincts about Jack that *he* was the problem and not me.

During this time when three men were living under the same roof, I noticed Jack's mood swings accelerating. What I didn't know was that the swings (which everyone witnessed) were symptomatic of bi-polar disorder, and something I knew nothing about. Another later discovery was that marijuana was a daily as well as nightly) event. Jack's mind was constantly racing and he complained about it often. Eventually, I began to figure out that the pot smoking slowed down his discomforting racing thoughts. There was a constant supply of alcohol available, too – beer, wine, rum and vodka (a Jack favorite) –which made a regular appearance just before dusk. All the while, the prototype composter was being built and it impressed me as an incredible creation. My feelings were mixed as I saw this new wonder alongside such an unhealthy lifestyle. For Jack, a multitude of stresses were at play—from the poor business climate to his deep seated conflict, again involving bitterness over two ex-wives. As much as I tried to push the negative things out of my mind and remain cheerful, they continued to gravitate back. They were the causes of the highs and lows of the relationship. There was one bit of good news in all of this. I did not ever get swallowed up by drugs and alcohol. Not only did I place a high priority on my health but it's just not me.

Two More Things…

One evening Jack revealed he had an older daughter. It sprung from a bottle of wine I saw sitting on top of his bedroom book shelf. The name of the wine had her name on the label. Now in her early twenties, she is his one and only biological daughter. Since she was nine, he told me she has had no contact with him. The story goes that Jack blamed his ex-wife for *brainwashing* his daughter against him (later on I found his story to be untrue and there was abuse involved). Without passing judgment on either side, I encouraged Jack to reach out after so many years. Unwittingly, I helped him craft an email to her which he said he never sent (for reasons only he knew too well). Another time, I found out that his second ex-wife had encouraged him to make a phone call to his daughter, which he did. She told him specifically not to ruin his single chance to re-establish relations with his daughter. Sadly, when he did contact her, the first words out of his mouth were to blame her mother for all that went wrong.

Then, Jack's road rage surfaced. The first signs occurred in July 2010 some six months into the relationship. Stunned by it, I voiced my disapproval over Jack's uncontrollable mission to get even with women drivers for minor things such as moving out of his way too slowly. His road rage extended to elderly people—he stared them down from his half open window.

The most poignant revelation to me about Jack was his inability to understand some core cultural codes of conduct and standard courtesies the majority of us live by. Jack had some missing links. Could this be attributed to what he claimed as having a genius IQ and ADD? This leads to the second incident in which his abuse turned physical. One of the most important things I learned about physical abuse is that regardless of who is at fault, a man should never put his hands on a woman or forcibly restrain her. Jack did both of those things in two independent incidents. His actions occurred over the most trivial of reasons: the first one below was over a complimentary hotel bathrobe. Like a spoiled child he later attempted to turn the blame on me!

Incident 2
The Wedding at Coral Gables, Florida

My nephew's wedding was to be the wedding of all weddings that one could imagine being invited to. I was excited and looking forward to attending. It was seven months into my relationship with Jack and thus far he had shown no signs of physical abuse. He was relentless about wanting to go with me and bringing with us his nine year old adopted daughter, Brianna from his second marriage. She lived on the West Coast and would be making a visit east to see her father during the week of the wedding. For now, Jack's business deals were not panning out and he was constantly stressed to the point of exhaustion. I didn't want him to attend the wedding with me because I wanted to enjoy the festivities of a 200 guest wedding held at the Biltmore Hotel. There would be family reunions with relatives I hadn't seen for almost two decades. There was a live Venezuelan Band scheduled to play into the wee hours of the morning. Finally, there would be fun outings: to Miami's South Beach and with the girls to have our hair and make-up done. In short, I wanted to have fun. Jack was relentless in wearing me down to the point of allowing him to come. I believe he did not want to be left alone in the company of his young daughter Brianna for four days. Knowing of my love for children, bringing Brianna to the wedding meant he would have some help. More important, and without my knowledge at the time, he was planning to use me to make important business contacts at the wedding.

Upon entering the lobby of the hotel we were presented with a complimentary glass of champagne. Two glasses was the hotel's cutoff point for newly arriving guests. Since one drink was my limit, Jack gladly helped himself to the server's tray for my second glass. It was as though the party had started before we had entered the lobby elevator to go up to our room.

During a wonderfully elegant family and friends dinner, Jack made a few social rounds in an effort to impress people. It was interesting to note that he spent a considerable amount of time that evening in the attempt to impress one of my beautiful nieces. Utilizing origami skills (the Japanese art of paper folding) acquired earlier in life, he worked hard to impress her. As she became disenchanted with Jack's preoccupation with her, to his distress, she eventually flipped him off. Two other things about Jack stood out that night: first, he was rarely by my side, and second, he made a most unexpected announcement to some members of my family that I was his fiancée! They were just as surprised as I was!

That same night there was a pool party that would last until 2 in the morning. Up in our rooms on the fifth floor, we changed into our bathing suits. As impatient as kids can be, Brianna left the room ahead of us to go down to the pool. The hotel had a strict dress code ensuring that guests wear their bathrobes over their bathing suits as they traveled between their rooms to the pool. Earlier that day, both Jack and Brianna lost their complimentary robes— Brianna spilled orange juice on hers and Jack left his somewhere. I got a replacement for Brianna but Jack did not bother to get a new one for himself. Thus, he would grab mine off the closet hook leaving me without one to wear down to the pool. As any normal girlfriend would do, I asked Jack if I could have my robe to wear. His reply was, *earlier you said I could borrow it, and you didn't need it.* I told him I needed it now because the hotel hallways were frigid. I added that I didn't understand why he thought he should have my robe and not offer it up, as any gentleman would, to his girlfriend. This was a common cultural code he didn't seem to compute. Again, Jack refused. Now, ticked off I said, *What? Do I have to do everything including wiping your rear end?* In a split second, Jack's face turned beet red, his cheeks began twitching, and in an angry rage retorted, I'm *not going to the pool party, I'm packing and leaving. I am getting a rental.* With that he flung his luggage bag onto the king sized bed, flipped it open and began throwing his clothes into it. I began crying and he began ranting non-stop making denigrating comments about me. He would repeat over and over again the same things in a loud tone that could be heard outside the room. I told him that I was leaving, and at that moment Jack grabbed me and threw me onto the bed. He pinned me down with his hands against my throat. The memory of four plus seconds (what seemed like forever) of not being able to breathe was among the most frightening moment of my life. He released me suddenly when the sound of our room door opening broke his hold on me. Brianna had forgotten something! In a panic, he ordered the nine year old into the bathroom. That way she would not understand what had happened. She was thoroughly frightened over his behavior, though. I tried reaching for my phone, and in less than a second Jack had knocked it out of my hand where it dropped to the floor. Brianna had been peeking through the partly cracked doorway and saw this. I pleaded for the nine year olds help. Jack ordered her to stay put (the bathroom was just three feet from the bed). He told her I was crazy and violent and that they were leaving to go home right away. Brianna froze in the bathroom. He ordered her to pack her things but she was too afraid to come out. He ordered her for a second time which she did not do. She had witnessed her father striking my arm so that I could not use my phone. I remain frozen in bed. When Jack went halfway into the bathroom, I saw my only chance for escape, and jumped out of bed. He ran after me and on the way out of the room, I grabbed a floor lamp and threw it behind in my path. I had made a successful escape to my older brother's room. I did not press charges because I was intent on not upsetting the wedding. My brother handled the situation that evening in best interests of the young child by getting a separate room for her and Jack. His gesture was confusing to me. Had Jack and his daughter left the hotel that evening I am certain that my relationship with Jack was over for good.

The next morning while still in shock, Jack called me on the phone. His response went, *You know, I have this pride.* In choosing that expression I thought he displayed the trait of a weak and fearful man along with the shaky voice that uttered it. To save face at such a grand wedding, we both pulled ourselves together, and I accepted him back to participate in the wedding. Looking back, what a fool I was! At the dance reception following the wedding, my brother asked why I was still with Jack. I responded that I was confused over the mixed signals represented by the extra room he got for Jack and Brianna. To me, it represented that it was acceptable for Jack and his daughter to stay. Added to that was the obvious embarrassment over Jack leaving that evening, and another factor back home complicating matters as well. At this point, I'm not sure exactly what my brother thought had transpired in our room. As siblings we were not that close. My description of the events that occurred in the hotel room, though was later confirmed by Jack's daughter to her mother. There were two things for sure: my brother never knew me to ever lie about anything and neither one of us really understood domestic violence. My brother was upset with Jack's behavior and emailed me to me a month following the wedding saying, *it was very unclassy of this guy to put the additional room charge on my credit card* (my brother paid for our original room). Again, another cultural code missing!

A week after the wedding, my niece was visiting a friend in Sanibel Island. She would stay with me in Ocala on the way down to pick up her dog, Lacy which was staying with me. She called me from the road, and it was then that I decided to tell her about the choking incident at the wedding. Her first words to me were, *Why where you still with him the next day at the wedding reception?* I replied that I was in so much shock that I think I was paralyzed from taking any action. It was then she told me that I was insane, referring to the commonly known definition of insanity—doing the same thing over and over again and expecting a different result. Aren't many of us guilty of that when it comes to matters of the heart? She followed, *you weren't ready to leave him then, but now you must leave him because he strangled you.* Still in denial over the shocking wedding incident, I responded, *he choked me not strangled me.* Suddenly I realized there was no difference! Over and over in my mind I began to understand the most frequently asked question: *why do women stay in abusive relationships?*

I put the wedding incident behind me by justifying it as an unusual one-time incident. Why? During the wedding Jack was extremely stressed over his business failures and was on his cell phone practically non-stop. He wasn't enjoying the festivities and I was oblivious to the increasing anger festering beneath the surface. It turns out that he was in the process of losing a funding opportunity for his business in the country of Sri Lanka. He chose not to tell me and instead internalized his frustrations. Looking back, the time he did spend socializing was in drawing attention to himself and his business in attempting to make important contacts through my family and guests. Unaware of this, I wanted desperately to forget about the choking incident. As uncomfortable as the drive home from Miami was, I did try to forget so that things might be restored between us. But another conflict was on the horizon.

Conflicts always revolved around Jack's refusal to discuss matters surrounding our relationship. There were numerous fallouts over the most trivial of things and Jack had a way of reeling me back to him after a week using half apologies for his behavior. This recurring theme became dynamic in our relationship. When he thought he was really losing me, he sent emails with a more desperate tone, pleading his case. Too *proud* to take responsibility for his inappropriate behavior, the apologies were not forthcoming until he realized I would be gone for good. He worked his charms successfully by saying the right things. Add strong chemistry between us and eventually I would be drawn back. I felt alone where I was living, too. For a time, there was no further physical abuse but I felt the pressure whenever he copped a mood. In fact, it got to the point where I felt like I was walking on eggshells. Tiring of all of this one day I told him that I wished to date other men. I made this decision to distance myself from him after reading an article about women abusers and began connecting the dots. The next two voicemails below represent the apology and jealousy factors characteristic of abusive men:

I owe u an apology. I did overreact and I apologize for it. uh I need to find better ways to express myself um, I'm not doing so well and, uh, you probably already know that uh ... I'm dealing w lots of fear ...and anger and stress and I'm not doing a lot right, and I guess I'm not right in the head, so, um ,I'm sorry. I think do have a right to be upset with ya but I don't think to that extent.

I didn't express myself well or in an acceptable way, so I wanted to call and say I'm sorry. Take care

Following this voicemail and 30 minutes later at 9:15 p.m. I wasn't aware that Jack had driven by my house with the intention of stopping in to have a talk. This was a first. Upon seeing a car in my driveway his jealousy got the better part of him and he left this vm:

Well, I, I, take my breath away... I came over um to see you and there was a car in your drive and I can only assume who it is. And it kind of confirmed a lot of some feelings I've been having for a long time and...and I'm just...

Wow Nancy, how could ya seriously, you missed a big one

We all live by our decisions and we all choose the path that we do

I'm sorry that you've chosen the path that you have

Be well be happy, I only wish the best for you. Take care

I had invited a girlfriend over for dinner that evening and Jack had driven by just before my friend was getting ready to leave. I called him back to inform him and he apologized for *assuming the worst* about me.

As strange as all of this might sound, once again my sympathy took over. This was the first time that I knew of that Jack had come to my home unannounced. I began to realize what a lost soul he was and felt pity on him. Perhaps this could be the start of a friendship and nothing more. Until this last voicemail, I did not realize how badly Jack had it for me. I admit to being an idiot, then! The first part of helping him was trying to get him to understand his abnormal behavior. I had tried to figure him out for the better part of a year and concluded that he lacked the willingness and ability to grow as a human being. Had I known he was incapable of change, I'm certain that I would not have wasted my time.

Incident 3
I Just Wanted to Take a Walk

There was good news on the horizon: Jack wanted to quit smoking for good! He had already visited a hypnotist once in the past year. This time represented a chance for us to work together as friends. Equally important, I saw it as a wonderful chance for him to improve his health. His first attempt had lasted less than a week. The second time around, he stood hard and fast to get past the painful withdrawal symptoms which lasted little more than a week. I thought he made a valiant attempt and this was the first time he asked for my help. I drove to his house every evening to go on healthy walks with him—something I had been encouraging for a year. This was a new beginning for us engaging in healthy outdoor activities. During our walks, I noticed the poor condition of his body from years of a sedentary life sitting in front of the computer. Then, after three weeks something happened, and just like that he decided to stop walking. Sadly, I discovered he had begun smoking again. Two weeks later, I tried encouraging him to get back on track. During a phone call Jack told me he did not want to go for a walk. I was welcome to his house though, and decided to visit in the hopes of cheering him up. When I arrived he was sitting in front of his computer preoccupied in thought and noticeably in a bad mood. It was obvious to me that Jack was in no mood to be around anyone so I asked him if I might take a walk myself before dusk and then head home. Suddenly, like the flip of a switch, Jack went into a rage shouting, *How many times do I have to tell you, No, I don't want to take a walk!* Had he not heard that I was going off on my own? Then he shouted, *You're in a bad mood, you're in a bad mood aren't you?* Replying, *I've been in a great mood*, he followed once more with the same harassing question. I became visibly upset and left crying out the door. Without a word from him that evening or the next day, I tried to reach him by phone worried that he had gone mad. He did not return my calls. What was I to think other than being done with him! Two days later I went over to his home to retrieve my things (including my garage door opener). When I arrived Jack appeared at the doorway entrance of his house. He had already lined up my things just inside. Standing in front of me outside on the deck, I asked him, *is this it?* Following a pause it became obvious to me that he had been enraged for some time before my arrival. To ease his stress I carried my pocket purse dog (which he was always happy to see) in one arm. Suddenly, in the next second, my canvas bag was being hurled at my chest and my tiny dog. Inside the bag was an old sunbeam mixer made of heavy glass and metal bottom (I lent this to him just the week before). I caught the bag before it hit us both. This was followed by the worst rantings I'd ever heard and similar to some celebrities of late. I rushed down the deck steps to leave and for a moment, I hesitated. I remembered my garage door opener on the visor of his car. As he disappeared back into his house, I brought my dog back to my vehicle and then I quickly ran into the open garage to retrieve my clicker from his car. As if in a flash, Jack came running out of the front door of his house once again continuing his ranting. He cornered me in the garage using his car and his body to block me from leaving! Then he threatened to call 911 if I did not leave his premises that very moment. How could I? Continuing in the same mode of behavior he began dialing on his phone. Facing him, I asked, *What's with you?* He responded that he was going to keep me from leaving until the police arrived, citing that I was trespassing. This was all so crazy! My garage door opener was already in my hand, staring him in the face. Upon realizing the folly of the situation Jack decided to let me go. Within a half mile of my drive home, a police car zoomed by on the opposite side of the road. Later on I found out that this was no coincidence. When the officer arrived at his home, Jack had barricaded himself in his house and would not answer the door. This bizarre incident represented the end of my romance with him. At the end of three weeks emails poured into my inbox from Jack. The first one went:

I apologize for my behavior. I fully understand if you do not want to talk to me again. I wish you only the best

A second one:
I love you I miss you
If we cant be lovers anymore I hope we can still be friends.

A third one followed:
I guess no response to my email sums it up. What can i say :(
I had hoped you would a come to your senses by now all things considered. My bad.
Just for the record - I never said I didn't want to see you anymore - that's what you said.
Sorry you feel that way.

I guess all that's left for me to do now is wish you well. I wish you well.

Bummer :(
sigh :(

Was hoping to do something this weekend - daytona or foghat concert at silver springs - guess its solo :(.

I replied back to Jack I'd had enough with him and his desire to be friends was no longer a possibility. His behavior typically ranged from puffed up pride and then to desperation when he refused own up to his irrational behavior. Normally, two people would attempt to talk things over. But Jack's style—when he was upset about something—was to launch a military strike. In the aftermath of an outburst, he always attempted to make me believe that, no matter how bad the circumstances, we were together for good, evident in this voicemail:

ya know I just don't get you Nancy. What do ya expect me to say to you... you expect me to listen to Oh I'm going to start dating again...Why are we even going through this and I hang up and then you get upset because I hang up on it. Come on that's not very nice Every great journey starts with a first step. Make the first step Nancy. Stop the nonsense. I haven't done anything to hurt you, seriously, you're acting horribly, seriously.

The phrase, *I haven't done anything to hurt you* was mind boggling. How did I make sense of this? Writing journal notes helped. In one, I referenced a talk he had with me involving his partner, Mike:

There has been something so bizarre about you. I have never experienced it with anyone in my life, and until this moment I haven't been able to put my finger on it. It's a void space in you—one that a long time ago might have been filled with compassion, love and empathy for others. Could I be so wrong?

I am beginning to see that you have more in common w your partner. You once told me that long ago he shut down with the outside world and that accounts for his anti-social behavior. But you are of the same cloth. I didn't want to believe this could be true when all the while you have been pressing me to open my heart to you as you say you have done for me?

After nearly a month of being apart from one another a barrage of emails, once again poured into my inbox. It was the week was leading up to his birthday and I would not be there to celebrate it with him. I knew how sad and lonely Jack was but he was no longer my concern. *I* was. From his emails, I realized just how poorly he was doing in his business dealings, and how much he was looking for a distraction away from his emotional lows. I was determined not to be his distraction. It was interesting to note that following three weeks of no communications, Jack attempted to pick up with me as if we had been together just yesterday. He texted the following three messages:

Hmmm…11 o'clock I guess I called to late oh well I missed you. sorry about that. Just checking in to see how ya were doing uhhm… was thinking about u so I thought I'd give ya a call aaand
Maybe you'll call me back sometime (awkward laugh)

*Hmm, well, don't **know** if you're ok. Just checking in. I thought I was going to hear from you yesterday. Umm it's Monday. Didn't hear from you so I um don't know what's going on so anyway give a call if you want. That would make my birthday complete.*

Hey it's me, um, it's uh it's 2 minutes to midnight, and I still haven't heard from you, um, it um be nice to.

Two days later there was this voicemail on my cell:

I'd like to know you're okay If you're not okay so…and if I don't hear from you by tomorrow I guess I'm going to start making calls so maybe u can give me a call or me a text or something. Let me know your okay send me a text or something it's all I care about anyways talk to ya later

Hey I'm really getting uh concerned about you. Um I don't know really what to do about it um hopefully you can just text me and... just say you're okay and I'll be fine, I'll leave you alone, whatever you want ,um, but I hate being this concerned. I haven't heard or seen ya (he never saw me) in a couple days. I drive by your house it doesn't look like anyone's been there and there's been no response to any kind of messages so itd be nice to hear your okay, that's all I care about
Talk to you later

Our Meeting at the Hilton Hotel

Once again, the alarm bell failed to ring and I remained the habitual push over who eventually returned Jack's call. At his request for a talk, I decided to meet him on neutral territory at the Hilton Hotel one last time— something he was well aware of. Seeing him for the first time in a month, there was a visible sadness to his face. He looked exhausted, similar to the rung out race horse that trails dead last through the finish line. Jack's birthday had just passed and he had had no one to celebrate it with.

This time, I gave him an ultimatum regarding his ongoing disrespect and temper flare-ups. Perhaps Jack needed this jolt to make some necessary changes. After all, he was the one now who wanted to have a discussion and would not let me go easily. This was his last chance to recognize friendship as a new beginning. At our meeting we both agreed to communicating when conflicts arose, not isolating me, and stopping the long term disrespect by his partner, Mike. Mike had never accepted me as Jack's girlfriend and from time to time he took the opportunity to sabotage our relationship through name calling behind my back. As much as I stayed away from Mike, Jack didn't take the required action to put a stop to his partner's disrespect for some time. Finally when I had had enough, and did demand from him that he do something Jack conveyed to me how much his resentment was growing by the week over the issue. Assuming Jack was the boss in his two man company I addressed that point with him and he was. But the truth was, Jack avoided any kind of confrontation with people was anything but a decision maker. At the same time, Jack would complain to me about Mike behind his back. They were like an unhappy, bickering married couple. There was no irony then when the last abusive act against me (incident 4 below) was a tag team effort by the two worthy of a wrestling match!

Incident 4
Held Up Like a Punching Bag

If the three incidents above did not put my mind through enough confusion and turmoil Incident 4 turned my world upside down. The incident amounted to shock, disbelief, betrayal and total fear. Regarding the latter, I do not ever recall feeling the kind of fear that has one visibly shaking as I did on the afternoon of May 21, 2011. With the exception of the wedding incident the physical abuse of this incident finally opened up my eyes to who this Match Man really was—*a sociopathic monster.* That Jack would forcibly restrain me in a bear hug while his partner and friend of forty years punched me in the face and mouth like a punching bag was devastating. More shocking was that they acted together in spontaneity with one another encouraging and approving each other's actions. Jack snapped like a stick of explosive dynamite, and partner Mike who was full of long term rage against the world, and me, instantly joined forces.

More startling was that incident 4 occurred barely a week after our meeting at the Hilton Hotel. Before that meeting, both Jack and Mike had left on a business trip for Puerto Rico made possible through me and my best friend. Jack had left for this first trip without informing me about it until his return ten days later. The two men were there exploring a new venture in waste management. Meetings were set up in advance through my friend's contact, and the two were staying at a resort owned and operated by the same. Jack was on a grand high because for years all of his business ventures amounted to nothing. Now, he had something concrete that he could look forward to pursuing. Without going into great length here's how the incident unfolded:

Upon returning from the island of PR Jack seemed like a new man with new beginnings. Just a day later during an outdoor walk we took together, there was the disappointing news of a former business venture going nowhere. The bad news set Jack back to his moody and depressed self despite his having a new focus for business in the islands. Also, there was a trip planned for both of us to travel together on the second trip there. I was scheduled to be interviewed for a potential employment opportunity with the same contact. You would think that this would cheer up Jack based on his *friend* (me) attempting to help him out. Before leaving for the second trip to PR the following week, on Thursday we planned dinner out and a movie. Thursday came and we shared a wonderful evening out to dinner, a special trip to an ice cream parlor, and to the opening of the movie, *Pirates of the Caribbean, On Stranger Tides*. As the evening came to a close, Jack dropped me off at my home before midnight. As we sat in the driveway for a moment I remembered he was planning to borrow my truck for a business related transport the next morning. This was something I had done for him before. Upon asking if he still needed to use it, a troubled expression came over his face. Avoiding eye contact with me, he said, *Mike insists on renting a truck because he doesn't want to be around yours*. In total surprise I responded, *You have got to be kidding*. Instead of putting a stop to Mike's nonsense Jack's excuse was that he did not want to cause any upset to his business. Too tired to debate the subject, I got out of his car and went inside. An interesting side note—this was the first time Jack did not get out of his vehicle to open the car door for me as he regularly did in the past. The next morning I called Jack to discuss the disrespect matter involving Mike. In his usual fashion, Jack tried shrugging it off by not answering to it. He was barely out of bed by 10:30 a.m. (a frequent rising time) and said he'd call me back in five minutes. He called an hour later. Right there, I asked him to handle the matter once and for all because it was one of the agreements we made at the Hilton. Still groggy, he muttered, *I'll think about it, I haven't taken a shower*. I never heard back from him. Again, this was fast becoming Jack's MO—avoidance. Just the night before (and many times before) he said more than once that I was the most important thing in his life and he wanted to be with me for the rest of my life. Now I was presented with confusing contradictions. In trying to make sense of things I went over to his house to talk in person to ask him why he too was being disrespectful. If he refused to take action there was nothing left of a relationship already on skid row. My plan was to retrieve my garage door opener (still on his car's visor) and my personal belongings. To Jack the act of retrieving my garage door opener represented finality of our relationship, and once prior to this he had used possession of the device as a way to hold on to me.

When I arrived at Jack's place, he was out in the hanger behind his house drilling holes in plastic garden pots. When I entered the hangar he saw me and I waited for him to stop drilling. He did not so I asked him to stop, and then he did. The intense expression on his face carried the weight of his ongoing problems—both business and personal. I asked, *why are you allowing this strife in our relationship?* He continued to ignore me with no intention of communicating. I continued on about Mike's behavior when Mike suddenly walked into the hanger from a back door opening near us. He had overheard my conversation about him which by anyone's estimate was an accurate description of his lesser traits. Without hesitation, Mike walked up to within an inch of my face calling me a *whacko*. Looking to move away from him I found myself backed up to a table saw, machinery to my immediate right, and Jack to my left. So I placed my hand to his chest to push him back away from me. Mike stood his ground as if to intimidate me. Just before attempting to make another move to escape, Jack, who was standing just three feet from me instantly grabbed my entire body in a bear hug. Suddenly I felt the impact of a fist punching me on the right side of my face. Everything happened so fast—Jack grabbing hold of me and the impact of a man fist to my face. I never saw the first punch coming! With my face positioned above his left shoulder, Jack maintained his hold on me as a second punch was forth coming. To avoid more injury to the right side of my face my involuntary response was to raise my legs up from the ground to slide down so that my face would be covered behind Jack's left shoulder. As the weight of my body dropped Jack gripped harder with his arms and lifted all 100 pounds of me keeping me suspended up from the ground. The second punch came and I flipped back my head to try to lessen the impact. This time instead of impacting my eye, Mike's fist landed on my mouth splitting my lower lip against my upper teeth. Now holding my upper body in a lower position Jack dragged me twenty feet to the entrance of the hanger. Unable to support my feet on the ground my legs swept the ground as he dragged me. I pleaded, *please let me go!* Along the way, my cell phone dropped to the floor. Again, begging to be released Jack continued his tight hold. Over and over I begged to be let go. Then, Mike picked up my phone and with Jack looking on, he slammed it onto the cement floor where it exploded before my eyes. Mike walked out of the hangar and Jack continued to maintain his bear hold on me.

Physically shaking me, he shouted, *Mike is right, Mike is right, and you deserve it.* With that Jack released his grip on me with a sudden jolt that sent me twisting and falling on my knees. Traumatized and in pain, I watched Jack walk away without the least bit of concern. As he walked away I will remember the unforgettable moment when he turned his head for a quick glance back at me as I lay stunned on the ground. He muttered, *I can't be around a person like you,* as if to justify what had just happened. Meanwhile, Mike disappeared for good. Unable to get up off of the hangar floor, I cried, *how could you do this to the one you claim to love?* After a few minutes I slowly collected myself enough to rise up off of the ground, pick up the pieces of my phone and get to my vehicle to attempt the drive home.

Without any form of communications I was not able to call the police. My cell phone was in a hundred pieces, I did not have a land line at home, and pay phones today are difficult to locate. All I could think about was getting out of there. Dazed and in shock, I wasn't road worthy to drive to a police station. I crawled towards home at 25 mph. I could not make the short drive and pulled into a friend's farm near the half way mark. My friend was busy holding a private graduation party for her daughter when I arrived but she came out to my vehicle to be with me. After a time she had to leave and so I continued my drive home. During the remainder of my drive everything appeared blurred and in slow motion. The surreal sound of white noise consumed my space. Upon arriving home I was relieved to be in a safe haven. Still reeling in the full effects of emotional trauma I had difficulty trying to gather my senses. I knew I must get a replacement phone but I was incapable of leaving my house. I had never felt so vulnerable in my life. What if something should happen to me? My heart was beating so fast, at my age I was worried. For a long while I was immobilized by the trauma and the disbelief of what had happened to me. The next evening was already here and still, I was in shock. I decided that I would call the Marion County Sheriff's Office the following morning to report the crime.

The next morning, Jack had already left the country for PR when the interviewing Officer arrived to my house to make a report. Therefore, she interviewed Mike only. Mike hid from the police when they arrived at his house but later that day, he was interviewed by phone. In the police report, Mike denied ever touching me and said that I must have fallen on some equipment in the hanger. Within minutes after the Officer finished questioning Mike I received the following text messages from Jack who was already in PR:

2:34 pm I have been informed you have initiated some
        silly action against Mike.
2:35 pm In 1 hour I will do a few things.
2:36 pm Sort it out fast or deal with a lot of stuff that will
        be most unpleasant.

Upon receiving these TM's I called the Officer to notify her about them. She told me that Jack was using intimidate tactics and I should keep a record of them on my phone so that they could be submitted at an upcoming meeting scheduled at State's Attorney's office. A first time victim of physical abuse, I was learning how slowly the wheels of the legal system worked. Had I reported the incident at the scene, things would have moved swiftly and the two would have been arrested and sent to jail. Smashing my cell phone, though prevented that. Later, I learned that many victims of physical abuse do not make it to the initial meeting at the State Attorney's office because they are not strong enough to pursue it to court, or they end up going back to their abuser. I was determined to follow through with my case. I believed that these two men must be held accountable for their actions no matter what the end result.

For sure, Jack had never been held accountable for his past abusive behavior against women and children which he had successfully kept under wraps for decades.

As this book goes to print my case is still pending a small claims court hearing for the damage to my front teeth. Moving on with my life and closing out this chapter of my life are my foremost priorities.

There are many things I learned from both my Match journey and my last Match Man. Regarding the latter, the most important was about the brain abnormality of a man leading to violent rages and worsened through decades of an unhealthy lifestyle of drugs and alcohol. I also learned about the grave dangers these men present to women who stay with them. As for my Match journey, one of the most important things I learned about chemistry is that it can be highly over-rated when it comes to finding a soul mate. There is no question that for many, chemistry between two humans reigns. But the overpowering role that it sometimes plays for those passionate human beings can contribute to destroying lives, too, as it almost did mine. I have learned some things about love that are obvious to some of us but not all—that love thrives best when based on trust, mutual respect, and a line of open communications that are accepted by both. Only then can two people have a better chance at remaining better bound through conflict. This kind of love allows partners to better tolerate each other's quirks and idiosyncrasies and accept the good and the not so good. It should allow both to reach out to one another, to look out for each other's best interests and be supportive of each other. Contrary to lending support I had observed Jack being in competition with everyone he crossed paths with, including family. His competitive attitude was one which harbored the negative sort of jealousy that we are all familiar with—the kind which attempts to kill the spirit. Finally, real love is the kind that motivates and perpetuates the best in each other. Again, these are things we all know too well but do not always put into practice in our relationships.

Lastly, I learned about the irrational, faulty thinking that leads to the snap of anger and how fortunate I am to be alive today. I was reminded of it on the Oprah Winfrey show in an interview with David Arquette who said, on the subject of anger:

Anger is like drinking poison and expecting the other person to die because you have no control over them. You must look into yourself to get grounded before you can heal. You can't expect that from others.

From that insight, I discovered that I indeed had become Jack's *poison*. At the same time I was his only true friend!

— CHAPTER THIRTY-ONE —

A Curve Ball Leads to This

When I set out to write this book, I never considered how the ending might turn out. Every one of us would like to have our own success story. As a realist, though, I was well aware of how difficult my journey might turn out. All of us have been reminded at one time or another in our lives that when it comes to matters of the heart things are not so clear.

And then there are the curveballs life throws us. The domestic violence of, *My Last Match Man* was just that. For a time, he pressed me into believing that he *was* my soul mate. Cleverly, he painted himself as a man with a bright future during less than the best of times. As a result, he resonated differently from all the men before him. Similar to me and many others he was busy working on new opportunities despite how bad things were economically. How cool was that? But there were obvious reasons behind his lack of success in both his business and personal endeavors. Most notable was his odd behavior and a bad temper. Incomprehensible to me at the time, I still cast all doubt aside that he could be dangerous. Always looking for the good in people, I perceived our individual differences in a more positive light to find my own personal success. It is similar to the Seinfeld episode where George Castanza sets out to behave in the total opposite manner of his past with women thinking it will lead to newfound success in affairs of the heart.

Despite my last Match Man's clever and cunning ways, it still remains a wonder to me how I allowed myself to fall victim to domestic violence. Remember, Jack did some things that most women only dream about—writing lyrics to songs for a girlfriend and singing them to her. In time, I discovered that Jack wrote the songs more to draw attention to himself. It was no surprise then, when I discovered that he was a pathological liar, too. His love was of his own invention, and eventually this Match Man would come to a self-admission in an earlier voicemail saying, *I'm not right in the head.* So, I got taken in just as many others have. It was only after several reviews of this chapter and much research that I discovered how Jack fit the profile of a dangerous...YES... sociopath!

There is the old adage: *When you look for something you'll never find it until you stop looking.* In giving up on Jack what I found was truth in his identity. A month before being physically beaten, my *idiot hat* was just beginning to come off. I had no idea I was dating a sociopath, yet romantically speaking I was done with him. I was done with his obsessive and jealous love, temper tantrums, and smoke and mirror tactics. Not ever wanting to be enemies with anyone though, at the end I gave in to his last request to be friends. Knowing he was losing me was one thing but I had no idea about the huge rage lurking beneath his veneer. I never imagined being primed for a beating on the most beautiful sunny day in Florida! Looking back, it all makes sense when I think about one song in particular Jack wrote about how *lost* he was without me. His convincing powers via this song were waning and he realized he had lost the challenge in maintaining his grip on me. As difficult as it was for me to give up, that little voice in my head was in high decibel. Simultaneously, I felt a deep black cloud lifting. My instincts, finally were in charge!

Feeling free for the first time in over a year, I began making new friends with *normal* people who I could trust and respect. I looked up an old friend of mine with whom I was previously romantically involved. Despite the end of our relationship we continued to remain good friends. Connecting with a trusted friend was a way of reaching out to the familiarity of my past and reminiscing about the good ole times. Just like me, my friend was now single and cyberdating on another site. I called him and told him of my humiliating predicament just before the last incident. Immediately following the incident, my friend drove over one hundred miles every weekend to be by my side to help see me through my recovery. Keeping me safe and protected for months, we developed a special bond of friendship that I did not think possible between men and women. He continues to hold a special place for me in his heart as I do for him. That men and women *can* have that kind of bonded friendship is truly rewarding. The question arises, are we to remain friends, or could he be my soul mate? Just as I've said to men many times before, *time will tell.* For now, and for the right reasons, I couldn't be in a better place where romance is not the lead role. My journey will continue and I am relieved to know that *my idiot hat has finally come off!*

Why I Went Back On Match

Just days before Incident 4, I had already written off Jack and taken out a three month subscription to Match. You might ask, why? One might think that I was hardly ready to plunge into the dating scene after my experiences with him. I was, though, because I was not willing to give up so easily on the human race. Also, there was the urgent need to forget about my recent past. Moving forward and meeting new people strictly as friends was the best way for me to do that, and do it on Match.

After Incident 4, time needed for healing was of paramount importance in getting back to my mental, emotional and physical well being. Resisting thoughts of retreating, I was determined to overcome the fear factor which was now transparent in my every behavior. So many alerts were racing through my mind. What to do and where to start? One thing I knew for sure—I had an unquenchable thirst to know that there were normal people of the opposite sex out there, and in particular on Match. In coming to terms with the crazy Match Man who had disrupted my life, I wanted to find a way to reduce the impression he left in my mind. Initially, my first reaction was to terminate my newly subscribed Match membership. A refund was not possible, but hiding my profile was. Averse to hiding from anything in life, I chose to take the initiative and informed Match about the status of one of their members. In doing so, they removed my last Match Man from the site within forty-eight hours. The fact that he was out of sight and no longer viewing me was a big relief. From those actions, I discovered that my way to heal was to remain on Match. It felt analogous to climbing back onto a horse after hitting the dust, and I had experienced that more than once as a horsewoman. A short time later, if things began to shine brighter, they did. Some of the most heartwarming emails landed in my inbox from several Match Men. What healers and confidence boosters they were! A favorite went:

Goodness! If your name is not beside the comment "gentle warmth", then something...somewhere...is terribly wrong. Wow! Just...wow!

In disbelief I questioned his compliment and received this:

The whole truth is, I did not so much see the "gentle warmth" you carry so well, as I felt it. Upon first spying your breath-taking smile, in combination with the depth I also see in your eyes....I don't know how anyone could miss it. That is, unless they are blind, completely unfeeling...or just moronic.

You know, I have to admit, it kinda saddens me that no one else see's this "specialness" in you...which tells me many things, but mostly that people, males in particular, or not looking beyond the obvious. It is in the "unobvious" aspects of life, and of a person's character, in which we find the reasonings why some love lasts and others do not.

Still, I think all one has to do is look...for only a precious moment...at your primary profile photo alone...and it is as plain as the nose on their face. I assure you this is true.

And, by the way, I believe as you do...life without passion...for something...is a wasted life. Be safe.

Another factor about going back on Match was my determined effort to learn once and for all, how to more expertly read match profiles and separate the real ones from the not so real. In numerous match profiles the same things can be said, and *are* said, in over a hundred different ways. Then, how does one know the difference between a person who *says what they mean* versus, *mean what they say?* What I learned is to pay close attention to the subconscious note inherent in our written profiles. Call it the unique approach each of us takes in the way we reveal ourselves. As a collective whole they might well be seen as clues to our hidden agendas. Could I have seen the signs of my last Match Man? Yes…had I paid closer attention to what he wrote. Among others, his approach was more to the negative side in describing the kind of woman he was looking for in noting: *I'm not looking for a woman who wants to be rescued.* Still, I have found that the only way to find more tell tale markers of a person is through meeting them live. From there your instincts should guide you. Then, you might come back to read their profiles again to compare your own impressions to their own descriptions. Finally, I believe that the expression*, the eyes have it!*...came about for good reason. Wouldn't you rather see pleasing eyes and the curl of a welcome smile?

Below are three match profiles of men whom I have known. The first two represent short written profiles, and the third is a lengthier style. Test yourself on who you think is real:

Headliner:
I love to relax and laugh. I am looking for someone who likes to share their feelings

I am looking for someone who wants to just get to know each other. I am secure and am looking for the same. I love to just sit and talk about hopes and dreams. I like to relax. I like energetic people who love to laugh.

Headliner:
Romantic Dreamer Waiting to Be Captured

Nothing complicated. Someone honest, loving, giving, smart, funny, adventurous, wordly, creative, beautiful, talented, sincere, passionate, romantic woman who is easy going and not looking to be rescued. Someone comfortable.

Headliner:
It's not how you start, it's how you finish...

Those close to me would describe me as strong, ambitious, smart, independent, quick witted, successful and fiercely loyal to friends and loved ones - with an open mind and big heart!

My entrepreneurial spirit has taught me to be good at taking risks when appropriate, being decisive when necessary, and being able to focus or concentrate in order to get things done. It also means being good at figuring out how to get out of life what is desired; figuring out how to operate responsibly, and how to reason without distorting reality.

Let me close by saying that I tend to live life with a great amount of humility and appreciation. I believe we create the life we want and I'm only interested in living a meaningful, rich and fulfilling life, with a lot of fun... I suppose I could wax on poetically about how great of a catch I am but truthfully, that is something you should decide for yourself. Attracting someone really isn't the hard part, but meeting your match certainly is. That said if you think we might be compatible then I do look forward to your reply.

Having become friends with the first Match Man, I can attest to the genuineness of what he says—*he means what he says* instead of, *says what he means*. I found his most notable qualities to be intelligence, kindness, generosity, and an easy communicator. The second profile, Jack's, is self-explanatory. A newer version it was posted for a short time before being removed. Finally, the third one, like the first, was genuine, too. He was a lively thinker, a good communicator and had a decided air of confidence. It was no surprise, then that this Match Man also emphasized the importance of good values.

In closing, there is the knowledge I have gained about humans in judging their best measure. The first has to do with the everlasting remembrance of how they make others feel. I have provided many examples in this book—both good and otherwise—of the things men say which show us who they really are. Second is the sage advice from a friend of mine who said to me recently:

Pick a man who likes a woman and not just loves her.

To that I would add:

Pick a man who likes women, period...because they will accept you for YOU!

Finally, that men can become inspired over the beautiful smile of a woman and establish beautiful memories to go around for some time is truly as uplifting as the heavens. Most of us relish having that kind of attention paid to us, as long as it is in the normal range of acceptance. It validates us as individuals.

Whatever the meaning of the Match Man's story below, that it may have been inspired from his own soulful journey is all that really matters:

U R THE BEST LOOKING LADY ON HERE.

HERE'S A STORY I WROTE, HOPE U LIKE IT *This story is about young love or new love. What happens in the beginning and what happens in the end.*

In the beginning of the love it is like a tree – two trees together. As they fall deeper and deeper in love the trees start to flourish. These are beautiful flowering trees – spring flowering trees. You have your young love and then you marry. Or you get into a deep relationship.

As time goes by the trees continue to flourish. For as many years as can be. And your love for one another nourish these two trees and they continue to grow and grow into big beautiful trees with flowers everywhere. If you don't keep the trees nourished with your love for one another the trees will begin to lose leaves.

In the beginning you will pick up the leaves and care for your tree. But as things start to deteriorate in the relationship the leaves fall more and more. When that relationship dies, the leaves are gone and all you have are two intertwined trees. The trees are dead, the love is gone.

In order to get over the pain, the hurt and the fear the trees must be untangled. Sometimes we turn to everything outside to help us heal but we cannot heal until we unwind the trees branch by branch. Sometimes when you start to unwind the trees, it takes you a long time to get one branch unwound. You continue to unwind, there are stickers on the trees and you have to unwind it very carefully. Some days you cannot unwind one branch. The more you unwind these trees, the less pain, anger and fear continues to go away.

CONCLUSION

My Battery Case

On Friday, December 30, 2011 I won my Battery court case. Co-defendant Mark Olsen was charged with battery and the Judge awarded me monetary damages for injuries I suffered by Mr. Olsen. I have not been paid. As for ex-boyfriend and co-defendant, Brian Donnelly, in closing comments, the Judge spoke volumes about his reprehensible testimony saying that she did not believe one word of Mr. Donnelly's testimony.

— CHAPTER THIRTY-TWO —

The Journey Continues

What *About* Match.com?

I believe Match.com remains one of the better dating sites for two major reasons: first, for ease of navigation; and second, being the largest site it has a wider audience to choose from. In addition to success stories posted by Match, I have heard of several who have been successful in meeting their match. One, a doctor says that it took him more than a year and a great effort to eventually land the woman of his dreams. Now married, they have beautiful twin daughters. Recently, during a plane trip to North Carolina I sat next to a woman who told me she, too, met her husband on Match. Finally, I know of another successfully paired couple who are neighbors of a family relative. As for my Poetry Match Man, *Here There and Everywhere,* he hasn't been back on Match since landing his *head-turner*!

For those who complain about on-line dating, their frustration has more to do with a *concept* that is designed to work with one hundred percent success. In practice, though, one cannot expect to find that degree of success when humans are involved. After all, *we* are the imperfections of life who generate all those interesting and crazy life experiences best known as, *the good, the bad, and the ugly.* I have tried to capture all those things in this book including our biggest concerns and fears associated with cyberdating.

In giving an overall rating to the Men of Match, *behavior* speaks volumes. There is no question that there are some genuinely good men on Match. If you are fortunate enough to find one, consider yourself blessed. Keep in mind though, that people are people—the good ones and bad ones. One Match Man from New Mexico summed it up this way: *none of us are angels, and none of us are perfect.* Then the biggest challenge is having the ability to decipher between the two, and literally finding the lid that matches your pot.

The Men of Match are not much different from those who do not use the internet. Remember, at the beginning of this book I said that one of the major things separating Match Men from the rest is *the anonymity of the web.* Simply put, I believe that anonymity has the potential to encourage deception, and makes for lesser beings. Without trying to place more than a fair share of blame on Match Men, I would note that they have expressed similar frustrations with Match Women. If you ask me why, I would answer: *why does so much war exist?* As in real life, the human condition responds the same way in cyberspace.

A final observation I have made from my adventures with the Men of Match is that there are quite a few broken souls out there. It is no fun that these men carry their baggage over into their on-line relationships while they make similar cases against women. Add to that today's troubling economic times in which the almighty dollar has many egos depressed. This makes for extra challenging times in the dating world.

With every date that I've been on or close to going on, I have tried to use the experience to become wiser for the next. Deciphering profiles is one thing, going on a date is another, but the quest for compatibility in finding a soul mate is the mission. All those higher attributes we call virtues have been tested to the extreme—patience, tolerance, faith, and continuing hope for humans. Wouldn't we all like to become more perfect human beings? In my own best attempts to improve, I am becoming more aware of just how my communications with men affect the differing style and tone of their communications back to me. The saga as we know it continues to remain a never ending dilemma between the sexes.

What About Soul Mates? Final Thoughts...

One of two persons compatible with each other in disposition, point of view, or sensitivity
                                        American Heritage Dictionary

An affinity one has for another
                                        The Random House Dictionary

In defining a soul mate there are many more specifics that come to mind than the two dictionary definitions above. How about: *life-mate, attraction, compatibility, chemistry, friend, comfort, other half, the one* and others? I especially like one of my friend's expression: *it's a feeling that you just have about another person.* Based on my own experiences in cyberdating, the definition doesn't stop there. Soul mates mean different things to different people. There are other important parts through which we measure human beings which help us determine our choice in a lasting soul mate. They include past baggage we have accumulated in our lives. There is no question we allow some of this to invade our otherwise precious relationships. And, what about the degree to which we manifest ourselves as spiritual beings in how we treat one another? These questions lie at the crux of whether or not we find a soul mate or remain with one through the difficulties they present. These factors certainly raised havoc in my last relationship on match. Just how many times have we had our hearts broken because we loved so naturally and so hard only to find that our perceived soul mate wasn't all those things the dictionary defines as *affinity for one another?* Whatever definition you choose to use I believe a soul mate is as unique to its definition as we are as individuals.

What about finding a soul mate? I believe my soul mate is out there somewhere at this moment just as all of your soul mates are, too waiting to find *you.* In using the plural, I believe that each of us have *multiple* soul mates in the course of our lives. That some of us find each other's sooner has much to do with timing. Where we live, what we are doing in our lives at the moment, and our individual passions and motivations which drive us loom large in shining or dimming the light on finding our other half.

What about chemistry? I have found that the power of chemistry more often than not overwhelms in the true meaning of love for many of us. As powerful as chemistry may be, it is not self sustaining on its own especially when other factors intrude upon love. It is more evident that during our younger years chemistry plays a more noticeable role than it does as we become older. Like many in their twenties, thirties, and even forties, I would like to think that chemistry is at the top of my list when it comes to a soul mate. Don't we all revel in the rapture of it as that magic that rings gloriously in our minds? However, as we get older, I believe chemistry remains vital, but it doesn't necessarily make the top slot. More gratifying and sustaining are friendship, comfort, and familiarity. For me, chemistry is a close third behind friendship and comfort. This leads me to friendship.

Must we be friends to be soul mates? YES! Is it the same for young people as it is for the older group? YES, too. The maxim: *with friends like these, who needs enemies?*...applies well to the unnecessary strife created between couples who don't behave as friends. It would be hard to refute that the older you get friendship takes on even greater importance for success as soul mates. There's this, too: without being friends the stress in our lives becomes increasingly stressful for every year that passes! For me, liking your other half as a friend adds to happiness.

Is passion a necessary ingredient in finding your soul mate? YES and NO. This is because there are those of us who live their lives through passion alone, and there are others who have passion for specific things in their lives. Therefore, I believe it is possible for two people *not* to have passion for one another as soul mates just as it is impossible for those with loads of passion to survive without it. The truth lies in finding our true identities—in knowing who we really are so that we can better define what makes each of us compatible with another. After throwing in all of the key ingredients each of us deems important to a soul mate, there is the romantic element which I believe is the glue binding one another together as soul mates.

In my two year journey on Match I might have found my soul mate recently. It is too early to tell, and so my journey continues. Like many of us, I continue to be a work in progress. As a result of two years of cyberdating, I can say that my personal transformation has led me now to a more clear understanding of, *who I really am, what I want in a mate, and what defines a true soul mate.* Some of the desperation that I have experienced along with many others in their efforts to find their other half is a bygone, and I am pleased to say that my journey continues in a more relaxed and concerted manner.

In celebration of both men and women, I think this Match Man—and yes, he truly *likes* women—says all in his message to women about finding your true soul mate:

Find a guy who calls you beautiful instead of hot, who calls you back when you hang up on him, who will lie under the stars and listen to your heartbeat, or will stay awake just to watch you sleep... wait for the boy who kisses your forehead, who wants to show you off to the world when you are in sweats, who holds your hand in front of his friends, who thinks you're just as pretty without makeup on. One who is constantly reminding you of how much he cares and how lucky his is to have you.... The one who turns to his friends and says, 'that's her.'

In continuing this cyberdating journey, I welcome readers to share your stories by emailing me at Nancybeckons@gmail.com. Or, please visit my website and comment on my blog page at www.nancybeckons.com. Friend me on Facebook too! Together, let's share funny, sad and success stories!

— CHAPTER THIRTY-THREE —

The ABCs of Signing Up on Match.com

If you are considering Match.com for the first time, you are signing onto a site that is, in my opinion, one of the easier dating sites to navigate. The creators of Match put a lot of time and thought into this site to make it one of the largest dating sites on the internet. Of particular note is the fact that every month that I was on match the site conducted a super short painless survey (two questions) of their members about their level of satisfaction. The first states, *periodically, we check in with members like you to see how we're doing. Take a second to tell us, how likely is it that you would recommend Match.com to a friend?* The second, *what specifically would you tell someone to get him or her to try Match.com?* Not wasting members' valuable time with a longer survey, and continually looking for ways to improve the site are most likely the key reasons why so many people find match popular and become repeat subscribers. A repeater myself, I've tried several other dating sites only to return.

Membership

A six-month membership runs around $60.00. If you prefer a shorter time, you can join for a month. If you are really uncertain, there is a free trial period. It really serves as the hook to paid membership. The reason is that you cannot send or access emails in your pre-established message inbox after you have taken all the time and trouble to set up your profile. In the free trial period, once you discover that you are being viewed and sent emails by members of the opposite sex, it is not possible to communicating back without a paid subscription. The influx of emails sitting idle in your inbox serves so much of a temptation that in no time at all your credit card is out of the wallet.

There is also the question you might ask yourself: Why pay for a membership when you can sign onto other dating sites for free? My answer is, *you get what you pay for.* You might want to look at it from the following perspective, also: Do you want quality or do you want the cheapest method to bare your soul? And perhaps the cheapest people, too. Unless they are super lucky anyone who disputes this point is only fooling themselves. I have investigated several free sites and found many of those sites to be inclined toward casual affairs.

Username and Password

To get started on Match.com you will need a username and password. I have changed my username several times, the most recent being *goodvibesonly.* Sometimes you will not be able to get the username of your choice because it has been taken. I wanted the name *good vibes* but I could not get it so I was forced to add *only.* There's a good chance no one else will ever get a name once it has been taken because even after a membership is canceled, that username can still be accessed. However, the profile attached to a cancelled membership will be *hidden* to would be viewers. It remains that way because there are those who decide to become a member again, sometimes months or even a year later. Some members (including myself), decide to take a leave of absence. I did exactly that after becoming discouraged when I did not find potentially suitable matches. After a stint of trying other dating sites, eventually I found myself back with Match.com. My old username was still in their system, even after signing up with a new user name and creating an entirely new profile. What I learned quickly is that I should have hidden my old profile to prevent it from being viewed in my absence.

There are quite a few Match subscribers who have been members for more than two years (some continuously and some intermittently). The reasons are many. For example, when you haven't found someone worthwhile to go out with sometimes it is necessary to take a break before considering going off for good. For some others, a reason might be the desire to find a casual relationship or, to make new friends.

Writing a Good Profile

After you have subscribed to Match and created your user name and password, you are ready to write an introduction about yourself and the type of person you are seeking. One of the great things about Match is that they supply a blueprint which is extremely flexible in terms of how much or how little information you want to furnish. The paragraphs you write will determine what types of persons respond. There are additional items that are fill-in-the-blank, and/or checklists.

Two important categories are *About My Date* and *Background/Values.* Do you want someone with blue eyes or brown eyes only or is any color alright? There are many individual items to check off. What I really like about Match is that if you don't feel like going through the entire list, there is a default box already for choosing *any* or *none.*

I have found that by not limiting my tastes to one or two choices, I am afforded a broader range of men when conducting a search. This means a greater number of men will eventually match up. In the *Background Values* section there is a question whose answer is included in the face page specs. It is your faith or religion. Even though you may not choose to reveal information about this subject, it remains important to many in the dating process. If you are adamant about not wanting to go out with a person who checks *agnostic,* the religious faith question will definitely keep you from wasting your time reviewing that profile.

One of the great things about filling out the blueprint is that if you do not want to reveal your persuasion or you find a category to be not to your liking, Match always gives the option to check *none* or bypass it altogether.

Primary Photo

There are three very important parts of a profile: the written summary about yourself, your headshot photo (called the primary photo), and a headliner at the top of your face page. The headliner you create is a catchy one-liner followed by your stats which uniquely identify you in a short sentence. They can all be found on your profile page.

The quality of your primary photo is key. It is a looking-glass. If you have decided to go without a face photo, you are severely limiting your chances of finding people to date. Ask yourself why *you* would take a risk with someone whom you can't see. Dating is risky enough without that added factor. Match Men who do not post photos have given me a variety of reasons such as, *I haven't learned how to do it on the computer; I don't want my friends to know I'm on here; I'm getting ready to;* or *send me your private e-mail and I'll send you pictures right away.* Just as bad are primary photos that are so fuzzy that they belie the true age of a person or mask otherwise noticeable facial imperfections. My advice here is to go with the men who post quality headshots without sunglasses. The eyes and the expression tell all.

Profile Page

When you first sign into Match, the page entitled *My Profile* appears. From this page there's the option of finding out such things as who has viewed your information and who has winked at you. Also on that page is your access to the messages inbox and your profile. From this page you can act on a variety of options. There is your public profile and there is your private profile which reflects any spur of the moment editing changes immediately for you to see. There are also *Connections* and the *Daily 5 Match*.

One interesting thing Match has done is give the ability to hide your profile whenever the mood strikes. There are good reasons to do that. First, if you are getting inundated with emails and want to hide yourself from public view, you can put a stop to the email madness. Second, you might want to take a short break from Match. Third, when you are viewing other's profiles, Match uses that information to give to the viewers. It's called the domino effect. The person you have viewed will discover the next time he/she signs in that you have viewed his or her profile. Match considers that to be the interest between two people. The information is reflected both in *Who's Viewed You* as well as future matches. The process quickly turns into a numbers game using the member base as a huge pool of potential mates. Match uses the information from member profiles to find matches for you. It is a constant process which continues to expand into larger and larger numbers of possible matches. When the membership base has been exhausted you'll know because the same matches repeatedly come up. The longer you remain on Match the number of new matches sometimes winds down to a trickle. Every week new members appear and they will find you through their own searches or Match presents them with a *Daily 5 Match*.

Connections

Connections is a place where you can see the status of your emails, who's winked at you and favorite matches all at the same time and in one location. The Match photos create a navigational visual for getting around quickly and easily. One of my favorite things about *Connections* is that

I never have to remember who emailed me or who I emailed last as well as any winking activity.

A quick note on winking: I think that getting a wink from a man makes more sense than the other way around. As a matter of personal taste I think that the wink thing is a bit corny. However it does provide a vehicle for men who are not ready to make the leap into emailing a woman right away. Also, rejection is tougher for some and giving a wink to feel out a person's interest is much tamer than exchanging emails. Personally, I do not choose to wink at men.

Conducting Searches

Last and most important on *My Profile* page is the search key used to conduct a variety of different searches. There are a number of different methods to come up with the most selective search of matches. Aside from inputting zip codes, there are searches by region, city, age and key words relating to a desirable mate. Reverse matches are possible, too. The more options Match affords gives better access to the larger database. After conducting a search you can save it to finish viewing at a later date. A time-saving feature of searching is that as you wade through pages of results, the headshot and first few sentences of a profile appear with numerous others on the same page. If you want to view just the face photos, it is possible to get that format by clicking on gallery view. You can view photos at one time and if one interests you, you can click on it to view the complete profile. There is even a form to see how well he matches you and a reverse match. There you have it.

(Changes on the match website since the time of printing are not reflected here).

— CHAPTER THIRTY-FOUR —

"Life is a romantic business. It is painting a picture, not doing a sum."

— *Oliver Wendell Holmes*

Author's Profile

Welcome Timelessbty

Timelessbty

"One person with passion is better than ninety nine who only have and interest"

IM me now!

- 47-year-old woman
- Ocala, Florida, United States
- seeking men 35-55
- in United States

Relationships: Divorced
Have Kids: None
Want Kids: Do not want to have kids
Ethnicity: White/Caucasian
Body type: Slender
Height: 5' 3" (160 cm)
Religion: Spiritual but not religious
Smoke: No way
Drink: Social drinker, maybe one or two

About My Life and
Who I Am Looking For

I am an all around athletic girl and love working out outdoors to keep myself looking great. Swimming, walk/running, and riding horses are my top three. Well-educated and traveled I like to do exciting and interesting things. Call it the challenge of learning and growing. Having a New England background, I'm still a country girl at heart.

An experience of a lifetime was encircling the entire globe by ship. Looking back, the funniest moment was getting my ears pierced on upper deck while making transit through the Suez Canal. The army guys, for a moment were on a different watch. Some of my grandest moments were in standing before the Taj Mahal, the Pyramids, the City of Karnack, and the Nile River.

About you: Be yourself. There must be chemistry and compatibility between us. You're a gentleman with class who is honest and has values. You're in line with my own youth and fitness levels. You are open to growth, are spiritual, and have a calming effect. Finally, if we can become pals, then, *I'm there*.

Smiles…

Luckyglobalgirl
Headliner: You might... have created me... in your profile

IMAGINE... the idyllic picture of jogging around the perimeter of a farmer's hayfield, the wonderful smell of huge roles of hay that have just been baled? The footing soft, the going, easy... NOW...envision soaking up the gorgeous views and smells of nature that span 1 1/2 miles in either direction. Open your eyes, and there I am...

What of my man? He has similar character traits and values. He has ethics and manners, has a good heart, kind, generous and considerate of others. Similar to me, he's in great shape, has good energy (mentally and physically) is attractive to me, and dresses well.
Turn ons: He enjoys learning what's important to her, appreciates her differences & understands the importance of the emotional connect. He can laugh at her flaws.
Turn offs: not following through on promises (unless he has a good reason) and cocky men. If you are the one, I'm confident that you'll experience the feeling of being the most special man there is. No currently separateds, please. Smiles...

Goodvibesonly
Headliner: Quality, good taste, manners, and a little swagger...have it?
About My Life and Who I am Looking For
A timeless beauty who enjoys spending time with her special mate whether it be outdoor sport activities, attending a concert, or cuddling on the couch to watch a home movie. I love keeping fit by eating right and working

out preferably outdoors - swimming, walk/running, and riding horses. I have a worldly outlook having traveled around the world, yet remain a kind of sophisticated country girl at heart. Dress me up or down, casually, without trying, I always seem to turn heads. Lol.

About Him: Aside from all those things many of us desire in a mate, it would be important that you have most of your act together. No *currently separateds*, please. Consideration for others and having a calming affect with your special woman would be a top priority, also. You can probably tell that my standards are on the higher side. Hopefully, yours are, too, and especially regarding yourself and the effort you put forth on a continuous basis to improve yourself. Smiles....

— Author's Biography —

A lifelong observer of the human condition, Nancy Beckons worked as a news broadcast journalist in radio, and as a news correspondent for the Waterbury Republican newspaper in her home state of Connecticut. In radio she won an award from national AP Radio for a news breaking story on the 1980 Reagan presidential campaign over the John Anderson delegates. She has covered numerous human interest stories as a journalist.

As a junior, Nancy was a top-ranked equestrian athlete, having won the United State's Equestrian Federation's (USEF) *Horse of the Year Award* national titles for eight consecutive years. She was featured in *Sports Illustrated Magazine, Faces in the Crowd,* twice. She has taught riding as a highly accredited instructor and was nationally licensed in the English Hunter & Jumper disciplines as a top ranked A-rated Horse Show Judge.

Nancy graduated from Tufts University in Medford, Massachusetts with a B.A. in Political Science. She worked in sales and marketing for two Fortune 100 companies, followed by a legislative research analyst position assisting in the interpretation of state statutes. She also worked on several statewide political campaigns during which time she had access to a greater database of interpretive information and statistics on gender behavior.

An avid sports enthusiast, when she is not working you can find Nancy walk/running, swimming, riding, or playing softball at Wrigley Fields in Citra Florida. In every one of her endeavors, Nancy has excelled at her craft. Now she has parlayed all of her talents and experiences into her first book, *The Men of Match: Memoirs of a CyberDating Maven.*